THE EVIL HISTORY OF REPLACEMENT THEOLOGY

An Illustrated History of the Church's Dark and Shameful Treatment of the Jews

J.P. Sloane, D.Min., Ph.D.

AvingtonHouse
Publishing

MINA YANKO
(Ianco Mina)

The Former Deputy Director for the Department of

"Righteous Among the Nations"
at the *Yad Vashem* Memorial Institute Writes:

Having originally come from a European Jewish background in Romania and later relocating to Israel, I would like to share my thoughts on this powerful and historically accurate work. I find this book's sad history of European (and some Middle Eastern) Jewry accurate and compelling. It is apparent Dr. Sloane has gone to a great deal of insightful research and documentation on a very delicate and sensitive subject.

I would highly recommend this captivating and compelling filled with surprising, little-known facts for anyone who wants to enlighten themselves about the misguided treatment of the Jewish people for over the past 2,000 years.

—Mina Yanko
International Speaker & Educator
Jerusalem, Israel

A Holocaust survivor herself, Mina Yanko served 30 years as Deputy Director for the Department of "The Righteous Among the Nations" at the *Yad Vashem* Memorial Institute for Holocaust Studies in Jerusalem. The institute does research for the State of Israel to honor *Righteous Gentiles* like Oskar Schindler and other gentiles who risked their lives, during WWII, trying to protect the Jews from extermination during the Holocaust.

Mrs. Yanko speaks several languages and is a highly sought-after *international lecturer and educator* speaking at universities, churches, synagogues, and other venues regarding the Holocaust and the *Righteous Among the Nations*.

When Mrs. Yanko is not involved with her speaking engagements, she provides her time and expertise to the Hebrew University in Jerusalem.

Mina Yanko, in a photo taken with her close friend and associate, the late Shimon Peres (circa 1990s). Shimon Peres (1923-2016) was the Prime Minister of Israel twice, and he also served as the Interim Prime Minister of Israel during the 1970s to the 1990s. He similarly served as the ninth President of Israel (2007-2014).

DEDICATED TO

Liselotte ("Liselle") Sego, who, as a young Jewish girl, saw Adolf Hitler at the opera sitting in a private box adjacent to that of her family—unaware of the Holocaust about to be unleashed on her people. By the grace of God, Liselle lived to tell about it.

AND TO THE MEMORY OF

Zola Levitt, Ph.D.
A pioneer in educating Christians
about our Jewish roots.

Beware lest any man spoil you through philosophy and vain deceit, after the tradition of men, after the rudiments of the world and not after Christ (Colossians 2:8).

At various times throughout the ages in Christendom, the Jews were forced to wear pointed hats (usually yellow to stand out) and identification badges depicting the Ten Commandments or the Star of David. One of the badges forced on the Jews by the Nazis in twentieth-century Germany is shown above.

THE EVIL HISTORY OF REPLACEMENT THEOLOGY
An Illustrated History of the Church's
Dark and Shameful Treatment of the Jews

By J.P. Sloane, D. Min., Ph.D.

ISBN-13: 978-0692692981
ISBN-10: 0692692983

AvingtonHouse Publishers, Dallas

All Koran passages, unless otherwise designated, are taken from Marmaduke Pickthall's translation of the Koran, which is in the public domain in the United States because the author died in 1936. Works by this author are also in the public domain in countries and areas where the copyright term is the author's life plus 60 years or less.

All Scriptures, unless otherwise designated, are taken from the King James Version of the Bible with "thee," "ye," and "thou" converted to modern English. The use of "you" and the Old English words "thy" and "thine" have sometimes been translated into the contemporary word "your." For further clarification, with words ending in the archaic plural suffixes "t," "est," and "eth," the archaic suffix has been deleted, and the modern ending substituted. Because not all verses benefit from these changes, a few exceptions have kept their archaic words intact to retain the poetic essence of the King James Bible and the various translations of the Koran, which have also been, for whatever reason, rendered in the English of the seventeenth century.

We also believe that Heaven and Hell are proper nouns that describe actual places; therefore, they are capitalized in this work.

Illustrations are from public domain sources except the Israeli landscape taken from space ("MAP 7.S-AB," *The Holy Land Satellite Atlas*, by Edward Campbell et al., volume 1, RØHR, 1999, page 81).

Because of age and degradation, some pictures have been enhanced. The photographs from the Holocaust period are also in the public domain in the United States because they meet three requirements:

1. They were first published outside the United States (and *not* published in the U.S. within 30 days).

2. They were first published before 1 March 1989 without copyright notice or before 1964 without copyright renewal or before the source country established copyright relations with the United States.

3. They were in the public domain in its home country (Poland/Germany/Bosnia) on the URAA date (1 January 1996).

The cover is adapted from D.W. Griffith's 1915 silent film, *The Birth of a Nation*. The film was about the secret organization, which began in the nineteenth century, known as the "Knights of the Ku Klux Klan," comprised of Protestants. They terrorized Blacks, Catholics and—like the original Crusaders—they despised the Jews.

Much of the secular history cited throughout this book, unless otherwise noted, is taken from Bernard Grun, *The Timetables of History* 3rd revised edition, New York: Simon & Schuster/Touchstone Book, 1991.

The Hanukkah Menorah that we show in the *Post-Levitical Feast* section is Public Domaine from PublicDomainVectors.org. While this book is not exhaustive documentation of the evil history of replacement theology and the crimes perpetrated against the Jewish people, we have documented most of the events which happened to them throughout the 2,000 years of the European Christian Era. Due to the confines of space and to keep the number of pages to a reasonable limit, not all events are footnoted. Therefore, in addition to the over 300 footnotes and 160 sources that we do refference, all the non-footnoted events may be corroborated by doing an Internet search including: "Jewish Persecution | Timeline of Judaism | History of Anti-Semitism;" "A Brief Chronology of Antisemitism | The Jewish Agency;" "Timeline of antisemitism - Wikipedia," etc. We also suggest doing a library search. One excellent source is P.E. Grosser & E. G. Halpern's book, *Anti-Semitism: Causes and Effects*, 2nd ed. (New York: Philosophical Library, 1983).

CONTENTS

INTRODUCTION

Is God Finished with the Jews?

Scripture tells us that a demonic and evil-union will occur at the End of the Age among nations united in their hatred against the Jews. This demonic union will climax with the whole world coming against the Jews in the City of God—Jerusalem—and the land God gave them—Israel.

I was born in California during WWII, so naturally—at a very early age—I became aware of the Nazi atrocities against the Jews. As a child, I remember asking my father why people hated the Jews so much. My father said it was because they killed Jesus. At the time, I did not know my dad was just repeating the centuries-old Christian heresy known as "supersessionism," also known as "replacement theology." Based on what my father told me, I eventually came to believe that the Jews killed Jesus, and the Church (Christians) had replaced Israel as the chosen people of God.

After the war, California began to grow rapidly. Housing developments had taken off with returning WWII vets, thanks to a bill passed by Congress—the Servicemen's Readjustment Act—also known as the Servicemen's Readjustment Act of 1944. It was commonly referred to as the "GI Bill of Rights," a law that gave benefits to vets, including low-cost mortgages.

I still remember one afternoon around the years 1946-47, when my parents and I drove to El Segundo, California (a suburb of Los Angeles), to visit friends. As our car entered the town, we came across a new housing development. At the entrance to the tract homes, it advertised the benefits of living there, but with the caution, "Jews Not Welcome." I asked my father why Jews were not allowed to buy a house there; he said it was because many people hated the Jews and did not want to live next door to them. I thought that was very strange and found it hard to grasp, of course, since I was a child. I will never forget how it troubled me; it still does to this day.

As I grew older, I remained troubled with the idea that every Jew was responsible for Jesus' death. It seemed to me there was something wrong with the concept of replacement theology. I could not shake the nagging questions, "Is God done with the Jews as many theologians insist? Where in the Bible is there such a proclamation, if any? If God had not disowned the Jews, from where did that notion come? What has been the effect of that theory's impact on the Jews?"

First, terms need to be clarified. The Jews are one of the twelve tribes of the descendants of Jacob whom God renamed "Israel." The name "Jew" comes from the tribe of Judah (those who lived in the land revisionist historians refer to as the "West Bank"). The Bible refers to it as "Judea," the Hebrew tribal land where Jerusalem is located.

The Jews are descended from the Hebrew patriarch, Abraham (Genesis 17:5), to whom the Covenant with God was given through the lineage of his son, Isaac (Genesis 17:19-21); however, for the sake of simplicity, we will refer to all the tribes of Jacob (Genesis 32:38) collectively as "Jews."

Down through the ages, it has generally been accepted that the Church replaced Israel as the receiver of divine mercy and election; consequently, whenever Israel is mentioned in biblical prophecy, many theologians have wrongly substituted the Church for Israel and Heaven for Jerusalem. Has that always been the case? Is God through with Israel? Let's begin with the New Testament to see how God regarded His commitment to the children of Israel and the Holy Land in connection with the events surrounding the death, burial, and resurrection of His Son, Jesus, and how

20

the Gentiles were brought into God's preordained New Covenant (Jeremiah 31:31) with Israel.

The main argument used for allowing God to forsake His Chosen People, the Israelites, is that the Jews killed Jesus. That argument says they were given the opportunity to establish God's kingdom on earth, but killed His Son rather than accept Him as their long-awaited Messiah; yet for that to be true, then all the Jews who were followers of Jesus during His life, death, and resurrection in the Holy Land must be ignored. Also, we know that 50 days after Passover (the time when Jesus was crucified, died, buried, and rose from the dead) was the Feast of Pentecost when approximately 3,000 additional Jews received Jesus as their Messiah and were baptized (Acts 2:41).

A little-known fact lost on many of us today is how people were counted in the first-century Middle East. In those days, when crowds of people were counted, they usually did not count the women and children; so when the Bible recorded a crowd of 5,000, there might have easily been double or even triple the five thousand![1] In Matthew 16:10, we read that Jesus had a crowd of four thousand men and—at the very least—double that amount when women and children were included.

Because we are conditioned to only think about the original twelve disciples who were with Jesus, we typically overlook the additional 72.

> After this, the Lord appointed seventy-two others and sent them two by two ahead of Him to every town and place where He was about to go (Luke 10:1).

We see the strong attraction of Jesus to the common Jewish people when we read about the feeding of the 5,000 in the Gospel of Matthew:

> When Jesus landed [in the boat] and saw a large crowd, He had compassion on them and healed their sick.

> As evening approached, the disciples came to Him and said, "This is a

---

[1]Kenneth Barker, Gen. Ed., the *New International Version Study Bible* (Grand Rapids: Zondervan, 1983), #1463 footnote.

remote place, and it's already getting late. Send the crowds away, so they can go to the villages and buy themselves some food."

Jesus replied, "They do not need to go away. You give them something to eat." "We have here only five loaves of bread and two fish," they answered.

"Bring them here to me," He said. And He directed the people to sit down on the grass. Taking the five loaves and the two fish and looking up to Heaven, He gave thanks and broke the loaves. Then He gave them to the disciples, and the disciples gave them to the people. They all ate and were satisfied, and the disciples picked up twelve basketfuls of broken pieces that were leftover. The number of those who ate was about five thousand men, besides women and children (Matthew 14:14-21, NIV, bracketed clarification mine).

Some argue that many of those thousands of people who were followers of Jesus might have fallen away during His trial and execution. What we do know is this: After Christ's resurrection in Jerusalem, in addition to the women who were present (Mary Magdalene, Mary (mother of Jesus), Mary Salome (mother of James and John), Miriam and Martha (sisters of Lazarus), and eleven of His disciples[2]), there were an additional 500 of His followers who all saw Him at the same time![3] In addition to them, there is no reason to believe there were not even more followers of Christ in the territories of Galilee and Samaria at that time. Many of them were still alive around 55 A.D.[4] (1 Corinthians 15:6-7.)

After Jesus ascended to be with the Father, about a week before the day of Pentecost (Acts 1:9), Peter and the other disciples (approximately 120 men, Acts 1:15) stayed and prayed in the upper room. When the day of Pentecost finally arrived, and they were gathered together in Jerusalem, the Holy Spirit came upon them, and they began speaking and praying in various foreign languages (Acts 2:1-7), which resulted in thousands of additional Jews becoming Christians:

---

[2]Judas had hung himself (Matthew 27:5).

[3]1 Corinthians 15:5-6.

[4]Merrill C. Tenney, revised by Walter M. Dunnett, *New Testament Survey, Revised* (Grand Rapids: Wm. B. Eerdmans Publ., 1988), 297.

Those who accepted His message were baptized, and about three thousand men [women and children were not counted] were added to their number that day (Acts 2:41, clarification mine).

This Scripture is biblically documented proof there were thousands of thousands of first-century Jewish believers in Christ who were *not* responsible for the death of Jesus.

These facts are ignored by many replacement theologians who believe the Church has replaced Israel. In an attempt to show a Gentile influence in the first century, they focus on Luke, who authored two New Testament letters, the Gospel of Luke and the Book of Acts. Are these replacement theologians correct? Was Luke a Gentile

When Paul traveled, it was his custom to go to Jewish places of worship first and preach the gospel just as Jesus did. Through the custom of "to the Jew first" (Romans 1:16; 2:9-10; 3:2), Paul found many Jews, throughout the Roman Empire, who accepted Yeshua (Jesus) as their Messiah.

Many Jews in the Bible had Latin and Greek names, such as Simon, who Jesus called "Peter." The name Peter or *Petros* (πέτρος) is a Greek name which means "small rock" (pebble), while the word *petra* (πέτρα) means "rock." There were also many Jews in Paul's Messianic communities, throughout the world, who had Greco-Roman names. Luke was probably one of them. Dr. Arnold G. Fruchtenbaum states:

> There is no reason to assume that Luke was not a Jew, and all biblical evidence is that he was a Jew. One key statement is found in Romans 3:1-2, which clearly says, "The oracles of God" (the written Scripture) were committed specifically to Jewish people. That alone points out that Luke would have to be a Jew.

> Furthermore, in my own exegesis [critical study] of the Book of Acts, written by Luke as well, he clearly writes as a Jew. He has many "Hebrew-isms" in both Luke and Acts, and that means he is writing Greek by using a Hebrew word order. This is often done when a

person writes in one language while thinking in another[5] (bracketed clarification mine).

An example of this, which you might be familiar with, is the order of words when referring to America's White House. English speaking Americans would say, "The President of the United States lives in the 'White House.' " The French would refer to the president's home as "Maison Blanc." The order of words in French is just the opposite of English: Maison = house and blanc = white, so the correct order of words in French is "House White."

English-speaking Americans, if they were speaking French while thinking in English, would not use the French order of words; rather, they would say, "Blanc Maison." The words are correct, and any Frenchman hearing them would know what the person is talking about, yet the American reveals that French is not his native language because he speaks French using the English sentence structure.

The second example of people speaking in English—but revealing that English is not their first language—through the use of a foreign language sentence structure, is apparent in the 1956 song recorded by Patti Page titled, "Throw Mama from the Train." The opening verse is, "Throw Mama from the train a kiss, a kiss." At first, it sounds like someone is going to throw Mama off a moving train—that's the hook (i.e., attention-getter) of the song—but what is really being said is just the opposite! We finally realize that Mama is not on the train, but that the person on the train wishes to throw a goodbye kiss to Mama; nevertheless, the order of words is a dead giveaway that English is not that person's first language because—while speaking in English—the person is using a German word order. These examples are the arguments Dr. Fruchtenbaum is making for Luke being a Jew by explaining how, even though he was writing in Greek, Luke was using the Hebrew/Aramaic word order.

While the last two examples were mine, Fruchtenbaum continues to give several more convincing examples in his dissertation; however, the point

---

[5]Email correspondence dated June 29, 1999, to this author from Roxanne at Ariel Ministries regarding a previous response by Arnold G. Fruchtenbaum, Th.M., Ph.D., as to whether or not Luke was a Jew.

here is to show that many of the people cited in the New Testament were Jews with Latin or Greek names. Consider Saul in the Bible—a Hebrew name—whose other name was Paul.[6] He was a Roman citizen born in Asia Minor.[7] Paul's name in Greek was *Paulos* or in Latin, *Paulus,* meaning "small" or "modest." Luke's name in Greek was *Loukas* or in Latin, *Lucas,* which means "from Lucania."[8] We must not forget the first-century, well-known Jewish historian, Flavius Josephus; therefore, we can see four Hebrews (Peter, Paul, Luke, and Flavius) using Greco-Roman names.

Consider: Paul and Luke knew each other (Acts 21:18), and Luke wrote profusely about Paul throughout Acts. He affectionately referred to Luke as the "beloved physician" (Colossians 4:14). For that reason, when Paul wrote that the oracles of God are delivered through the Jews, he made no exception for Luke, who not only wrote the Book of Acts but the Gospel of Luke as well. Certainly, if Luke were a Gentile, God—who cannot lie (Titus 1:2)—would have had to instruct Paul to make an exception for Luke's Gospel and the Book of Acts as having been written by a Gentile when the Holy Spirit directed Paul to write:

> What advantage, then, is there in being a Jew? .... Much in every way! First of all, the Jews have been entrusted with the very words of God ... (Romans 3:1-2, NIV).

Signs in the Heavens Never Ceased Concerning the Jews

It is important to know that God continued to manifest heavenly events, which showed that He was not finished with His people. Those events were either misunderstood or ignored by the Church, and they not only occurred during biblical times, but also continued after the death, burial,

---

[6]*The Analytical Greek Lexicon,* 7th ed. (Grand Rapids: Zondervan, 1972), 323. In Greek, "Peter" is *Petros,* which means "rock" (pebble). In Hebrew, the name is *Kefa.*

[7]Saul, known as "Paul" (Acts 13:9), was not born in Israel or Babylon, but in Asia Minor in the south coastal region of Cilicia in a town called "Tarsus" (Acts 21:39). It was located in what is now Turkey (*Wikipedia.org*). Cilicia is the province where the Roman Emperor, Trajan, died in August of 117 A.D. (*Encyclopedia Britannica*).

[8]The name "Luke" might be derived from the name of a region in Italy, Lucania, through the ancient Greek name, *Loukas* (Gk. Λουκᾶς), which means "a native of Lucania." Mike Campbell, "Meaning, Origin and History of the Name Luke," n.p. Web. October 26, 2011.

and resurrection of Jesus.[9] God's orchestrated, heavenly events, which coincided with earthly events, had a direct effect on the fate of the Jews, along with countries or powerful people dealing with the Jews. One such event in the twentieth century concurred with the High Holidays of the Jewish calendar and the re-establishment of the Nation of Israel after a 2,500-year absence. Unfortunately, the "wise" Church scholars neither fully understood their relevance in the Scriptures nor realized what those events were when they happened, just like the Pharisees and Sadducees, who asked Jesus for a sign.

> He replied, "When evening comes, you say, 'It will be fair weather, for the sky is red,' and in the morning, 'Today it will be stormy, for the sky is red and overcast.' You know how to interpret the appearance of the sky, *but you cannot interpret the signs of the times*" (Matthew 16:1-3, NIV, emphasis added).

One of the heavenly signs of Jesus' return is told to us by the Apostle John:

> And I beheld when he had opened the sixth seal, and, lo, there was a great earthquake; and the sun became black as sackcloth of hair, and the moon became as blood (Revelation 6:12).

Paul also confirmed:

> For since the creation of the world God's invisible qualities—His eternal power and divine nature—have been clearly seen, being understood from what has been made, so that people are without excuse (Romans 1:20, NIV).

Consequently, because of God's biblical and natural revelations, those who promote the false doctrine of replacement theology—according to God Himself—are without excuse!

---

[9]When Jesus was crucified, the sun went dark for three hours (Matthew 27:45), during which time Jesus cried out, "My God, My God why have you forsaken me?" (Matthew 27:46; Psalm 22:1.)

Now lest we fall into heresy ourselves, we must be careful not to confuse the signs God gives us through the heavenly bodies with astrology, a form of divination used to see into the future through the various stars and houses of the zodiac. God repeatedly forbids divination (Deuteronomy 18:10-142; Kings 17:16-18; Jeremiah 10:2).

Nevertheless, there is a difference between astrology and God-sent, rare signs not seen every night in the starry heavens. The signs God places in the heavens are to make us aware of special events unfolding according to His agenda—not unlike the Star of Bethlehem—which heralded the birth of Jesus (Matthew 2:1-2).

One such occasional event mentioned in the Bible is a phenomenon known as the "blood moon," which announces the great and notable Day of the Lord:

> The sun will be turned to darkness and the moon to blood before the coming of the great and dreadful day of the LORD (Joel 2:31; Acts 2:20, NIV).

Of course, the scriptural reference to a blood moon is not a moon covered in blood; rather, it is a rare solar event, which happens around every six years. The occurrence happens as a full moon appears after the first harvest moon when the moon is nearest to the fall equinox.[10] The blood moon event occurs because the sun is closer to the earth, not when it is farther away, as it usually is when the moon turns black. Because the sun is closer to the earth and in line with the earth's equator—sunlight bends through the prism of the earth's atmosphere and projects a blood-red hue on the moon, giving it the illusion of being covered in blood. It is similar to the occasional fiery-red sunsets. Traditionally, readers of the Bible have thought of the blood moons mentioned in the Scriptures as a sign for the

---

[10]An Equinox happens twice a year (every six months) when the earth's equator lines up with the center of the sun, which results with day and night being approximately equal in length. We also have two Solstices twice a year (every six months). The Equinox and Solstices are separated by three-month periods (Equinox-Solstice-Equinox-Solstice). These heavenly events are timed to one of our four seasons.

End of the Age, yet down through history, we have seen the appearance of other blood moons. It is interesting to note that blood moons have accompanied monumental events in connection with Israel, the nation— the people of Israel, as we will see.

There is another heavenly event called a "Tetrad," a rare event of four, full, blood-moon eclipses in a row, falling exactly on the Jewish holidays with six full moons and four solar eclipses in between them without any partial lunar eclipses. This sign is always an omen of events that will affect a nation or the dispersed people of Israel. Sometimes it includes those nations who do harm to the Jews or are being used by God to either bless or bring down His judgment on Israel.

There were only 62 Tetrad events between 1 A.D. and 2000 A.D., and of those, only seven fell on or near biblical feast days; accordingly, they are referred to as "biblical Tetrads." In our current century, during the years 2014-2015, a biblical Tetrad occurred. It was the last such event for that century, and it is believed that it will not be repeated for another 600 years (2582-83)!

That order of four blood moons (a Tetrad), *without* any partial eclipse, would occur six more times during the twentieth century, but not during the Hebrew holy days of Passover and the Feast of Tabernacles; those occurred in 1967, the year of the Jubilee. The year 1968 brought a conclusion to the "times of the Gentiles," which was prophesied by Jesus in Luke 21:24.

For the first time after 2,500 years—Israel, once again, became in control of Jerusalem as predicted by Jesus in Luke 21:24. (Two thousand years ago, Jerusalem was part of the Southern Kingdom known as "Judea.") It is apparent that God is still watching over the Jews!

Throughout the history of the Church, blood-moon Tetrads have continued to accompany events that surrounded the Hebrew people during their dispersion throughout Europe and the world for the last 2,000 years. If God is done with the Jews, then why do we still see this divine, heavenly interaction, and the timing of major events involving the Jewish people still being manifested within a year surrounding—or even during—the blood-moon appearances? Despite all these signs and biblical passages, which clearly show that God is not through with His people, many mainline Christian denominations will not repent from this ancient heresy of replacement theology; consequently, as God warned us when speaking of events surrounding Israel in the Last Days:

> And in that day will I make Jerusalem a burdensome stone for all people: all that burden themselves with it shall be cut in pieces, though all the people of the earth be gathered together against it (Zechariah 12:3).

God further warned us:

> I will gather all nations and bring them down to the valley of Jehoshaphat.[11] There I will put them on trial for what they did to My inheritance, My people Israel, because they scattered My people among the nations *and divided up my land* (Joel 3:2, NIV, emphasis added).

Jerusalem is in the news almost every day. Muslim countries and the neo-Palestinians—with worldwide support—want to divide the small country of Israel who has already given up most of her land for peace, yet Israel's neighbors are still demanding more "land for peace!" Never mind that since 1967, Israel has given up 90% of her land for peace and received only bombs in return.[12]

---

[11]Jehoshaphat literally means "God judges." The valley of Jehoshaphat is also known as the "Kidron Valley," which is located directly east of the Old City of Jerusalem between the city and the Mount of Olives.

[12]Israel has already given up more than 90% of her land for peace in addition to almost half of Israel proper to the Palestinian Organization. Ref: Andrew Glass, "Egypt, Israel Finnish Peace Treaty, March 26, 1979." *POLITICO,* 26 March 2014. Web. 2 December 2015.

In 2014, Israel's Prime Minister, Benjamin Netanyahu, offered to give up another 90% of land for peace as a means of bringing back the Palestinians to the peace table. Ref: Gavriel Fiske. "Israel Said Willing to Give up 90% of West Bank." *The Times of Israel,* 6 February 2014. Web. 2 December 2015.

This ignores the fact that the Palestinian Organization has never declared peace with Israel or recognized Israel's right to exist, despite promising to so many times over the past decades. Ref: Oren Dorell. "Israel: Peace Deal Requires Recognition of

Daily, we hear calls from many politicians in Washington to divest holdings in Israel. We hear on the radio, television, and read on social media and in newspapers about businesses divesting their financial holdings in Israeli companies. It seems like the whole world is calling for boycotts (BDS[13]) against the tiny nation of Israel, a country so small it could fit about two and a half times in California's San Bernardino County. It is interesting to note, if we were to combine the Muslim nations surrounding Israel, they would be almost equal to the size of the United States (3.8 million square miles), yet they still demand that Israel continue to give up even more land for "peace!" Calls to boycott Israel can also be heard from various sources, including sovereign nations, colleges, various Christian denominations, the World Council of Churches, etc. Under the Obama Administration, we saw how—the United States of America—Israel's last major supporter, also turned its back on Israel and made nuclear aggression against her from Iran a real probability. At the time of this writing, a very large number of people think God might still give the United States and Israel a bit of a reprieve under the Trump Administration—but according to Scripture, that will only be temporary.

While you read this book and learn about the repetitive atrocities committed against the Jews throughout the world in the name of Christianity, it must be pointed out that due to the accuracy of our historical timeline, it might seem like déjà vu. However, it is essential for us to fully report the unrelenting nature of the 2,000 years of seemingly never-ending genocides against these innocent people by the Church against those God calls His children[14]—all in the name of replacement theology. As repetitive as these atrocities appear in our historical timeline, the savagery against the Jews really did happen—and sadly—it continues to this very day.

Please keep in mind, as you read these historical accounts of the Jews, you are witnessing the actual atrocities throughout the history of how Jews were forced to live, suffer, and die at the hands of those who

---

Jewish State." *USA TODAY,* December, 2015. "PLO Chairman Mahmoud Abbas told the *New York Times* over the weekend that recognition of Israel as a Jewish state 'is out of the question.' Web. 3 February 2014.

[13]BDS stands for the Palestinian led, "Boycott, Divestment, Sanctions" against the nation of Israel.

[14]Deuteronomy 14:1; Hosea 1:10.

claimed to be serving Jesus, the Prince of Peace.

To help you relate to the time when those various and horrific atrocities against the Jews occurred, we have included other important historical events that happened around the same time.

Finally, we must advise you that because the first few chapters necessarily deal with the early Latin Church Fathers, their names and writing styles are unavoidable. They might be a little difficult to understand and follow (not to mention trying to pronounce their names); however, we have tried to simplify it with bracketed clarifications. As we move along through the centuries, it becomes easier to understand. The subject matter itself is, at times, very disturbing, to say the least, but we must present it to accurately cover the shameful treatment of God's chosen people by the Church throughout the centuries.

Again, we reiterate that since we have a moral obligation to accurately and impartially look at the historical relationship between the Christians and Jews fairly, it is unavoidable that we have to provide details and examples of what occurred, "warts" and all.

CHAPTER 1

THE FIRST CENTURY JEWISH CHURCH: HOW IT WAS TAKEN OVER BY GENTILES IN THE SECOND CENTURY

Ironically, the Question of the First Century Was, "Could Gentiles Become Christians?"

The irony in all this is that the debate in the first century A.D. Church centered on whether or not Gentiles should be allowed to become Christians, and if so, could they remain Gentiles? Then after Gentiles were allowed to become Christians, the question reversed itself in the second century A.D. to, "Should the Jews be allowed to become Christians, and if so, could they remain Jews?"

Consider how—in the first century A.D.—the Jews who followed the Messiah (Gk. *Christos*) were understood to be a Jewish Messianic sect— or as the Greeks rudely referred to them in the city of Antioch— "Christians" (Acts 11:26). In fact, for the first half of the first century, the Church consisted mainly of Jews! It was not until the second half of the first century, with the advent of the conversion of Saul of Tarsus—who became the Apostle Paul—that the good news of eternal salvation, through the Jewish Messiah, was made available to the Gentiles in fulfillment of Genesis 12:3b where God promised Abraham that all the people of the world would be blessed through him (i.e., Israel). However, even though the gospel was made available to the Gentiles, it remained, and still does "... to the Jew first ..." (Romans 1:16; 2:9; 2:10). Paul instructed us, "... First of all, the Jews have been entrusted with the very words of God" (Romans 3:2, NIV).

Sadly, problems arose when Gentiles were allowed into the Messianic Jewish group of believers. The Bible gives the example of how Paul had to deal with other Messianic Jews, who were telling the newly received Gentiles, they needed to be circumcised and Judaized to be accepted as Messianic converts. Paul relates how he had to go to the early Church Fathers in Jerusalem and present his case against the Judaizing of the Gentile converts:

> Then after fourteen years, I went up again to Jerusalem, this time with Barnabas. I took Titus along also. I went in response to a revelation and, meeting privately with those esteemed as leaders; I presented to them the gospel that I preach among the Gentiles. I wanted to be sure I was not running [in the wrong direction] and had not been running my race in vain [in conflict with the teachings of the Church Fathers in Jerusalem] and yet, not even Titus, who was with me, was compelled to be circumcised, even though he was a Greek. This matter arose because some false believers [Judaizers] who had infiltrated our ranks to spy on the freedom we have in Christ Jesus and to make us [Gentile members of the Church] slaves [conform to Hebrew Law and circumcision]. We did not give in to them for a moment so that the truth of the gospel might be preserved for you (Galatians 2:1-5, NIV, bracketed clarifications mine).

> When Cephas (Peter) came to Antioch, I opposed him to his face, because he stood condemned. For before certain men came from James, he used to eat with the Gentiles. But when they [Jewish believers sent by James] arrived, he began to draw back and separate himself from the Gentiles because he was afraid of those who belonged to the circumcision group [Jews]. The other Jews joined him in his hypocrisy, so that by their hypocrisy even Barnabas was led astray [and avoided Gentiles]. When I saw that they were not acting in line with the truth of the gospel, I said to Cephas in front of them all, "You are a Jew, yet you live like a Gentile and not like a Jew. How is it, then, that you force Gentiles to follow Jewish customs?" (Galatians 2:11-14, NIV, bracketed clarifications mine.)

The customs Paul was probably speaking about refers to the 613 additional Laws, including the ritual sacrifice, circumcision, and kosher

Laws, which were no longer needed after Christ fulfilled them (Matthew 5:17-18).

The Early Church Still Observed the Seven Levitical Feasts of Israel and Hanukkah, a Fact Ignored for Nineteen Centuries

In the Church of the first century, Jesus observed the seven Hebrew feasts, a practice that was continued by all of His followers after He went to be with the Father. In the Gospel of John, Jesus went to the Temple in Jerusalem for the specific purpose of celebrating the Feast of Dedication (i.e., *Hanukkah).*

> And it was at Jerusalem, the Feast of the Dedication, and it was winter. And Jesus walked in the Temple in Solomon's porch (John 10:22-23).

Jesus' disciples continued observing all the celebrations, only with a new emphasis. Jesus never suggested that at any point, He or His followers were to discontinue celebrating the seven holy feasts of Israel or Hanukkah; therefore, His disciples continued observing the celebrations, only with a new emphasis.

Background: Hanukkah (the post-Levitical feast) celebrates Israel overthrowing the Seleucids and taking back their holy Temple. The Greek ruler, Antiochus Epiphanes, desecrated the Temple by sacrificing pigs[15] on the altar.

After the Israeli victory, the Levitical priests went to rededicate the Temple of God, but there was only enough sacred oil to light the Menorah (a large, seven-branch, oil lampstand) for one day, yet it miraculously lasted for eight days. That event, also known as the "Festival of Lights," occurred after the Old Testament was written and before the time of Jesus and the writing of the New Testament. John told us about Jesus celebrating this holy day and how He fulfilled it when He said,

> ... I am the light of the world: he that follows Me shall not walk in darkness, but shall have the light of life (John 8:12).

---

[15]God considers pigs/swine as unclean and an abomination; therefore, they are forbidden as food (Leviticus 11:7; Isaiah 65:4).

The Passover set in motion the Hebrew slaves being freed from Egyptian slavery by Pharaoh due to God's judgment on Egypt, which took the lives of every firstborn. As the Angel of Death went throughout the land of Egypt, he only spared the firstborn in the homes of the Hebrew slaves who "... put it on the sides and tops of the doorframes of the houses ...." (Exodus 12:7, NIV). Jesus is for us the Passover Lamb (John 1:29; 36).

This event, known as the "Passover Seder" (ritual feast), is still celebrated today/ One of the curious things regarding this event is that during the ceremony, when three matzos are chosen, the one in the middle, referred to as the *afikomen* (meaning "that which comes after"[16]), is broken in half. There are several ideas about why this is done, but no one really knows when it began. Regarding Jesus, it might be at this point where we read in the Bible, "and when He had given thanks, He broke *it* and said, 'Take, eat; this is My body which is broken for you; do this in remembrance of Me' " (1 Corinthians 11:24,NKJV). Then the broken matzo is wrapped in a cloth and hidden away until after the meal when the children search for it. Usually, the child who finds it receives a gift. Consider that Jesus was broken on the cross between two thieves (Matthew 27:38), and when taken down, He was wrapped in a grave cloth made of linen and then hidden in Joseph of Arimathea's grave (Matthew 27:59; Mark 15:46). When the women went to the grave three days later, He was gone, and they ran to tell Peter and the others. Then, like the children searching for the broken matzo, they all went to look for Him, but it was Mary Magdalena who found Him, and when Jesus spoke to her, she was joyful to know He had risen from the dead (John 20:1-18)!

There is still another symbol of Jesus and the three matzos with one on either side of the crushed one in the middle, and that is represented by the Trinity, God the Father, God the Son who was crushed for our iniquities (Isaiah 53:5), and God the Holy Spirit.

As we just read, Jesus was the Passover Lamb (John 1:29, 36) and even though that would be Jesus' last Passover Seder before He went to be

---

[16]Jesus is the afikomen, "that which comes after" (i.e., the prophesied Messiah): "And I will put enmity Between you [Satan] and the woman, And between your seed and her Seed [the Messiah]; He shall bruise your head, And you shall bruise His heel" (Genesis 3:15, NKJV, bracketed clarification mine).

with the Father. The Passover Seder is a ritual dinner filled with symbolisms. Jesus expected His disciples to honor the Passover after He was gone, only He modified the service and some of the symbols for them. First, some background information: At the beginning of the Passover Seder meal, it was customary to break a matzo, which would then be called the *afikomen,* אֲפִיקוֹמָן.

At the Last Supper, before His crucifixion, it was Jesus who conducted the Passover service: "And He took bread, and gave thanks, and broke it, and gave [it] unto them, saying, 'This is my body which is given for you: this do in remembrance of Me' " (Luke 22:19). At the beginning of the service after the *afikomen* is broken, it is then wrapped in a cloth and hidden away until after the Seder is over—just like Jesus would be taken from the cross and wrapped in a grave cloth and hidden in the earth until three days had passed. Then after the meal, the children would look for the hidden *afikomen.* When they found it, there was a great rejoicing just like the disciples rejoiced when they found Jesus had risen from the dead! It is important to understand that Jesus never canceled observing the Passover Seder; His disciples continued going to Jerusalem and celebrating it long after He was gone.

There are misunderstandings among some regarding Jesus and the Passover Seder. One is why Passover is so important regarding Jesus. The eating of the *afikomen* matzo is not to be misinterpreted as a cannibalistic ceremony, as some Pagans and Jews during that time often claimed. Many of us know that leaven, which is also called "yeast," affects the bread and causes it to change. In the Bible, leaven represents sin, which causes people to change (i.e., become sinful). That is why, a full month *before the Passover,* a wife in a Jewish home begins her spring cleaning by removing all traces of leaven in her kitchen; therefore, Jesus was comparing His body to the matzo, which was *pierced, bore stripes, had no yeast/sin, and was broken for all.*

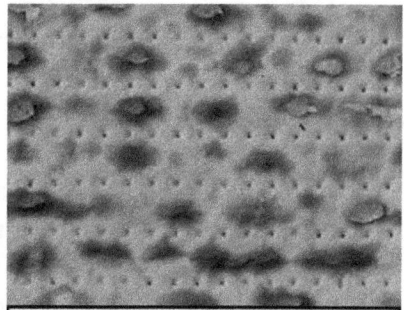

This is a section of a typical piece of Matzo Looking at it, we can see why Jesus identified it with what was about to happen to His own body.

When we eat matzo, it symbolizes that Jesus lives in us. Because Jesus was sinless, He was the fulfillment of Scripture. His willing sacrifice on the cross would deliver us from our sin. "So it is written: 'The first man Adam became a living being;' the last Adam, a life-giving spirit" (1 Corinthians 15:45, NKJV). "For as in Adam all die, even so in Christ all shall be made alive" (1 Corinthians 15:22, NKJV). Jesus was merely transferring the symbolism from the unleavened bread, which has no yeast, thus represented no sin to Himself. Likewise, the symbolism of the Passover lamb is also suggestive of the sinless life of Jesus, who had to be a spotless sacrifice in order to cover our sins once and for all. In Exodus, we read:

> The LORD said to Moses and Aaron in Egypt, "This month is to be for you the first month, the first month of your year. Tell the whole community of Israel that on the tenth day of this month each man is to take a lamb for his family, one for each household; if any household is too small for a whole lamb, they must share one with their nearest neighbor, having taken into account the number of people there are. You are to determine the amount of lamb needed in accordance with what each person will eat. The animals you choose must be year-old males *without defect*, and you may take them from the sheep or the goats" (Exodus 12:1-5, NIV, emphasis added).

The lamb offered had to be a lamb without any defect. The King James Version says, "blemish." For a human, that would mean never having sinned; only Jesus fulfilled that requirement. Some correctly argue that when eating the Passover Lamb is scriptural, drinking its blood is not. They cite Deuteronomy, which clearly states:

> Only be sure to refrain from eating blood, because blood is the source of life and you must not consume blood with the meat (Deuteronomy 12:23).

That is exactly the point Jesus is making—the blood is the life—and those who drink the wine are to remember that Jesus shed His blood to give us *everlasting life*! Alternatively, to put it another way, it is only through the blood of Jesus that we can have everlasting life. Jesus said:

> I am the way the truth and the *life*: no one comes to the Father, but by me (John 14:6, emphasis added).

Many decades later, Paul reminded the Church in the Pagan city of Corinth about the Passover observance and how it was fulfilled through Christ when he repeated Jesus' words:

> For whenever you eat this [Passover] bread and drink this [Passover] cup, you proclaim the Lord's death until He comes (1 Corinthians 11:26, NIV, bracketed clarifications mine).

Paul also observed the Feast of Unleavened Bread (not to be confused with the Passover[17]) at the Church at Philippi *before* he set sail again on his journey:

> But we sailed from Philippi after the Festival of Unleavened Bread, and five days later joined the others at Troas, where we stayed seven days (Acts 20:6, NIV).

The disciples and followers of Jesus gathered at the Temple to celebrate the "Feast of Weeks" or "Pentecost," unaware that the Church was about to be born:

> And when the day of Pentecost was fully come, they were all with one accord in one place. And suddenly there came a sound from Heaven as of a rushing, mighty wind, and it filled all the house where they were sitting. And there appeared unto them cloven tongues like as of fire, and it sat upon each of them. And they were all filled with the Holy Ghost and began to speak with other tongues, as the Spirit gave them utterance (Acts2:1-4).

Remember, although Jesus had already gone to be with the Father by that time, the Church was still observing the established Hebrew traditions

---

[17]The Feast of Unleavened Bread begins immediately following the day after Passover and lasts for seven days as opposed to the Passover, which is only one day. Although it is tied to the events of the Passover, it is not the Passover Feast. God told the children of Israel they had to be prepared to leave quickly after the Passover event occurred. To do that, they had to bake their bread without any leaven (yeast) added to the dough because it takes time for the dough to rise. Leaven is also associated with sin; it only takes a little to affect everything around it. For that reason, the Jews only eat Matza (unleavened bread) and make sure their homes are free of any yeast or yeast products during the Feast of Unleavened Bread, which begins on the evening following Passover.

and feasts. Coming together, "...they were all with one accord," which, in this case, was to celebrate the Hebrew Feast of *Shavuot* (Gk. *Pentecost*). They had no idea what was about to happen, which was the birth of the Church! Was that the end of it? Did the early Church suddenly stop celebrating Pentecost because the Church was born on that day, and because of that event, there was no longer a need to celebrate Hebrew feasts?

Presumably, all Gentile Churches (most of which were birthed through local synagogues) were aware of Pentecost because we read how the Apostle Paul prepared to celebrate it during his missionary travels throughout the Pagan world—and he did that after the birth of the Church at Pentecost:

> Paul had decided to sail past Ephesus to avoid spending time in the province of Asia, for he was in a hurry to reach Jerusalem, if possible, by *the day of Pentecost* (Acts 20:16, NIV, emphasis added).

The undeniable truth is that the disciples continued to observe the Jewish rituals of worship (as Jesus had done) in the Temple at Jerusalem long after Jesus had gone to be with the Father.

The Bible states:

> Now Peter and John went up together into the Temple at the hour of prayer, being the ninth hour (Acts 3:1).

Remember that Jesus came to fulfill the Law, not to abolish it (Matthew 5:17), so what does the Bible mean when it says that we are not under the Law anymore?

> For sin shall not have dominion over you: for you are not under the Law, but under grace. What then? Shall we sin because we are not under the Law, but under grace? God forbid! (Romans 6:14-15).

The only difference between the Old Testament Hebrew religion and the New Testament Hebrew religion is that in the New Testament, the Hebrew religion had become complete through the prophesied Messiah and the blessings promised to Abraham: "...in you shall all families of the earth be blessed" (Genesis 12:3b). With the arrival of Jesus, the Gentiles would be allowed to be grafted into Israel's covenant with God (Romans

11:17, 19, 24). The old kosher (e.g., meets the standards of traditional Jewish dietary restrictions) food laws were canceled (Acts 10:12-16), as well as the rest of 613 Laws (Romans 6:14); however, the Ten Commandments are still to be used as a guidepost. For example, reflect for a moment why the Ten Commandments are still important, even though Christians are no longer under those Laws. Exodus 20:13 tells us, "Thou shalt not kill." In the original Hebrew, the word translated into English for "kill" is the word *ratsach* (Heb. תִּרְצָח), which is more closely aligned with the word "murder."

We have the same civil law against murder. I am not a murderer, and I even loathe to cause someone pain, much less kill them; therefore, the laws against murder would not apply to me. However, for someone who is hot-tempered and wantonly violent, even to the point of desiring to murder someone, then this law would apply.

The same is true with the rest of the Ten Commandments. If we are in Christ and truly desire to please Him, then there is no need for the Law because it does not apply to us. On the other hand, if we continually break one or more Laws just because we "feel like it," then it is obvious we are not a true follower of Christ. By unrepentantly continuing to do the things the Ten Commandments warn us not to do, we place ourselves back under the Law. Make no mistake; if we flaunt our sin in the face of God's Law, then there will be consequences to pay—if not in this life—then in the other! We must also be careful not to confuse the Law with the feasts of the Hebrew calendar because they are not thought of in the same way.

As for observing all the Jewish feasts, surely, the disciples who studied directly under Jesus knew how the Church should conduct its worship services and what feasts—if any—the Church should observe. Certainly, the Apostle Paul, who was the apostle to the Gentiles (Romans 11:13; Galatians 2:8)—and warned them against the Judaizers[18]—would not

---

[18]The term "Judaizers" is not often referred to in the New Testament (Galatians 2:14), but is inferred because some were told that obeying the Torah (Jewish Written Law) of Moses, along with circumcision, was part of their salvation; however, that is an example of works. Christians are not saved by works, but by faith. Paul went against such teachings, but in no way does that mean the Jews' observances of the holy feast days (including Christ, the disciples and Paul) were to no longer be observed.

41

have observed any Jewish feasts if such observances could be misconstrued as Judaizing the Gentiles who joined the faith. It is undeniable that in the first century Church, all of the seven were included as a part of Messianic worship.

The following chart shows the seven Levitical feasts in the Old and New Testaments and how some of them were fulfilled through the ministry, death, burial, and resurrection of Jesus. It is anticipated that those prophecies, which have not yet been completed, will be fulfilled through Christ at some point in the future.

JESUS WAS REVEALED THROUGHOUT THE LEVITICAL FEASTS

Table 1: The Levitical Feasts of Israel As Found in the Old Testament

APPLICATION OF THE LEVITICAL FEASTS IN THE OLD TESTAMENT	JESUS REVEALED IN THE LEVITICAL FEASTS IN THE NEW TESTAMENT
PASSOVER The Passover is celebrated on Nisan 14 (Jewish calendar). That was when God delivered Israel from the angel of death and Egyptian slavery; a sin offering of a male lamb is to be sacrificed (Deuteronomy	John said, "Behold the Lamb of God who takes away the sin of the world" (John 1:29). Jesus was crucified the day of the Passover preparation (John 19:14). He gave us eternal life (John 3:15).
UNLEAVENED BREAD And on the fifteenth day of the same month is the Feast of Unleavened Bread unto the LORD: seven days you must eat unleavened bread (Leviticus 23:6). NOTE: Leaven (yeast)	Jesus' life was without sin [leaven]: "For He [God the Father] had made Him [Jesus the Son] to be sin for us, who knew no sin; that we might be made the righteousness of God in Him" (2 Corinthians 5:21, bracketed clarifications mine).
FIRSTFRUITS (Leviticus 23:10) The first fruits of one's labor are dedicated to God. This cele-brates the Fall Festival with the first fruits of the harvest. After the first fruits, many more will follow.	Jesus was the FIRSTFRUITS of those who died and will be raised to life again through His death, burial, and resurrection. "But now is Christ risen from the dead, and became the first fruits of them that slept" (1 Corinthians 15:20).

FEAST OF WEEKS (Heb. Shavuot; Gk. *Pentecost*) (Leviticus 23:16) This feast begins 50 days after the Feast of Unleavened Bread.	Before Jesus went to be with the Father, He promised His disciples they would be baptized by the Holy Spirit (Acts 1:5), and then He ascended into Heaven (Acts 9). Days later, on Pentecost (Acts2:2-3), the Church was born, which is a good reason to celebrate it.
TRUMPETS (Leviticus 23:24) This is the first feast of the fall season.	Many associate this feast with the Lord's return and the Rapture. "For the Lord Himself shall descend from Heaven with a shout, with the voice of the archangel, and with the trump(et) of God: and the dead in Christ shall rise first" (1 Thessalonians 4:16), and "...We shall not all sleep, but we shall all be changed, In a moment, in the twinkling of an eye, at the last trump" (1 Corinthians 15:51-52a).
DAY OF ATONEMENT (Yom Kippur) Two similar male goats are brought before the high priest. Both have the sins of the people placed on their heads. One will escape death; the other will be a sacrifice for the sins of all the people of the congregation (Leviticus 16:5-10). "They will look on Me whom they pierced. Yes, they will mourn for Him as one mourns for *his* only *son,* and grieve for Him as one grieves for a firstborn" (Zechariah 12:10b, NIV).	With Jesus, instead of two goats bearing strong similarities, there were two humans also bearing strong similarities: both males, both Judeans, both named Jesus. Pilot, offered the criminal, Jesus Barabbas, to be punished, but the High priest said to release him and chose the other Jesus because He referred to God as His Father. One would be a scapegoat with sin on his head who would be set free, but like the other goat, the High priest chose Jesus to be the one to shed blood, although unknowingly, also for the atone-ment of our sins.

TABERNACLES (Leviticus 23: 34) The Lord promised His people that He would, one day, tabernacle (dwell) with them. "In that day," says the LORD, "I will assemble the lame, I will gather the outcast And those whom I have afflicted...And the outcast a strong nation; So the LORD will reign over them in Mount Zion From now on, even forever" (Micah 4:6-7, NKJV).	Jesus tabernacle/dwelt among us. "And the Word became flesh and dwelt [tabernacle] among us, and we beheld His glory, the glory as of the only begotten of the Father, full of grace and truth" (John 1:14, bracketed clarification mine NKJV). We look forward to the day when Jesus will return and again tabernacle among His people.

JESUS WAS ALSO REVEALED THROUGH THE
POST-LEVITICAL FEASTS

The Feast of Hanukkah is a non-biblical holiday that was established between the writings of the Old and New Testaments. It is a very joyous time of year and is celebrated alongside Christmas (also a non-biblical feast or holiday); yet, despite the fact that Hanukkah was not established in the Old or the New Testaments, but rather during the period in between, Jesus celebrated Hanukkah with His disciples just as He did the other feasts of Israel.

Table 2: The Post-Levitical Feast of Hanukkah (Dedication) also known as the "Festival of Lights"

APPLICATION OF HANUKKAH (FEAST OF DEDICATION) KNOWN AS "THE FESTIVAL OF LIGHTS" INTER-TESTAMENTAL PERIOD	JESUS REVEALED IN HANUKKAH (FEAST OF DEDICATION) KNOWN AS "THE FESTIVAL OF LIGHTS" NEW TESTAMENT
During the intertestamental period, the Greek-Seleucid ruler, Antiochus IV Epiphanes, attacked the Southern Kingdom of Judah. The small, orthodox, Maccabee family, bravely fought and defeated the powerful Antiochus. After Judas Maccabeus' victory, when the Maccabees went to rededicate the Temple—the same Temple where Antiochus had sacrificed a pig and thereby desecrated the holy sanctuary—there was not enough oil to light the candelabra. Still, the small amount of oil on hand miraculously lasted for a full eight days instead of only one.	Jesus' involvement in and through Hanukkah: "Then came the Festival of Dedication at Jerusalem. It was winter, and Jesus was in the Temple courts walking in Solomon's Colonnade" (John 10:22-23, emphasis added, NIV). We can see Jesus represented on this feast day, too, throughout several Scriptures as the "Light of the World." "Then spoke Jesus again unto them, saying, 'I am the light of the world: he that follows me shall not walk in darkness, but shall have the light of life' " (John 8:12; John 9:5; Matthew 5:14).

After the first century and the passing of Jesus' disciples—Peter, John, Paul, and the other Founding Church Fathers—things Jewish were not only discouraged but were gradually purged from the Church.

We have seen how Jesus' sacrifice on the cross was foreshadowed by the Passover, but while one sacrificial lamb could not atone for the entire Hebrew congregation because it was relegated to individual families, the children of Israel had another sacrificial tradition, which consisted of one blood sacrifice (like Jesus would become) for the whole nation. That sacrifice occurred on Israel's holiest holiday, Yom Kippur (also known as the "Day of Atonement") when the High priest took two identical goats; one would be a blood sacrifice, and the other one would be set free. The first time that ritual was performed was during the time Moses' brother, Aaron, was the High priest. In the Bible, we read the story of when God ordained Aaron to do the following:

> [You]...shall take from the congregation of the children of Israel two kids of the goats as a sin offering, and one ram as a burnt offering.... He shall take the two goats and present them before the LORD *at* the door of the tabernacle of meeting. Then Aaron shall cast lots for the two goats: one lot for the LORD and the other lot for the scapegoat. And Aaron shall bring the goat on which the LORD's lot fell, and offer it *as* a sin offering. But the goat on which the lot fell to be the scapegoat shall be presented alive before the LORD, to make atonement upon it, *and* to let it go as the scapegoat into the wilderness (Leviticus 16:5-10, NKJV, bracketed clarification mine).

The two goats had to be alike, but unlike the Passover Lamb, each goat carried sin on its head for all the people. The high priest chose which one would then be killed and sent to God for the sins of the people, while the other goat was turned loose in the desert.

"Okay," you might say, "but just taking another sacrificial holiday and substituting Jesus, or anyone else for that matter, as the stand-in sacrifice does not mean that Jesus had anything to do with a pair of twin goats who were sacrificed. Why should we believe this has anything to do with Jesus?" That is a great question and to answer it, we are providing some background information.

When Abraham was preparing to sacrifice his son, Isaac, God provided a ram as a sacrificial substitute in Isaac's place. Likewise, instead of one animal for the sin of one person, which would soon become ineffective because we all continue to sin, God offered His Son as a sacrifice, but not just for one person or one family. When Jesus' time came, He would atone for the sins of everyone, just like the goat chosen as the blood sacrifice between those two identical goats on the Day of Atonement.

The day when Jesus was brought before the Roman governor, Pontius Pilate, he could find no wrong in Him and, therefore, wanted

Jesus to be set free. At that time, there was a Passover tradition[19] that allowed one prisoner to be set free. Pilate reasoned that if he could offer the people a choice between Jesus and a vicious Zealot, the people would jump at the chance to take the lesser of two evils; Pilate thought they would choose Jesus. He stated:

> But you have a custom that I should release someone to you at the Passover. Do you, therefore, want me to release to you the King of the Jews? Then they all cried again, saying, "Not this Man, but Barabbas!" Now Barabbas was a robber (John 18:39-40, NKJV).

Pilate must have been surprised and very frustrated with their response. Thinking the people in the courtyard might take pity on Him if they saw Him broken and bloodied, Pilate had Jesus removed and brutally beaten. To Pilate's surprise, when the soldiers brought Jesus back, the chief priest and the people—who followed the chief priest's lead—cried out against Jesus yelling, "Crucify Him, crucify Him!" Pilate then washed his hands of the matter and turned Jesus over to the chief priest and the Roman soldiers to be crucified (John 19:1-7).

Yom Kippur, Two Identical Goats, Two Identical Men, and the Cross

Now we have a troublesome question concerning how Jesus and Barabbas, as the two goats of Yom Kippur, also known as the "Day of Atonement," are identical. As we showed in table one, (1) both were believed to have been from the tribe of Judah; (2) both were males; (3) both were under arrest—Barabbas for being an insurrectionist and a thief and Jesus for claiming to be the Son of God, and (4) they had something else identical as well.

We know Jesus claimed He was the Son of God, and He often referred to

---

[19]The Mishnah (Jewish oral tradition committed to written form and completed around 190 A.D.) records, "they may slaughter the Passover lamb for one...whom they have promised to bring out of prison," William L. Lane. *The Gospel According to Mark, the English Text with Introduction, Exposition, and Notes*, 2nd ed. (Grand Rapids: Eerdmans, 1974), 553. Regarding a prisoner being released at the Passover, Lane observes: "There is however, a parallel in Roman law which indicates that an imperial magistrate could pardon and acquit individual prisoners in response to the shouts of the populace."

God as His "Father" or "Abba;" therefore, Jesus became known as the "Son of the Father." Jews considered the title of YAWA (Jehovah) to be too sacred to be pronounced, so they referred to God as "HaShem," meaning "the Name" or as Jesus referred to YAWA many times throughout Scripture, "Father."[20] As for Barabbas, many people are unaware that the name Barabbas in Hebrew is בר אבא, which is "bar" (son) and "Abba" (father) or "son of the father." When the gospel writers translated Barabbas into Greek, they wrote it as Βαραββᾶς, ᾶ, ὁ, which we pronounce as buh-RAB-uhss in English; yet his whole name in Hebrew was actually ישוע בר אבא or Yeshua bar Abba—literally, Yeshua son of the Father. Why was this important connection to Yom Kippur and the twin goats changed? We will examine how this passage came to be revised when we look at one of the early anti-Semitic church fathers by the name of Origen.

Christ's name was also Yeshua, and He too was known as "Yeshua Bar Abba" or "Jesus Son of the Father!" You will not see this comparison revealed, except possibly in some obscure biblical footnote, if at all.

"A key part of the Day of Atonement liturgy at the Tabernacle and Temple was a sin offering involving two goats. They were chosen to be as similar as possible to one another."[21] In the case of Jesus and Barabbas, as we read earlier, both were identical. As we previously explained, during Yom Kippur, there was one goat with sin on its head, which was released. He was called the "scapegoat." The other goat, also bearing the sins of the people on its head, was chosen by the high priest as a blood sacrifice for the sins of the people.

---

[20]Some estimate there are 449 Scriptures referring to YAWA as Jesus' father.

[21]Julia Blum, "TWO GOATS OF YOM KIPPUR," Biblical Hebrew and Holy Land Studies Blog - IIBS.com. 13 Oct. 2016, "The tradition tells us that during the Second Temple period [530 B.C.-70 A.D.] these two goats had to be purchased at the same time and for the same price: they had to be almost identical in appearance and value (bracketed clarification added)." Julia Blum is a teacher and an author of several books on biblical topics. She teaches two biblical courses at the Israel Institute of Biblical Studies: "Discovering the Hebrew Bible" and "Jewish Background of the New Testament." She also writes Hebrew insights for those courses.

And Now, the Rest of the Story:

Like the two sacrificial goats during Yom Kippur, we have one man named "Jesus" who was a criminal with sin on his head, and like the scapegoat, he escaped Roman law and was released. The other man, also known as "Jesus," was sinless and not guilty of any crime; but was the one chosen by the high priest to be killed—and just like the other innocent sacrificial goat chosen by the high priest during Yom Kippur, Jesus also became a blood sacrifice for the atonement of the people's sins.

When arguing that Jesus should be put to death:

> "... Caiaphas, who was high priest that year, spoke up: 'Do you not realize that it is better for you that one man die for the people?' " (John 11:50a).

How ironic that Caiaphas made that statement without even realizing the significance of what he was saying. Jesus was bruised[22] not only for their iniquities but for *our* sins as well (Isaiah 53:7; 1 Peter 2:24). Inexcusably, this strange parallel between the Day of Atonement and its connection to the Day of Jesus' Atonement for our sins—on the cross—would be forever purged from the Church's memory by Origen in the third century, which we will read about later.

The purpose of sharing how the early Church continued celebrating the Hebrew festivals is not intended to suggest that the Church should return to observing them, although there would be nothing wrong in doing that. As the Apostle Paul traveled throughout the Pagan world, it would not have been uncommon for him to be on the receiving end of anti-Semitism; on the other hand, he also had to deal with the Judaizers. It is not a far stretch to imagine that some of the Gentile converts criticized Paul and the other Messianic Jews because they continued to keep the Jewish feasts and traditions, which might have caused some of the Jewish converts to feel intimidated. Those conflicting viewpoints most likely created a lot of discourse in the Gentile Churches. In the face of such criticism, it became necessary for Paul to intercede and write to the

---

[22]"Bruised" is a euphemism for "being killed." One prophetic example directly pointing to this event is in Genesis 3:15.

Gentile and Jewish converts with the following clarification:

> Therefore do not let anyone judge you by what you eat or drink or with regard to a religious festival, a New Moon celebration or a Sabbath day [Jewish feast days are considered Sabbath days] (Colossians 2:16, bracketed clarification mine).

New moon celebrations are tied directly to the Hebrew calendar and the feast days connected to them. If the Messianic Jews, like the Apostle Paul, wanted to continue celebrating the feasts of Israel, so be it, but if the Gentile converts were uncomfortable in doing so, they could abstain from participating. As we stated earlier—in the first century—the question was, "How can a Gentile become a Christian?"

Replacement theology has become commonplace. It is revisionist history that was taught by many of the theologians the Church held in high esteem, and many continue to do so today.

Ignatius

Ignatius was a Pagan convert to Christianity who was born in Syria sometime after the death and resurrection of Jesus (around 35 to 50 A.D.) and martyred somewhere around 98 to 117 A.D.[23] He was the first to use the phrase "Catholic (i.e., universal) Church"[24] and later became the bishop of Antioch where the term "Christian" was first used (Acts 11:26). Ignatius lived the majority of his life in the first century, His dislike of Jews and their feasts were characteristic of many Pagans and even some of his fellow Pagan converts. Unfortunately, Ignatius' resentment of the Jews was also a harbinger of things to come. So, it was in the second century—after the passing of the Jewish Fathers of the Faith—when anti-Semitism, through the influence of Pagan converts, really began to take hold.

---

[23]Philip Schaff, D.D., LL.D. and Henry Wace, D.D., *Nicene and Post-Nicene Fathers: A Select Library of the Christian Church, Second Series,* vol. 1 (Hendrickson Publishers, 2004. Ft. Nt.), 169. According to Clement of Rome, after Ignatius was martyred, Heros became the Bishop of Antioch in the tenth year of Trajan (107 A.D.).

[24]Herbert Thurston, the Catholic Encyclopedia, vol. 3 (New York: Robert Appleton Company, 1908). Web 28 June 2016.

Ignatius was one of the first to declare that it was forbidden for Christians to participate in the Passover alongside the Jews because they participated in the murder of Jesus.[25]

Jesus never accused the Jews of His impending doom:

> Therefore, does My Father love me, because *I lay down my life*, that I might take it again. *No man takes it from Me,* but *I lay it down of myself*. I have power to lay it down, and I have power to take it again. This commandment have I received of my Father (John 10:17-18, emphases added).

Could it be that Jesus was a liar? Of course not! Jesus went to the cross voluntarily. He could have easily disappeared if He wanted to, just like the time when His enemies grabbed Him to prepare to stone Him, and He walked through their midst unseen (Luke 4:29-30), or the time after His resurrection when He suddenly appeared in the midst of His followers, even though the door was locked (John 20:19).

As for the Passover, if anything, Jesus made it clear that the Passover would be an ongoing observance. He even modified the Passover for us. (He was considered the fulfillment of the Hebrew Scriptures and was never intended as the founder of another separate religion):

> When the hour came, Jesus and His apostles reclined at the table. And He said to them, "I have eagerly desired to eat this Passover with you before I suffer. For I tell you, I will not eat it again until it finds fulfillment in the kingdom of God" (Luke 22:14-16, NIV).

"Eat it again?" How could Jesus do that if He was putting a stop to the Passover? The answer is simple. Jesus did not cancel the Passover; on the contrary, He was re-emphasizing its importance as a feast, a feast that He looked forward to sharing with His disciples. Even so, it makes more sense that Jesus was referring to His impending crucifixion when He said, "I will not eat it [the Passover meal] again until it [the Passover] finds fulfillment in the kingdom of God" (bracketed clarifications mine). Jesus did not stop there and made it crystal clear to His disciples that He would, at some

---

[25]Ibid. 119., Chapter 14: *The Epistle of Ignatius to the Philippians.*

point in the future, once again share the Passover Seder with them:

> After taking the cup, He gave thanks and said, "Take this and divide it among you. For I tell you I will not drink again from the fruit of the vine until the kingdom of God comes."

> And He took bread, gave thanks and broke it, and gave it to them, saying, "This is my body given for you; do this in remembrance of me" (Luke 22:17-20, NIV).

Note: When Jesus celebrated His last Passover meal in the first century, and He broke the unleavened (no yeast) bread (matzah) saying, "Do this in remembrance of me," He was instituting a new Passover revision and not a new type of meal observance. On the other hand, the commemoration of the Last Supper in church (Holy Communion) throughout the year is, by no means, to be avoided and is indeed beneficial for Christians.

Another reason we know that Jesus meant for us to observe the wine and breaking of matzo as His blood and body, specifically during the Passover Seder, was because He intended for the Passover celebration to be continued after He went to be with the Father. How do we know this? We know because His disciples, including Paul, the apostle to the Gentiles, continued observing the Passover meal every year, long after Jesus was gone.[26]

What was and remains so important about the bread used at Passover? The unleavened bread had no leaven, which symbolized sin. The unleavened bread at the Passover Seder represented Jesus' body, which likewise, had no sin, yet bore stripes and piercings. As for the wine served at Passover, each of the four cups also had a meaning: (1) Cup of Sanctification; (2) Cup of Deliverance; (3) Cup of Redemption, and (4) Cup of Restoration. It is the third Cup of Redemption, which now signifies the blood Jesus shed as the means for our redemption (Matthew 26:27-39).

Sometime after the death, burial, and resurrection of Jesus, the Apostle Paul, who was ministering in the Pagan city of Corinth, specifically told us to be observant of the Passover:

---

[26]Acts 20:6.

Your boasting is not good. Don't you know that a little yeast leavens the whole batch of dough? Get rid of the old yeast, so that you may be a new unleavened batch—as you really are. For Christ, our Passover lamb, has been sacrificed. Therefore *let us keep the festival,* not with the old bread leavened with malice and wickedness, but with the unleavened bread of sincerity and truth (1 Corinthians 5:6-8, NIV, emphasis added).

As far as the Jews killing Jesus, it appears that Ignatius not only misunderstood the observance of Passover, but was either ignorant or ignored Jesus' proclamation that no man takes His life from Him, but that He would lay it down Himself (John 10:17b-18a). Remember, Jesus had to die for every one of us because we all sin and fall short of the glory of God (Romans 3:23).

As the number of Gentiles grew—the Jews became the minority—and as a consequence, they were outcast by the Gentiles. Many Gentiles based their belief on the idea God was finished with the Jews—in part—by having observed the destruction of the Jewish Temple in 70 A.D. by Titus.

At the same time, Titus captured and killed over one million Jews and captured 100,000 more who were scattered throughout the Roman Empire, where they had managed to survive.

Second Century

Ironically, the Question of the Second Century Was, "Could Jews Become Christians?"

During the years of 115-117 A.D., many Jews were more motivated to throw off their Roman yoke, so they revolted once again against Rome. However, that time the Jews revolted not only in Judea but throughout the Roman Empire—from Cyrene (near present-day Libya) and Egypt in the west—to sections of Mesopotamia (in the Tigris/Euphrates river system area)—to the east, including the island of Cyprus near Turkey in the Mediterranean Sea. That revolt is known as the "*Kitos War*," which is the Hebrew version of "Quietus," the last name of the Roman general, Lusius Quietus. During that revolt, hundreds of thousands of Greeks, Romans, and Jews were killed or murdered. The Jewish uprising continued, so in 135 A.D. the Roman Emperor, Hadrian, completely destroyed Judea and—as an insult— renamed all of what was once Israel,

"Syrio-Palæstina" in memory of Israel's ancient and by then extinct adversaries, the Philistines.

Irenaeus

Irenaeus (125-202 A.D.), Bishop of Lugdunum in Gaul and a disciple of Polycarp—who was a disciple of Jesus' apostle, John, who was also known as "St. John the Revelator" because it was he who wrote the book of Revelation also known by its Latin name the Apocalypse. Irenaeus wrote in his book, *Against Heresies,* that St. John's Revelation "was seen not very long ago, almost in our own generation, at the close of the reign of [Roman Emperor] Domitian" (bracketed clarification mine).[27] That would place the writing of Book of Revelation containing the End of the Age prophecies around 96 A.D. It would be good to remember this when we study in Chapter 4 about a man named "Alcasar" who developed the theory of Preterism, which is a philosophy regulating most End Times prophecy to the first-century when he alleges that Jesus returned spiritually to begin His millennial reign on earth in 70 A.D. The obvious problem with that is those prophecies were given a quarter of a century *after* the events of 70 A.D.

In 132 A.D., a messianic figure named, "Shimon (Simon) Bar Kochba," began another failed three-year revolt against Rome in Judea. The result was the defeat of Kochba's forces, with over half a million Jews killed and thousands sold into slavery; many were dispersed throughout the empire. Judaism was no longer recognized as an acceptable religion and, therefore, its practice was outlawed in Rome. (At that time, Christianity was still considered a branch of Judaism).

Judeo-Christian Revisionist History Began with Rome and Institutionalized with Emperor Hadrian

With the onset of the second century, relationships between the ethnic Jews and Gentiles began to change. In the words of the Reverend John

---

[27]Alexander Roberts, James Donaldson, A. Cleveland Coxe, Allan Menzies, Ernest Cushing Richardson, and Bernhard Pick. *The Ante-Nicene Fathers: Translations of the Writings of the Fathers down to A.D. 325.,* vol. V. (Buffalo: Christian Literature, 1885), Chapter 30, Verse 4.

Pawlikowski, Professor of Social Ethics at the Catholic Theological Union in Chicago, Illinois:

> In the second century and beyond, many of the principal Fathers of the Church began to write of Jews as a "rejected people" who were doomed to a life of marginality and misery. Jews were to wander the world as a "despised people." This image persisted in Christian preaching, art and popular teachings for centuries to come. In certain countries, it often led to civil and political discrimination against Jews and in some instances to physical attacks on Jews, which resulted in death. While some popes, bishops, and Christian princes stepped up to protect Jews, they were clearly a minority. It was only in the mid-twentieth century that the Catholic Church and many Protestant denominations issued major statements repudiating this anti-Judaic theology and began a process of constructive Christian-Jewish interaction.

It was during the second century in 135 A.D., when the Roman Emperor, Hadrian, destroyed Judea and renamed the area "Syria-Palæstina" in remembrance of Israel's old—and by then—extinct enemy, the Philistines. Hadrian built a temple on the then-vacant Temple Mount to the god Jupiter.[28] That undoubtedly contributed to the false myth God was finished with the Jews and reinforced the belief Hadrian was justified in what he did because God used him to destroy those hated Jewish "Christ-killers!"

Because of ethnic pride and the desire to feel superior to those *arrogant Jews*—who claimed to be God's chosen people—more and more Gentiles enthusiastically bought into the false claims the Jews had somehow permanently lost God's favor. It is a historical fact that once a country has been conquered and its people dispersed—if they don't return to reconquer their land by the third generation—that country is lost forever! When pondering why God would allow such devastation to befall His chosen people, the Gentile world wrongly assumed it was because the Jews killed Jesus.

---

[28]Cassius Dio (164-235 A.D.), Roman senator and historian in his book *ROMAN HISTORY*, 69.12 (Cassius. *Roman History*. Harvard Univ. Press, 2001.).

What made matters even worse was that the Gentile Fathers of the Church also exposed their ignorance and bigotry by allowing that teaching to be promoted.

THE FIRST BLOOD MOON TETRAD OF THE
CHRISTIAN ERA (162-163 A.D.)

On the evening of 161 A.D., the Roman Emperor, Marcus Aurelius, began the horrendous persecutions of Jews and Christians. During that same year, the Parthians invaded Armenia, a Roman province. Following shortly on the heels of those events in 162-163 A.D.—just 27 years after the events of 135 A.D., once again, Rome devastated Judea. The generation who saw that devastation was also able to witness a biblical Tetrad (four blood moons falling on Hebrew feast days). With the onset of those blood moons and its solar eclipse, it appeared as though God had not forgotten His people, the Jews, and was retaliating against Rome for the destruction of the Southern Kingdom of Judah and the accompanying great diaspora (dispersion) of Jews throughout the Roman world. Almost simultaneously, a great plague occurred that wiped out nearly 10% of the entire Roman population.

Tertullian

Tertullian (155-240 A.D.) lived in the (Roman) African province of Carthage and is credited with being the first Christian author to produce an extensive body of Latin Christian literature. In his thesis, *An Answer to the Jews*, which he wrote toward the end of the second century in 198 A.D., Tertullian focused on all the negative renderings of Hebrew history that are recorded in the Scriptures.[29] While no one can refute Tertullian's creative imagination, which he combines with formidable insight and observational prose, we have to read Tertullian with discretion and view his writings with a cautious eye toward those erroneous, proof texts he used to bolster his equally flawed conclusions.

Tertullian began with his observation of God's promise to Abraham. "He

---

[29]Alexander Roberts, D.D., James Donaldson, LL.D., eds, *Ante-Nicene Fathers*, *vol. 3, Tertullian, An Answer to the Jews* (Peabody: Hendrickson Publ., 2004), 151.

promised to Abraham that 'in his seed should be blest all nations of the earth...' " (Genesis 22:18), and out of the womb of Rebekah, "two nations were about to proceed" (Genesis 25:23).

Tertullian continued:

>...of course those of the Jews, that is, of Israel; and of the Gentiles, that is, ours.[30]

From conception, the Bible tells us that the twins in Rebecca's womb were two nations (Genesis 25:23)—one child being the father of the Israelites and the other one a Gentile; but when Tertullian referred to the twins, he did so with a broad brush. He painted himself and all non-Jews as being related to each other through Esau; therefore, according to him, all Gentiles are the same kin.

The first male twin born to Rebekah was not Jacob (who God later renamed "Israel"), as Tertullian would have us believe, but Esau, who later became the father of the Edomites (Genesis 36:9). Although they were a Semitic tribe like the Hebrews, his descendants were Gentiles and Pagans through their religious beliefs.

By using an old geometry saying—"a square is always a rectangle, but a rectangle is not always a square," we will revisit Tertullian's argument about the two nations who Rebekah gave birth to by contrasting his questionable conclusion that all Gentile nations come from Esau. Likewise, it can be said that while the Edomites became Pagans, not all Pagans became Edomites. Tertullian, a Carthaginian,[31] would still have all of us (Gentiles and Edomites) be against the Jews.

Tertullian cleverly changed the meaning of Scripture when he commented on his proof texts regarding God's revelations, where he cited Genesis 25:23 when God tells Rebekah:

>"Two nations *are* in your womb, Two peoples shall be separated

---

[30]Ibid.

[31]Robert L. Wilken, "Tertullian," *Encyclopedia Britannica Online*, n.p. Web. 11 Nov. 2015. Tertullian was born to a Pagan family in Cartage in 155 A.D. and died there in 222 A.D. His father might have been a Roman centurion.

from your body; *One* people shall be stronger [greater] than the other, And the older shall serve the younger [lesser]" (Genesis 25:23, NKJV, bracketed clarifications mine).

Now we will look at how Tertullian revised the Scripture in order to use it as a proof text. Tertullian wrote:

Accordingly, since the *people or nation* of the Jews is anterior [Jacob being the first out] in time and "greater" through the grace of primary favor in the Law.

Because the Jews were first [in Tertullian's misreading of the birth order in Scripture], they should thereby be the ones who normally inherit the blessings through the undeserved favor given to them by the law of inheritance (bracketed clarification mine).

At that point, Tertullian proposed his allegorical stretch as he incorrectly continued to insist that Esau—who Tertullian identified as representing the future Christian Gentiles—was *born last*:

...whereas ours [we Gentiles] is understood to be "less" in the age of times beyond doubt, through the edict of the divine utterance...

Tertullian argued that Esau, who he identified with the Gentile Church, should be the greater because he mistakenly believed Jacob was the first-born and the oldest. (Traditionally, it was the oldest son who inherited the family estate.) Based on that incorrect birth order, observe how Tertullian built his replacement theology case:

... the *prior* and "greater" people—that is, the Jewish Jacob who became known as Israel must necessarily serve the "less;" and the "less" people—that—is, the Christian[s] who by now can only be Gentiles—overcome the "greater" (i.e., the Jews).[32]

There are two problems with this argument: First, Jacob was not Jewish, but a Hebrew. It was one of Jacob's sons, by the name of Judah, who was the patriarch of the tribe of Jews. Second, it was Esau who was born first,

---

[32]Alexander Roberts, D.D., James Donaldson, LL.D., eds, *Ante-Nicene Fathers, vol. 3, An Answer to the Jews,* 151.

not Jacob, which was also misinterpreted by Tertullian; consequently, he made the false argument that Jacob was the "greater who would serve the lesser" because Jacob was the coveted "firstborn" who would inherit all the blessings and fortunes of his father, Isaac. This is a false conclusion on Tertullian's part because the Bible teaches just the opposite:

> And when her [Rebekah's] days to be delivered were fulfilled, behold, there were twins in her womb.
>
> And the first came out red, all over like a hairy garment; and they called his name Esau.
>
> And after that came his brother out, and his hand took hold on Esau's heel; and his name was called Jacob: and Isaac [their father] was threescore years old when she bore them (Genesis 25:24-26, bracketed clarifications mine).

We cannot find anywhere in Scripture where it is even hinted that the descendants of Jacob would ever serve the descendants of Esau (Jacob representing the Hebrew tribes, which include the Jews), and Esau substituted for all Gentiles (including the Gentile Church), with the possible exception of a brief interlude found in Genesis 33:5 and 15.[33] That is a pure fabrication out of an *eisegetical* (reading into Scripture something that is not there) whole cloth!

There are many instances where Tertullian took liberty in his interpretation of Scripture. Another example of Tertullian's inaccuracy is the passage found in Chapter 9 in his book, *An Answer to the Jews*, where he wrote:

> So too, Egypt is something understood to mean the whole world in

---

[33]In order to appease Jacob's brother, Esau, Jacob patronized his brother with flattery: "Then Esau looked up and saw the women and children, 'Who are these with you?' he asked. Jacob answered, 'They are the children God has graciously given *your servant*' " (Genesis 33:5, NIV, bracketed clarification mine, emphasis added). Again, in verse 15, Esau said, "Then let me leave some of my men with you." "But why do that?" Jacob asked. "Just let me find favor in the eyes of *my lord*" (Genesis 33:15, NIV, emphasis added). After that, the brothers went their own ways (Genesis 33:16-17) but were only temporarily reunited again by the death of their father, Isaac (Genesis 35:29).

that prophet [prophecy], on the count of superstition and malediction [curse or hex]. So, again, Babylon, in our own *gospel of John*, is a figure of the city Rome, as being equally great and proud of her sway, and triumphant over the saints (bracketed clarifications mine, emphasis added).

The truth is that John never mentioned Babylon in his gospel. Tertullian must have been referring to the Book of Revelation—which was given to us by John—wherein there is a person he referred to as the "Whore of Babylon" who sat on the city of seven hills (Revelation 17:5, 9), which is understood by biblical scholars to be Rome.

Many have used the example of *allegorical* reasoning (i.e., double meaning) developed by Tertullian, including Augustine. It continued through Luther and Calvin's time right up to today. It is important to realize, when we allow for more than one meaning to a verse of Scripture, we fall into the trap—which Bible critics claim—we can make the Bible say anything we want. Down through the ages, the Orthodox Churches have allegorized away the special relationship God proclaimed in His Word toward Israel to nullify His special relationship with the Jews. God means what He says and says what He means; there is no room for loopholes.

With the Protestant Reformation of the Church, replacement theology prevailed when other problematic Catholic doctrines did not—much to the shame of the Protestant Church. It resulted in tyranny and bloodshed being inflicted on innocent Jews.

It is believed by most biblical scholars that John's Revelation was written toward the end of the first century based, in part, on the observations of Irenaeus when he stated that the imprisonment on the island of Patmos was "toward the end of Domitian's reign" (81-96 A.D.). Irenaeus (120-202 A.D.) was a disciple of Polycarp of Smyrna, who not only knew the Apostle John but was his disciple as well; so who in the second century—other than Polycarp and Irenaeus—would be better able to pass down firsthand information regarding the teachings of Christ and His disciples and how they lived?

Another writing of the second century was a work known as the *Shepherd* of Hermas,[34] wherein the author warned the Church about "the great tribulation that was coming" at some future point, contrary to the sixteenth century Roman Catholic Church's revision of the Book of Revelation. We will explore that in greater detail in Chapter 4.

Meanwhile, we know that the early Church Fathers were looking for a future return of Christ, as documented by the early Church writings, including a publication known as the *Teaching of the Twelve Apostles*. The work is sometimes referred to as the *Didache* (Gk. Διδαχή), written toward the end of the first century or the beginning of the second century. In *Didache XVI*, we read this future-looking passage:

> Watch for your life's sake. Let not your lamps be quenched, nor your loins unloosed; but be ye ready, for ye know not the hour in which our Lord comes.... *For in the last days* false prophets and corrupters shall be multiplied, and the sheep shall be turned into wolves, and love shall be turned into hate; *for when lawlessness increases, they shall hate and persecute and betray one another, and then shall appear the world-deceiver as Son of God, and shall do signs and wonders, and the earth shall be delivered into his hands, and he shall do iniquitous [wicked, sinful] things which have never yet come to pass since the beginning....* And then shall appear the signs of the truth; first, the sign of an out-spreading in Heaven; then the sign of the sound of the trumpet; and the third, the resurrection of the dead; yet not of all, but as it is said: The Lord shall come and all His saints with Him. Then shall the world see the Lord coming upon the clouds of Heaven (bracketed clarification mine, emphases added).

Around that time—at the turn of the first century (the years immediately before and immediately after 100 A.D.)—John, the apostle, passed away. It was in the middle of that second century when our misguided acquaintance, Tertullian, was born (155 A.D.) who, despite some of his inaccurate interpretations of Scripture as we just read, became

---

[34]Robert Davidson and Alfred Robert Clare Leaney, *Biblical Criticism* (Harmondsworth: Penguin, 1970), 230. The *Shepherd of Hermas* was a Christian literary work of the late first or mid-second century, which was considered a part of Scripture by many Christians and Church fathers of the time, including Irenaeus, Tertullian, and Origen.

distinguished as the first Christian author to produce volumes of Christian literature in Latin.

Origen

Toward the end of the second century, a man named Origen (184? - 254? A.D.), a contemporary of Tertullian, was born in Alexandria, Egypt, and— like Tertullian—he lived during the second and third centuries.

How Origen Destroyed the Prophetic Connection between Jesus, Barabbas, and Yom Kippur

In the Gentile Church, many things were attempted to sever any connection to the Church's Hebrew roots and make the Bible more palatable for the Gentiles. Because of Origen's hatred for the Jews, he destroyed the parallel between the death of Jesus on the cross and Israel's holiest holiday, the Day of Atonement. (Refer back to *Yom Kippur and the Two Identical Goat Connection to the Cross,* Chapter 1, page 42.) Why would Origen do such a thing? He did it because Barabbas's name in the original manuscripts was "Yeshua Bar Abba" (i.e., "Jesus Son of the Father"). Origin thought the name "Jesus" was too holy to be identified with Barabbas, so he stopped using it in copies of biblical manuscripts he had produced. He only referred to him by the Greek version of his name, "Barabbas;" thus, he destroyed a vital link between Barabbas and Christ with the twin goats of Yom Kippur. He probably encouraged other scribes to do likewise, effectively rewriting the Bible.[35] Like many of the Church's Early Fathers, Origen made abundant use of allegories in his interpretations of Scripture.

There is something else troubling about Origen. He was very instrumental in establishing the philosophical foundations of the Church. In doing so, he incorporated his self-serving belief that God was through with the Jews.[36] We can see further evidence of Origin's anti-Semitism in Chapter 8 of *Origen Against Celsus:*

---

[35]Ehrman, Bart D., and Daniel B. Wallace. *The Reliability of the New Testament.* Edited by Robert B. Stewart, (Minneapolis: Augsburg, Fortress Press, 2011), 118.
[36]Origen (c. 185–c. 253), n.p. Web. 13 June 2014.

For it is indeed manifest, that when they beheld Jesus, they did not see who He was; and when they heard Him, they did not understand from His words the divinity that was in Him, and which transferred God's providential care, hitherto exercised over the Jews, to His converts from the heathen. Therefore, we may see, that after the advent of Jesus, the Jews were altogether abandoned, and possess now none of what was considered their ancient glories, so that there is no indication of any Divinity abiding amongst them.[37]

To make such a statement, Origen had to ignore all the thousands and thousands of Jews who followed Jesus in the first century. Of course, Origen, like others of his ilk, failed to provide solid scriptural references to support his claim (which was impossible) that all Jews are evil and undeserving of God's love.

Again, Origen argued:

For what nation is an exile from their own metropolis, and from the place sacred to the worship of their fathers, save the Jews alone? And these calamities they have suffered, because they were a most wicked nation, which, although guilty of many other sins, yet has been punished so severely for none, as for those that were committed against our Jesus.

Apparently, Origen was unaware of the practice of the Babylonians and other Middle Eastern countries who routinely captured citizens from one country and displaced them into other areas of their vast empires to break all ties the indigenous people had with their historical lands and holy sites. The relocation of the conquered peoples usually destroyed their nationalism, but also made them loyal to their conquerors. It is true that God used Israel's enemies to punish them, for example, when He allowed them to be conquered and resettled in Babylon.[38] Origen

---

[37]Alexander Roberts, D.D., James Donaldson, LL.D. eds. *Ante-Nicene Fathers, vol. 3, Origen Against Celsus* (Peabody: Hendrickson Publ., 2004), 433.

[38]Relocation of conquered people: "Now the rest of the people that were left in the city, and the fugitives that fell away to the king of Babylon, with the remnant of the multitude, did Nebuzaradan [the captain of the guard] carry away" (2 Kings 25:11). Ancient conquerors destroyed holy sites of the conquered peoples in order

further developed his argument for replacement theology in Chapter 22 of his discourse when he stated:

> ... according to Celsus, "... the Son of God has been already sent on account of the sins of the Jews; and that the Jews having chastised Jesus, and given Him gall to drink [it was a Roman soldier, not a Jew who offered Jesus gall], have brought upon themselves the divine wrath." And anyone who likes may convict this statement of falsehood [Jesus came for the very reason that the sinful Jews who would torture Him were in need of redemption], if it be not the case [then why was it] that the whole Jewish nation was overthrown within one single generation after Jesus has undergone these sufferings at their hands. For forty and two years, I think, after the date of the crucifixion of Jesus, did the destruction of Jerusalem take place. Nor it has never been recorded, since the Jewish nation began to exist, that they have been expelled for so long a period from their venerable temple worship, and service, and enslaved by more powerful nations; for if at any time they appeared to be abandoned because of their sins, they were notwithstanding visited [by God], and returned to their own country, and recovered their possessions, and performed unhindered the observances of their law. Law[39] (bracketed clarifications mine).

It is understandable how Origin reached the same conclusion which he and others held regarding God's dismissal of the Jews. Historically, the Hebrew people were held captive in Babylon for 70 years before King Cyrus the Great allowed them to return to Judea (the Southern Kingdom of Israel) in 538 B.C. It would be 2,500 years before the Northern Kingdom of Israel would exist again. Why did it take 70 years before God allowed the Jews to return to Judea? It took that long because, for 490 years, the children of Israel ignored God's commandment to allow the land to rest

---

to show how their gods were more powerful and impotent compared to the conquered peoples' gods [not unlike today's Islamists]: "The Babylonians broke up the bronze pillars, the movable stands and the bronze sea that were at the temple of the LORD and they carried the bronze to Babylon..." (2 Kings 25:13, NIV, bracketed clarifications mine).

[39]Alexander Roberts, D.D., James Donaldson, LL.D., eds., Ante-Nicene Fathers, vol. 4, 506.

(not be plowed or planted) every Sabbath year.

> But in the seventh year, the land is to have a year of Sabbath rest, a Sabbath to the LORD. Do not sow your fields or prune your vineyards (Leviticus 25:5).

Because the Hebrews refused to observe that commandment, God would eventually make it compulsory for them to observe one year of punishment for every Sabbath year they ignored. We see God's constraint when He allowed Nebuchadnezzar to take Israel captive and relocate them to Babylon, which prevented them from being able to work the land they had refused to let stand idly every Sabbath year. That captivity lasted 70 years, which was one year for every Sabbath year the Israelites worked their land instead of allowing it to rest. It is important for all of us to remember that God is not mocked (Galatians 6:7).

We arrived at the 70-year figure by dividing the 490-year-period (the period when the disobedience took place) by 7 (the number of the Sabbath day), which came to 70. Because the Leviticus commandment was for a Sabbath that lasted a full year instead of a day, that brought the total of the Sabbath years to 70. Since it had been a collective total of 70 years that the Jews continued to work their land in defiance of God's ordinance, God made sure they would have to make restitution. Therefore, it was 70 years that the Israelis could not live or work the land they loved and—as further punishment—they were forced to serve a foreign king in a foreign land.

Why did God wait so long to bring judgment? The Bible teaches that God is slow to anger and quick to forgive, but it is the in-between period that's difficult! (Numbers 14:18; 2 Peter 3:9).

Because of the Israelis' almost half a millennium of disobedience, they would not be in control of Israel (the Northern Kingdom) for another 2,500 years when God allowed them to take their land back in 1948. That was a long time for the tribes of Israel, but it was only two and a half days by Heaven's time (Psalm 90:4; 2 Peter 3:8); however, in *Yehud Medinata* (Aramaic for Province of Judah), King Cyrus allowed the Southern Kingdom to enjoy a form of self-governance, as well as worshipping in the Second Temple, which he permitted them to rebuild in 538 B.C.

Some events can have unforeseen consequences, and many Israelites chose to remain in Babylon after they were free to leave. Perhaps one reason some of the Jews stayed in Babylon was that they were born there; it was the only home they ever knew. Another possible reason some stayed behind might have been because they were too old to relocate and start over again in a land that had mostly fallen into ruin.

Some good did come for those who stayed behind. One example is Ezekiel, who established a Torah academy in Sura, a city in southern Babylonia, which lasted for 1,600 years until 1001 A.D. The academy gave rise to the creation of the Talmud, which helped to sustain the Hebrews in Babylonia. The absence of many Israelites returning to their land, not to mention the Jews lack of control over Israel, helped reinforce the Gentile myth that God was finished with the Jews, despite the reassurance God gave His people when He promised Israel:

> For the Lord your God is a merciful God; he will not abandon or destroy you or forget the covenant with your ancestors, which he confirmed to them by oath (Deuteronomy 4:31).

At the time of Origen's birth in 185 A.D., the Northern Kingdom of Israel had not existed for some 740 years.[40] That, combined with Christ's Crucifixion around 33 A.D. and the destruction of the Temple in 70 A.D. (as prophesied by Jesus in Mark 13:1-2; 14:58; Luke 21:5-6), climaxed with the complete destruction of Judea, brought about the beginning of the predicted "times of the Gentiles." That occurred when the Romans dispersed all Jews throughout the Roman world (Luke 21:24a).

As stated earlier, those final events transpired at the pleasure of Rome's Emperor, Hadrian, who changed the name of Israel's Southern Kingdom from "Judea" to "Syria-Palæstina "[41] and renamed the city of Jerusalem to

---

[40]Israel's revolt against the Neo-Babylonian Empire led to its destruction in 586 B.C.; however, the Hebrews still referred to the area, including Judea, as Israel: "After Herod died, an angel of the Lord appeared in a dream to Joseph in Egypt and said, 'Get up, take the child and his mother and go to the land of Israel, for those who were trying to take the child's life [in Bethlehem of Judea] are dead' " (Matthew 2:20, NIV, bracketed clarification mine).

[41]The name change of the region was done in memory of Israel's ancient and by then extinct enemy—the Philistines—who were probably Phoenicians of Greek origin.

"Aelia Capitolina"[42] in 135 A.D.[43]

Understandably, it is no wonder it appeared to Origen as though God was finished with Israel, as well as the Jews of Judea because they were terrible sinners; however, it appears that Origen was not schooled with Romans 3:23 which states: "For all have sinned and fallen short of the glory of God." What part of "all" was not clear to Origen? Jesus taught that there is none good but God (Matthew 19:17),[44] and that includes not only Jews but Gentiles as well; however, Origen continued with his contrived commentary and non-biblical approach to Scripture when he taught:

> ... And we say with confidence that they [the Jews] will never be restored to their former condition. For they committed a crime of the most unhallowed kind, in conspiring against the Savior of the human race in that city where they offered up to God a worship containing the symbols of mighty mysteries (bracketed clarification mine).[45]

Perhaps Origen should have also reflected on the rhetorical question asked by Paul when he wrote on this very subject regarding the people of Israel:

> Does this mean that God has rejected His Jewish people forever? Of course not! His purpose was to make His salvation available to the Gentiles, and then the Jews would be jealous and begin to want God's salvation for themselves. Now if the whole world became rich as a result of God's offer of salvation, when the Jews stumbled over it and turned it down, think how much greater a blessing the world will share in later on

---

[42]Judea (2013 August 3), *Wikipedia*, n.p. Web. 14 June 2014.

[43]Syria Palaestina (2013, August 3), *Wikipedia*, n.p. Web. 14 June. 2014.

[44]This passage has been used by some cults as a "proof text" to show Jesus was a created being because He asked the rich, young ruler why he called Jesus good because there was none good but God. Cultists and other critics of Christ make the point that Jesus was admitting that He was a created being and not God. Putting that aside, the truth is that Jesus was actually giving the rich, young ruler an opportunity to confess that he was either flattering Jesus or that he *knew* Jesus was the Son of God and, therefore, not an ordinary human, but the one unique (GK. *monogeneses*) person who was worthy of being called good.

[45]Roberts and Donaldson, *Ante-Nicene Fathers,* vol. 4, 506.

when the Jews, too, come to Christ.

As you know, God has appointed me as a special messenger to you Gentiles. I lay great stress on this and remind the Jews about it as often as I can, so that if possible I can make them want what you Gentiles have and in that way save some of them. And how wonderful it will be when they become Christians! When God turned away from them it meant that he turned to the rest of the world to offer his salvation, and now it is even more wonderful when the Jews come to Christ. It will be like dead people coming back to life. And since Abraham and the prophets are God's people, their children will be too; for if the roots of the tree are holy, the branches will be too.

But some of these branches from Abraham's tree, some of the Jews, have been broken off. And you Gentiles who were branches from, we might say, a wild olive tree, were grafted in. So now you, too, receive the blessing God has promised Abraham and his children, sharing in God's rich nourishment of his own special olive tree.

But you must be careful not to brag about being put in to replace the branches that were broken off. Remember that you are important only because you are now a part of God's tree; you are just a branch, not a root.

"Well," you might be saying, "those branches were broken off to make room for me, so I must be pretty good."

Watch out! Remember that those branches, the Jews, were broken off because they didn't believe God, and you are there only because you do. Do not be proud; be humble and grateful—and careful. For if God did not spare the branches he put there in the first place, he won't spare you either.

Notice how God is both kind and severe. He is very hard on those who disobey, but very good to you if you continue to love and trust him. But if you don't, you too will be cut off (Romans 11:11-22, The Living Bible).

Justin Martyr

During the second century, Justin Martyr (100-165 A.D.), also known as "Saint Justin," was considered the leading interpreter of the "theory of the Logos," as well as a highly respected defender of the faith. His last name reflects how he died when he was beheaded for his faith. Nevertheless, despite all of his scholarly accolades and devotion to Christ, Justin Martyr insisted that God had broken His covenant with the Jews because he believed God had replaced them with Christians—as "the *new* spiritual Israel"—a concept that is not found in Romans 11 or anywhere else in Scripture.[46] That was despite the fact God made an everlasting covenant with the Jews. Perhaps he might have simply overlooked the following passage where God said to Abraham:

> And I will establish My covenant between Me and you [Abraham] and your seed [Israel] after you in their generations for an *everlasting covenant*, to be a God unto you, and to your seed after you (Genesis 17:7, bracketed clarification mine, emphasis added).

Keeping in mind, "God is not a man that He should lie...." (Numbers 23:19), what part of "everlasting covenant" did Justin Martyr not understand?

[46]Alexander Roberts, D.D., James Donaldson, LL.D., eds., *Ante-Nicene Fathers,* vol. 1 (Peabody: Hendrickson Publ., 2004), 199-200. Justin Martyr, *Dialogue with Trypho, a Jew,* Ch. 11.

CHAPTER 2

THE LIGHT OF BIBLICAL TRUTH
FADED INTO HERESY

Third Century

We have seen how the second century began with planting the destructive seeds of replacement theology. We have also read about the treatment of those who brought the blessings of God to the nations and the sad relationship displayed through Christendom's actions against their brothers, the children of Abraham and Sarah.[47]

With the onset of the third century and the Pagan emperor, Septimius Severus (who ruled Rome from 193-211 A.D), it became a crime to convert to Judaism. The momentum of anti-Semitism began to build strength among those in the Christian Church with the continued attacks into the third century from the recognized Father of Latin Christianity, Quintus Tertullian (155-240 A.D.), as well as others.

---

[47]"I will make your descendants as numerous as the stars in the sky and will give them all these lands, and *through your offspring all nations on earth will be blessed*" (Genesis 26:4, NIV, emphasis added).

"Therefore, the promise comes by faith, so that it may be by grace and may be guaranteed to all Abraham's offspring—not only to those who are of the Law but also to those who have the faith of Abraham. *He is the father of us all*. As it is written: 'I have made you a father of many nations.' *He is our father in the sight of God*, in whom he believed—the God who gives life to the dead and calls into being things that were not" (Romans 4:16-17, NIV, emphases added).

Marcus Minucius Felix

One of the earliest defenders of Christianity to write in Latin, and a contemporary of Tertullian, was the Roman Lawyer, Marcus Minucius Felix (?-250 A.D.).[48] He wrote the *Octavius*, which is believed to be the earliest piece of existing Latin Christian literature. Felix began applying Latin thought, language, and Greek philosophy to his critical analysis of Scripture, which incorporated the concept of an allegorical (i.e., a second) meaning of interpreting the Bible; in turn, that led to him reading into the Bible things that were not there (eisegesis). As we shared earlier, making the Bible a collection of *allegories* is twisting Scripture to make it mean *anything* one wants it to mean. The Bible does contain allegorical passages, some of which are found in the parables Jesus told; however, in each case, Jesus told His disciples what the hidden meaning of His parable was so there would be no misunderstanding or any additional occult (hidden) meaning attached to it.

Let's look at Felix's introduction to Chapter 33 in his book, the *Octavius of Minucius Felix,* where he writes:

ARGUMENT; THAT EVEN IF GOD BE SAID TO HAVE NOTHING AVAILED THE JEWS, CERTAINLY THE WRITERS OF THE JEWISH ANNALS ARE THE MOST SUFFICIENT WITNESSES THAT THEY FORSOOK GOD BEFORE THEY WERE FORSAKEN BY HIM (capitalization and punctuation Felix's).[49]

In his introduction, we already see the forming of anti-Semitism by his conclusion, "... that they forsook God before they were forsaken by Him."

During that same period, Tertullian—the son of Pagan parents who converted to Christianity and lived in the Roman, African province of

---

[48]The Editors of Encyclopædia Britannica, "Marcus Minucius Felix" *Encyclopædia Britannica Online*, Encyclopedia Britannica, n.p. Web. 19 June 2016. Marcus Minucius Felix ("Minucius Felix" for short) was a Christian apologist, believed to have been born in Africa in an unknown year. He died in Rome, Italy, in 250 A.D.

[49]Alexander Roberts, D.D., James Donaldson, LL.D., ed's, *Ante-Nicene Fathers*, vol. 4, *Tertullian, Part (IV), Minucius Felix, Commodian, Origen* (Peabody: Hendrickson Publ., 2004), 169.

Carthage—became the acknowledged "Father of Latin Christianity"[50] (as well as a "Father" of the hellish Church tradition of replacement theology). Tertullian expanded on Minucius Felix's opinion that God had somehow turned His back on *all* Jews and ignored God's everlasting covenants with them by developing the replacement (i.e., supersessionist) view. As we previously discussed, the replacement view argues that the Church has replaced the formerly-held position of the nation of Israel as being the Chosen People of God.[51] In other words, the Church became the "Spiritual Israel."

In Carthage, during the middle of that century (250-258 A.D.), the town's bishop, St. Cyprian, ordered all Jews to leave Carthage or die by the sword.[52]

FOURTH CENTURY

As we move into the fourth century, the *Christian Synod (*i.e., a council or an assembly*) of Elvira* decreed in 306 A.D. that marriage, intercourse, or even social contact between Jews and Christians was strictly forbidden. (One wonders how that would have set with members of the first-century Church, such as the Apostle Peter, who was married and is believed to have been the first pope.)

While the final dispersion of the Jews from their homeland happened during the events in 135 A.D., little is known about their penetration numbers on the continent of Europe during that period. We know, of course, they were dispersed throughout the Roman Empire, but the outlying areas are less documented. One such region is the barbarian land inhabited by the Germanic tribes in what we now refer to as "Germany." The earliest evidence of a Jewish presence in the area of modern-day Cologne was the discovery in the 1930s of a fourth-century Jewish cemetery. Because of that discovery, we know Germany has had a Jewish

---

[50]*Encyclopædia Britannica,* 1946 ed., s.v., "Tertullian."

[51]Quintus Septimius Florens Tertullianus anglicized as Tertullian (c. 160–c. 220 A.D.); *Adversus Judaeos (Eng. Against the Jews),* n.p. Web. November 7, 2011.

[52]Dagobert Runes, *The Jew and the Cross* (New York: Philosophical Library, 1966), 41.

presence for over 1700 years dating from 321 A.D.

It seems almost ironic that just three years later, over in Asia Minor during 325 A.D., the converted Christian Emperor, Constantine, would follow in Hadrian's footsteps by once again renewing the expulsion of the Jews from their beloved Jerusalem.

> **Note:** The year 325 A.D. was the 190th anniversary of when the Jews were expelled from Judea, and the Holy Land was renamed to Syria-Palæstina in 135 A.D. by Emperor Hadrian.

Eusebius

The Roman historian and Christian defender, Eusebius (263-339 A.D.), proclaimed, "Jews are always cursed by God and thus doomed to perpetual punishment;" never mind the fact that all the early Churches consisted of almost entirely Hebrew believers and the Churches in Jerusalem and its leaders were made up of Jews. They published all the letters that are included in the New Testament, which document the ministry of Christ and His Jewish apostles. Something else ignored by the Church's illustrious historians is that many of the Temple priests also became believers in the Messiah (i.e., Yeshua) in the first century after He had gone to be with the Father (Acts 6:7).

Unfortunately, the supposedly esteemed Gentile Church Fathers held onto—and promoted—the lie that the Jews were to blame for the death of Jesus because they did not—or refused to—understand the Scriptures, especially those passages regarding the fact that the Messiah would have to die. Those prophetic passages have been available to us since the very beginning of time. We can see the first biblical prophecy, regarding the sacrificial death of Jesus, recorded in Genesis, Chapter 3, where God prophesied—when speaking to Satan—Adam and Eve's fall from grace:

> And the LORD God said unto the serpent, "Because you have done this [tempt Adam and Eve into sin], you are cursed above all cattle, and above every beast of the field; upon your belly shall you go, and dust shall you eat all the days of your life: And I will put enmity [dislike] between you and the woman, and between your seed and

her seed; it [a descendant of Eve known as the Messiah] shall bruise your head [bruise is a euphemism for killing], and you shall bruise His heel." [Jesus was nailed to the cross and died only to be resurrected to life again.] (Genesis 3:14-15, bracketed clarifications mine).

It took the blood of Jesus—shed as the Passover Lamb of God—to cover, once and for all, our sins (John 1:29) on that Passover eve (John 19:14-18).

CONSTANTINE COMETH

The fourth century also brought a very unusual turn of events that would forever drive a demonic wedge between Christians and their Jewish brethren. It began when the Pagan Roman Emperor Constantine the Great (i.e., Flavius Valerius Aurelius Constantinus) had a miraculous vision on October 27, 312 A.D., while preparing for the *Battle of the Milvian Bridge.* In his vision, he saw a great cross appearing above the sun with the inscription, "In hoc signo vinces" (Eng. "In this sign thou shalt conquer"). Being the perceptive man that he was, plus knowing that Jesus was believed to be the Christ and that it was a Roman cross on which He was crucified, Constantine had a special monogram created, as we see on the shields in the painting above. It was a cross which incorporated the first two letters of the Greek word, *XPIΣTOΣ*, which means "Christ." The Greek letters are *Chi* (X) and *Rho* (P). When we put them together, they form what has become known in the Church as the *Chi-Rho*. It was with that

Constantine the Great preparing to lead his troops into Battle with the sign of the cross on their shields.
(Unknown Artist, Valaam Monastery, Smolensky Skete, Russia)

75

stylized cross—emblazoned on the shields of every one of his Pagan soldiers—who Constantine proceeded to march into battle and secure his position as Emperor of Rome.

There is some controversy as to whether or not Constantine made himself the head of the Church, but there can be no doubt he was very influential in running its affairs, and certainly no one ever opposed him.

It is beneficial to realize that the Church began as a Jewish Messianic movement, steeped in the traditions and teachings of the Hebrew Scriptures we refer to as the "Old Testament," yet with the coming of Constantine, the Church's shift away from its Hebrew roots would then be complete. No thanks to Constantine, the Church would be under the influence of a transitioning Pagan Rome, Plato, and the Gentiles.

It was in 325 A.D., at Emperor Constantine's luxurious villa in Nicaea, located in the Roman province of Bithynia (which is now located in the Islamic nation of Turkey), where Constantine held a special Church council made up of many of the empire's Christian bishops and leading clergy. However, in doing so, he deliberately ignored the 12 Jewish bishops of the Church by not inviting them. That intentional snub of the Jewish bishops had a predictable result—anti-Semitism became internalized within the Church.[53]

The *Council of Nicaea* also prohibited the celebration of any Jewish holidays and exchanged the Jewish lunar calendar in favor of the Roman solar calendar. In doing so, it not only changed the day when First Fruits— the feast on which Jesus rose from the dead—would fall, but it forever changed the way we celebrate the dating of Resurrection Sunday, also known by its unbiblical name—"Easter Sunday."

That intended result affected important holidays and their relationships with each other, as well as more accurately determining the time it takes

---

[53]Jeffrey Seif, Ph.D. <staff@levitt.com> (August 1, 2011), in a personal e-mail to the author re: *The Institute of Jewish Christian Studies* teaching on the Nicaea convention's refusal to invite the 12 Jewish bishops throughout the world to its convocation: Dr. Seif, of the *Institute of Jewish-Christian Studies* in Dallas, Texas, confirmed this information to be accurate. The late Louis Goldberg, Th.M., Th.D., Professor of Theology and Jewish Studies at the Moody Bible Institute, also confirmed its accuracy.

the earth to go around the sun. Unlike the Hebrew lunar calendar, the Roman solar calendar allows for Passover to fall in different months and on any day of the week. On the Hebrew lunar calendar, First Fruits (the actual day Jesus rose from the dead) follows on the first day of the week following the Sabbath (*Shabbat*), which follows the Passover (or as it was simply called on the Hebrew calendar, "first day," which follows the Paschal Full Moon).

For that reason, the Hebrews had "leap months" (not a leap year with only one day added),[54] which widened the gap between the relationship of the Passover and Easter holidays. They became separated by as much as a month in some years, and the prophetic meaning of Jesus as the sacrificial Passover Lamb—accompanied with His resurrection from the dead on the Feast of First Fruits—was lost from Christian and Jewish awareness.

The earliest evidence of a Christmas holiday was during 354 A.D. It appeared on a document called the "Chronography of 354," a fourth-century calendar, which is the first recorded account of the Christ-Mass (i.e., Messiah-celebration). It was also around that time when Christmas was acknowledged as a Roman Catholic liturgical feast.

St. Jerome

Beginning in 382 A.D., Jerome (347-420 A.D.) began translating the Bible into what has become the Latin Vulgate. He is considered one of the most learned of the Church Fathers, but unbelievably, Jerome insisted that the

---

[54]It takes the earth 365¼ (i.e., 365.2422) days to orbit the sun. The one-quarter of a day shortage is corrected by adding an extra day (February 29) every four years (the fourth year being the leap year. The Lunar calendar's accounting of days was less, which allowed for the shifting of seasons out of the months where they were supposed to be (a lunar cycle is 29 1/2 days); therefore, a lunar year is 12.4 months. After three lunar years, the months are out of sync with the solar year by about 1 1/3 months, which means it would take 36 years for the seasons and months to once again fall at the same time. After all, who wants snow in July? Various methods were incorporated by various cultures to correct the problem. One of the ways civilizations used the lunar year, coupled with the shift of months, was to have a thirteenth month every few years. Nevertheless, the months and year problem between solar and lunar was finally solved when they settled on the solar year with a leap year every four years to keep the seasons, events and months more accurately aligned.

Jews lacked the intelligence to understand the very Bible they produced; consequently, in his mind, they should be severely punished and tormented until they repented and converted to Christianity.[55]

The Biblical Link from Abraham to Jesus:
The Prophetic Lamb of God

Let's pause at this point and reflect on the foreshadowing of an important event found in Genesis, where we first saw the rehearsal sacrifice of a son—when Abraham, in obedience to God, prepared to sacrifice Isaac on a pile of wood before the Lord. It was at that point when God interceded by providing Abraham with a male lamb (i.e., ram) as a sin offering. Years later, God would provide, once and for all, His Son as the final sacrifice upon the wooden cross for the sins of all humanity (Genesis 22:11-13).

The Bible also gives us a foreshadowing of Christ shedding His blood for mankind's sins in the same manner as the sacrificed Passover Lamb's blood would be painted on the doorpost and lintel of each Hebrew's door. It formed the abstract shape of a cross (from left to right on the doorpost and on the lintel, but not on the threshold; that way, the sacrificial blood would not be trampled underfoot).

The story began when Pharaoh had stubbornly refused to let the children of Israel leave Egypt, despite all the plagues God had already sent. Finally, God had enough and warned Pharaoh to let His people go, or there would be a very high price to pay. God would require the firstborn of every living creature in Egypt (humans and animals) to be killed, including Pharaoh's own son.

God kept His word. That terrible incident took place around 1300 B.C., but to protect His people, God had forewarned the Israelites to sacrifice a lamb and dip the hyssop plant (its leaves were like a broom) in the blood of the lamb and use it to paint the top and sides of their doorposts. By doing that, God promised the children of Israel the Angel of Death would "pass over" them.

---

[55]Robert Michael, *A History of Catholic Antisemitism: The Dark Side of the Church* (New York: Palgrave Macmillan, 2011), 10, 20.

As we revealed on the previous page, if we were to draw lines connecting the blood from the left doorpost to the opposite right doorpost, and then draw a line from the blood at the top of the door to the blood that dripped onto the threshold of the door, they would form a cross. However, it would not be until about 780 years in the future when the Babylonians performed the first crossbeam crucifixion in 519 B.C., which was a radical departure from the usual impaling on a sharpened pole. That dramatic foreshadowing of a Messianic Lamb of God being crucified proves that event was seen and planned by God 1,300 years before it happened in Jerusalem; thus, begs the question, "Should they have begun blaming the Jews for the death of Christ over a millennium before the actual event occurred?" No, because Jesus died for the sins of everyone (John 3:16-17), and it fell to the chosen people of God to carry out His planned sacrifice (Isaiah 53; Psalm 22). Remember, a sacrifice performed by any Pagan would be in vain because God would never recognize a Pagan's blood sacrifice for the atonement of sins.

The Bible tells us the wages of sin are death (Romans 6:23); consequently, we need a blood sacrifice to cover our sins. The Bible also tells us about the unblemished Lamb—the One who can take away our sins once-and-for-all:

> ... John saw Jesus coming toward him and said, "Look, the Lamb of God, who takes away the sin of the world!" (John 1:29).

This is further confirmed in 1 Corinthians:

> ... For Christ, our Passover Lamb, has been sacrificed (1 Corinthians 5:7b).

With the onset of the fourth century A.D., various factions, which would ultimately become Christendom, came together under the Roman Emperor, Constantine. As we previously explained, in 325 A.D., Constantine sent a summons throughout the world for all pastors and bishops to convene in Nicaea. It would be good for us to remember, during that time, 12 Jewish bishops throughout the world were not invited to participate—sadly, it was intentional.

At the *Council of Nicaea in* 325 A.D., they changed the day of Christ's resurrection from the Feast of First Fruits and caused it to fall on different Sundays between March 22 and April 25. One obvious reason was that the Council changed the calendar from the Hebrew lunar calendar to the Roman solar calendar.

Earlier, we explored in detail how Christ rose on the celebration of First Fruits. The Feast of First Fruits fell on the first Sunday following the Hebrew Sabbath and came immediately following the Passover. Jesus and His disciples celebrated it; the Church refers to it as the "Last Supper." When the Nicaean Council intentionally changed that relationship regarding the Passover and the important day of First Fruits, it would have had a special significance for the Jews because it is possible that they might have noticed Jesus' prophetic connection to the Feast of First Fruits. Paul, who was a Hebrew from the tribe of Benjamin and was not a believer in Christ at the time when those events occurred. After he came to faith in Christ, he talked about the importance of the *First Fruits* connection—which would be deliberately done away with—less than 300 years later.

> For since by man came death, by man came also the resurrection of the dead. For as in Adam all die, even so in Christ shall all be made alive. But every man in his own order: Christ the *firstfruits*; afterward they that are Christ's at His coming (1 Corinthians 15:21-23, emphasis added).

As we discussed, the association between the Passover and the celebration of the Feast of First Fruits—which fell on the Hebrew day called "Yom Reeshone," literally the "First Day" and the actual day when Jesus rose from the dead—was intentionally replaced by the Roman and Greek Sun's day [Sunday]. That was the day of the week set aside to honor the early Greek and the Roman sun god, Apollo (Greek, *Aplon* [Απλουν]), (Latin, *Apollo*). Later, the Romans called him, "*Sol Invictus,*" who—at the time of Constantine—was the patron of soldiers and the god Constantine worshiped until his life-changing vision of the cross encounter.

Consider: Annual events are normally celebrated on the *actual date* of a particular event (birthdays, wedding anniversaries, hiring dates, etc.).

In the case of First Fruits—it fell on the first day after the Sabbath following the Passover, which always fell on the same day after the full moon on the Hebrew lunar calendar. However, with the change of calendars, it then fell on the day set aside to honor the sun god on the Pagan solar calendar, which rarely coincided with the Hebrew lunar calendar. Who would want to pervert the actual day Jesus rose from the dead and its connection to the Passover and First Fruits by placing it on the same day honoring a Pagan deity? This brings us to the second reason why the calendar was changed by *the Council of Nicaea*. The reason can be found in their decree:

> For it is unbecoming beyond measure that on this holiest of festivals we should follow the customs of the Jews. Henceforth let us have nothing in common with this odious people.... We ought not, therefore, to have anything in common with the Jews...our worship follows a...more convenient course...we desire dearest brethren, to separate ourselves from the detestable company of the Jews.... How, then, could we follow these Jews, who are almost certainly blinded...*it is our duty not to have anything in common with the murderers of our Lord* (emphasis added).[56]

Consequently, the changing of the dating system, which dictated when Easter would fall, was a direct result of anti-Semitism and was intended to distance the resurrection event from the prophetic connections which completed the Passover celebration. The *Council of Nicaea's* mission was complete—it not only severed the ties between the Christians and their Jewish brothers and sisters—but it also distanced the Jews from Christianity by driving a wedge of hatred between them. As a result, the Church Fathers guaranteed that the Messianic connection of the Passover Lamb would be lost forever on the Jews and the children of Israel, some of whom would have made the connection and, therefore, might have become saved. Christianity then embarked on becoming a Gentile religion that would be centered—not in Jerusalem where it was born—but in Rome.

---

[56]"On the Keeping of Easter," I. Nice, A.D. 325, *The Seven Ecumenical Councils of the Undivided Church*, ed. Henry R. Percival, M.A., D.D., 2nd ed., vol. 14. (Peabody: Hendrickson, 2004), 54. Nicene and Post Nicene Fathers.

Two years later, in 337 A.D., Constantine died, and his son, Constantius II became the new Christian Emperor of Rome. Shortly after becoming Emperor, Constantius II decreed that a marriage between a Jewish man and a Christian woman was punishable by death. Converting to Judaism became a criminal offense in 339 A.D.[57]

With the *Laodicea Synod* of 343-381 A.D. in its approved cannon (XXXVIII), we read: "It is not lawful [for Christians] to receive unleavened bread from the Jews, nor to be partakers of their impiety."

Consider: Everyone has knowingly or unknowingly conspired against God at one time or another. It is interesting how the fathers of replacement theology never portrayed their need for a Savior equally with that of the Jews' need of a Savior. If the Jews were as bad as the replacement theologians would have us believe, should not God's grace, given to us through the blood atonement by Jesus on the cross, give the Jews even more grace?

> The law was brought in so that the trespass might increase. But *where sin increased, grace increased all the more*, so that, just as sin reigned in death, so also grace might reign through righteousness to bring eternal life through Jesus Christ our Lord (Romans 5:20-21, emphasis added).

It is as if the Jews bore the greater sin, and could never be forgiven! Are some sins worse than others in God's eyes? The Bible teaches:

> For whoever keeps the whole Law and yet stumbles at just one point is guilty of breaking all of it (James 2:12, NIV).

> Therefore anyone who sets aside one of the least of these commands and teaches others accordingly will be called least in the kingdom of Heaven, but whoever practices and teaches these commands will be called great in the kingdom of Heaven (Matthew 5:19, NIV).

God tells us that all sin is equally bad; therefore, the small mob (which

---

[57]Will J. Durant, *The Story of Civilization: Part III Caesar and Christ* (New York: Simon & Schuster, 1944), 655.

was hardly the whole nation of Israel) who persuaded Pilate to have Jesus crucified, might have been guilty of bearing false witness. In the eyes of God, however, that sin was no worse than any sin we commit. Consider if there were never a Hebrew race. Would we still not need Jesus to offer a blood sacrifice for our sins? With Rome tolerant of Christianity and the empire Christianized, what would have become of the large class of Pagan priests? Some have suggested that the political and influential Pagan priesthood simply became Christian priests, and all of their Temple statues were rededicated to commemorate Christian saints. From the Roman Catholic perspective, the transformation of Pagan deities that were assimilated into the Catholic Church was not as problematic as it might have seemed. After all, Emperor Constantine was the head of the Church; who would argue with him?

When a culture is forced to reinvent their ancient belief system into a new religion, the more familiar the rituals and symbols are, the easier it is to encourage the populace into accepting something new. Islam did that as well by reinventing all the biblical prophets and Jesus into Muslim prophets, along with alleged biblical stories included in the Koran. (We see the same thing today with the current Catholic and many Protestant Churches trying to blend Christianity with Islam or—as it is now called by some—"Chrislam.") This is not meant to condemn those Catholics who lived during the Dark Ages. We know, because of Constantine, the Catholic Church became the only church at that time, and we are merely pointing out some of the historical problems and Pagan adaptations made by the Church to convert the Roman Empire to Christianity. To condemn all Catholics because the Church made some adjustments would be foolish since it would suggest that, for the reason of these compromises, not a single Catholic and thereby not a single Christian, went to Heaven— that would be irresponsible as well as irrational thinking. If that had happened, then *no one* would have gone to Heaven for over a thousand years until the Church's Reformation!

Twenty-nine years after the First *Council of Nicaea* in 345 A.D., Aurelius Augustinus, known as St. Augustine (354-430 A.D.), was born.

St. John Chrysostom

Deplorably, the attacks against the Jews by the scholarly fathers of the Church continued as we read John Chrysostom's (344-407 A.D.) statement:

> The Jews are the odious assassins of Christ and for killing God there is no expiation [atonement] possible, no indulgence or pardon. Christians may never cease vengeance and the Jews must live in servitude forever! God always hated the Jews, so it is incumbent upon all Christians to hate the Jews! (Bracketed clarifications mine.)

Chrysostom made that horrendous and revolting statement, despite the fact Jesus said, "Therefore does My Father love Me, because I lay down My life, that I might take it again. *No man takes it from Me*, but I lay it down of Myself" (John 10:17-18, emphasis added).

God made this promise to Israel: "... I have loved you with an everlasting love" (Jeremiah 31:3b). When referring to Abraham and Sarah's descendants, God also promised Abraham, "And I will make of you a great nation, and I will bless you... And I will bless them who bless you, and curse them who curse you" (Genesis 12:2-3). Remember, God cannot lie (Titus 1:2).

Continuing with Chrysostom's vicious rant against God's people:

> The Synagogue is worse than a brothel. It is the den of scoundrels. The temple of demons devoted to idolatrous cults...a place of meeting for the assassins of Christ...a house worse than a drinking shop...a den of thieves; a house of ill fame [whore house], a dwelling of iniquity, the refuge of devils, a gulf and abyss of perdition.... As for me, I hate the synagogue. I hate the Jews for the same reason (bracketed clarification mine).

This from a man whose own Church contains statues (graven images) to which its members pray! In all fairness, Catholics are never taught to pray *to* the statues, although back in the Dark Ages, the message was not always received by the faithful.

If the Synagogues were so evil, why did Jesus go to them on the Sabbath (Luke 4:16)? Why did the Banu Qurayza worship in the Synagogues and the Temple in Jerusalem *after* Jesus ascended to the Father (Acts 3:1-2)? The Apostle Paul always went to the Synagogue to worship, no matter what part of the world he was visiting (Acts 14:1). Again, we have an ignorant proclamation not based on any Scriptural reference. Because of that, Chrysostom continued to expose his narrow-minded views and fabricated even more false accusations against God's Chosen People:

> Jews are worse than wild beasts. They sacrifice their sons and daughters to devils! Not only every Synagogue, but every Jew as well, is a temple of the devil and I would say the same thing about their souls.

Never doubt the power of a lie or groundless propaganda; when it is said repeatedly, it becomes a fact. This works especially well if the public at large is illiterate and must depend on facts from those (the godly clergy) more educated than themselves.

Around that same time in 351 A.D., all Jewish books in Persia were ordered burned. Throughout Italy during 357, the Jews had all of their property confiscated, and during 379 in Milan, Jewish places of worship were burned to the ground by the Bishop of Milan, who claimed he was doing "an act pleasing to God."

It was in 386 A.D. when this same John Chrysostom delivered the Church's first Christmas Sermon.

St. Augustine, the Bishop of Hippo

Aurelius Augustine (334-430 A.D.) was a great theologian and early Church Father, and much of his doctrine is still respected today. Unfortunately, some of his teachings greatly added to the schism between the Church and its Jewish brethren. Like many of his contemporaries, Augustine knew that if the Bible could be shown to be false in one area, then how could others defend it as the Word of God?

One of the problems Augustine had to deal with was the Bible's numerous prophecies regarding the End of the Age—many which centered around the nation of Israel—but by the time of Augustine, Israel had not existed for more than a millennium. No nation in history has ever been revived after the third generation if its people had been conquered and dispersed. As the famous Chinese General, Sun Tzu, said in his book, *The Art of War,* "a kingdom that has once been destroyed can never come again into being: nor can the dead ever be brought back to life,"[58] a statement that has been historically proven. As we just pointed out, by Augustine's time, Israel had not existed for almost a thousand years, so how was he to solve that troublesome problem?

The answer was replacement theology, replacing the old with something new. Using the unbiblical theory that it was solely the Jews who killed Jesus—Augustine mistakenly reasoned that God was through with them. To believe that, we would have to ignore the fact that the New Testament is a Jewish publication written by Jews about a Jew. We would also have to ignore all the early Church Fathers along with the thousands and thousands of first-century believers of the Church since most of them were Jews—including many of the Levitical Priests (Acts 6:7)!

In Augustine's mind, the Jews had to be dealt with because they were a glaring problem. His way was to declare that after the crucifixion, the Jews inherited all God's curses, and the Church inherited all God's blessings. Augustine taught that the Church had superseded Israel, as well as the original covenants God had given to them. The Church had become "Spiritual Israel,"[59] and wherever anyone would read about Israel in the Last Days, they were to infer what was being spoken about was the "Church;" all references to Jerusalem were understood to mean "Heaven."

---

[58]Sun Tzu, *The Art of War* (restored translation), trans., Lionel Giles (n.p.: Pax Librorum, 2009), 53. Consider: In the Bible, God shows Ezekiel the Valley of Bones and asks, "Son of man, can these bones live?" "I [Ezekiel] said, 'Sovereign Lord, you alone know' " (Ezekiel 37:3, NIV, bracketed clarification mine). Sun Tzu's book and the Book of Ezekiel (both written approximately 2,500 years ago) implies that once a nation is dead, it can never be brought back again from the dead. The Church overlooked God's answer to His rhetorical question to Ezekiel, which was "yes." The early Church Fathers believed that as well; only God had more to say on this subject, as we will see later in Chapter 7.

[59]See Justin Martyr.

86

To further his revisionist, historical concept regarding the Jews, Augustine wrote his monumental and ethnocentric, theological effort, *The City of God*. In his book, Augustine developed more anti-Semitic dogma, which is still prevalent in some of today's churches. Augustine's reference to Jesus is accurate, but he lumps all the remaining Jews together without acknowledging the thousands of first-century Jewish followers of Christ who far outnumbered the small rent-a-mob calling for Pilate to crucify Jesus!

Augustine wrote:

> ... He did many miracles that He might commend God in Himself, some of which, even as many as seemed sufficient to proclaim Him, are contained in the evangelic Scripture. The first of these is that He was so wonderfully born, and the last, that with His body raised again from the dead He ascended into heaven. *But the Jews who slew Him, and would not believe in Him*, because it behooved Him to die and rise again were yet more miserably wasted by the Romans, and utterly rooted out from their kingdom [this includes all of the Jews— believers and nonbelievers alike] where aliens had already ruled over them, and were dispersed through the lands (so that indeed there is no place where they are not), and are thus by their own Scriptures a testimony to us that we have not forged [made up] the prophecies about Christ... (bracketed clarifications mine, emphasis added).[60]

And so it is. As we stated earlier, Augustine laid the entire blame of the crucifixion at the feet of the Jews, ignoring two facts: (1) There were many (i.e., tens of thousands) of Jews who followed Jesus before His crucifixion, and over 3,000 more were added just 50 days after Jesus returned to the Father at Pentecost. (2) the actual physical nailing of the Lord to that cross was performed by Romans (Tertullian's "righteous" Gentiles)—*not* the Jews. We must not forget, if it were not for the Jews, the New Testament, a Jewish publication written by Jews about a Jew, would never have been produced. Admittedly, this is something Augustine acknowledged, but disingenuously:

---

[60]Alexander Roberts, D.D., James Donaldson, LL.D. ed's, *Nicene and Post Nicene Fathers*, vol. 2. *The City of God,* 389.

... For us, indeed, those suffice which are quoted from the books [Hebrew biblical scrolls] of our enemies [the Jews], to whom we make our acknowledgment, on account of this testimony which, in spite of themselves, they contribute by their possession of these books, while they themselves are dispersed among all nations, wherever the Church of Christ is spread abroad... (bracketed clarifications mine).[61]

Notice how Augustine declared the Jews—as an ethnic group—"our enemies." Our enemies? We Gentiles owe our salvation to a Jew named Yeshua (Jesus), the Church in Rome owes its embryonic development to a Jew named Paul and if the Church tradition is accurate—the Jewish apostle, Peter (their first pope), as well.

Augustine attempted to make his point against the Jews:

Therefore God has shown the Church in her enemies, the Jews, the grace of His compassion, since, as saith the apostle, "their offence is the salvation of the Gentiles."[62]

While pointing out the apostle Paul's observation that "their offence is the salvation of the Gentiles" (Romans 11:11), Augustine conveniently leaves out the very first verse where Paul tells us that God has not cast away the Jews (Romans 1:1), and then tells us in Roman 11:25-27 that God has a plan for the Jews.

Once again, in the above quote, Augustine made the point that the Jews, as a whole, are enemies of the Church, and although he acknowledged that their offense (those relatively few rabble-rousers involved with the crucifixion) resulted in "the salvation of the Gentiles," he insisted on mingling all the various Jews together with that statement. That misguided interpretation eventually had dire consequences regarding the very existence and lives of future generations of the Jewish people.

Despite Augustine's momentous classic works, *Confessions of St. Augustine* and *City of God,* there are passages included in those works

---

[61]Roberts & Donaldson, *Nicene and Post Nicene Fathers, vol. 2.,* 389.
[62]Ibid.

that are intolerable toward the Jews. For Augustine to do that, he had to ignore the inconvenient fact that Jesus was a Jew and the culmination of the long-awaited Hebrew Messianic faith or, as the Greeks called it, the Christian faith. It was Jesus and His Jewish disciples who contributed all the foundational teachings given to the Church!

FIFTH CENTURY

At the beginning of the fifth century (400 A.D.), the Romans forced the Jews to convert to Christianity. Question: If the Jews were so evil and revolting, why would you want to force them to join you?

It was around that time (405 A.D.) when St. Jerome finished his famous work—the Latin Vulgate—a Bible revised from *Vetus Latina* (i.e., old Latin) to the common (i.e., *Vulgate*) language (i.e., Latin) of the day; yet it was that same pious Jerome who also piled on shocking and appalling comments, like many of his colleagues did, regarding the Jewish synagogue when he wrote:

> If you call it a brothel, a den of vice, the Devil's refuge, Satan's fortress, a place to deprave the soul, an abyss of every conceivable disaster or whatever you will, you are still saying less than it deserves.

In 415 A.D., the Jews were expelled from the Egyptian city of Alexandria. It was during that same year when Augustine wrote:

> The true image of the Hebrew is Judas Iscariot, who sells the Lord for silver. The Jew can never understand the Scriptures and forever will bear the guilt for the death of Jesus.

"The Jews can never understand the Scriptures"? Perhaps Augustine should have compared the Old Testament Book of Zechariah with the New Testament Book of Matthew. Had he done so, he might have noticed what occurred with Judas and the 30 pieces of silver was prophesied hundreds of years before that event actually happened. That is even more proof that God had ordained the betrayal of Christ and His sacrifice on the cross:

89

I told them, "If you think it best, give me my pay; but if not, keep it." So they paid me thirty pieces of silver.

And the LORD said to me, "Throw it to the potter—the handsome price at which they valued Me! So I took the thirty pieces of silver and threw them to the potter at the house [Temple] of the LORD" (Zechariah 11:12-13, NIV, bracketed clarification mine).

Compare this with Matthew's account of the fulfillment of this prophecy:

Then one of the Twelve—the one called Judas Iscariot—went to the chief priests and asked, "What are you willing to give me if I deliver him over to you?" So they counted out for him thirty pieces of silver. From then on, Judas watched for an opportunity to hand him over (Matthew 26:14-16, NIV).

After betraying Jesus, Judas was filled with remorse and tried to return the 30 pieces of silver to the chief priests and elders, but they wanted nothing to do with it:

So Judas threw the money into the Temple and left. Then he went away and hanged himself.

The chief priests picked up the coins and said, "It is against the law to put this into the treasury, since it is blood money." So they decided to use the money to buy the potter's field as a burial place for foreigners. That is why it has been called the Field of Blood to this day (Matthew 27:5-8, NIV).

Augustine insisted, "The Jews can never understand Scripture"? Who did Augustine think Peter, James, Matthew, Paul, and others of Jesus' disciples—all Jews—were? Who did Augustine think those 40 men were to whom God gave the Old and New Testaments? The answer is obvious; it was the children of Israel who wrote down the Scriptures as God gave it to them (2 Peter 1:20-21).

Augustine also wrote:

The Jews held Him; the Jews insulted Him, the Jews bound Him,[63] they crowned Him with thorns,[64] dishonored Him by spitting upon Him,[65] they heaped abuse upon Him, they hung Him on a tree,[66] they pierced Him with a lance.[67, 68]

The problem with St. Augustine's observation is that the Jews had nothing to do with everything he accuses them of doing, except the part which says the Jews spat on Jesus and abused Him (John 26:67), but it was the Romans who did all the rest.

While Augustine was brilliant and had many fine qualities to be admired, it would appear—strange as it might seem—that it was Augustine who did not fully understand the Scriptures!

Two years later, during 418 A.D., the Jews of Minorca (one of the Balearic Islands located in the Mediterranean Sea belonging to Spain) were forced to convert to Christianity in complete abandonment of what Jesus taught the Church. Jesus instructed His disciples they should only share the gospel with the Jews (Matthew 10:5-6). If the Jews rejected their message of Salvation through Him, Jesus said:

> And whosoever shall not receive you, nor hear your words, when you depart out of that [Jewish] house or city, shake off the dust off your feet (Matthew 10:14, bracketed clarification mine).

---

[63]"Then the detachment *of [Roman] troops* and the captain and the officers of the Jews arrested Jesus and bound Him" (John 18:12, NKJV, bracketed clarification mine).

[64]"So Pilate, wanting to gratify the crowd, released Barabbas to them; and he delivered Jesus, after he had scourged *Him*, to be crucified' " (Mark 15:15).

[65]"Then they [the Jews] spat in His face and beat Him; and others struck *Him* with the palms of their hands" (Matthew 26:67, NKJV, bracketed clarification mine).

[66]"So Pilate, wanting to gratify the crowd, released Barabbas to them; 'and he delivered Jesus, after he had scourged *Him*, to be crucified' " (Mark 15:15).

[67]"But one of the [Roman] soldiers pierced His side with a spear, and immediately blood and water came out" (John 19:34, NKJV, bracketed clarification mine).

[68]Jules Isaac, *The Teaching of Contempt Christian Roots of Anti-Semitism* (New York: McGraw Hill Book Co., 1961), 11.1.

Notice, Jesus never told His disciples to torture, curse, or force any Jew who refused to accept Him as their Savior—a fact that would be lost on the future Church. When we look at the following passage of Scripture in context, we can better understand that Jesus never intended for the Church to replace Israel:

> These twelve Jesus sent out with the following instructions: "*Do not go among the Gentiles* or enter any town of the Samaritans. *Go rather to the lost sheep of Israel.* As you go, proclaim this message: 'The kingdom of Heaven has come near.' Heal the sick, raise the dead, cleanse those who have leprosy, drive out demons. Freely you have received; freely give.

> Do not get any gold or silver or copper to take with you in your belts—no bag for the journey or extra shirt or sandals or a staff, for the worker is worth his keep. Whatever town or village you enter, search there for some worthy person and stay at their house until you leave. As you enter the home, give it your greeting. If the home is deserving, let your peace rest on it; if it is not, let your peace return to you. If anyone will not welcome you or listen to your words, leave that home or town and shake the dust off your feet' " (Matthew 10:5-14, NIV, emphasis added).

Remember, in the first verse of this passage, Jesus is acknowledging that some Jews were already lost, and it was—and still is—His desire that all Israel be saved through God's grace. (Grace is an *undeserved gift,* Ephesians 2:8.) Another point to bear in mind is that Jesus was only referring to Jewish towns and Jewish people. Jesus knew that some Jews would reject Him, but *He never rejected them,* nor did He ever intend that they should be forced into compliance. Even His dying words on the cross were, "... Father forgive them; for they know not what they do..." (Luke 23:34a), a fact lost by the Gentile Church.

With the onset of 431 A.D. at the *Council of Ephesus,* the title, "Mother of God,"[69] which once belonged to Ishtar, was officially decreed and bestowed on Mary, the mother of Jesus, by the Roman Catholic Church.

---

[69]Hebrew Roots/Neglected Commandments/Idolatry/Easter, Footnote 12, pg. 37.

(They ignored the fact that her name was Mariam, Hebrew for Mary, and the "inconvenient" fact that she too was Jewish.)

During 438-457 A.D. in pre-Islamic Persia (Iran), Jews fared no better. Beginning in 438, King Yazdgerd II thought it would be good to persecute the Jews. King Peroz, who kept up the persecutions in the city of Ispahan from 457 through 484 A.D., followed King Yazdgerd II.

The Jewish community of Ispahan was accused of having beaten and murdered two magi, and because of that false accusation, the king of Ispahan put to death half of the Jews living in that city. He also took all the Jewish children and forced them to be brought up in the temple of Horwom as fire-worshipers.[70] Ispahan is an Iranian city to this very day.

Five years later, in 489 A.D. in Antioch, where followers of Christ were first called Christians (Acts 11:26), the fifth-century followers of Christ torched their Jewish brethren's Synagogue. Apparently, while the Jewish Synagogues of Antioch were good enough for the Apostle Paul, Barnabas, and other Christians of the first century, it was not good enough for their beneficiaries who continued to be called Christians in that city five centuries later![71]

Toward the end of the fifth century, around 476 A.D., a period known as the "Dark Ages" began, and with it, more ages of darkness descended on the Jews.[72]

---

[70]"ISPAHAN," JewishEncyclopedia.com: *The unedited full-text of the 1906 Jewish Encyclopedia,* n.p. Web. 2 September 2014.

[71]Edward Flannery, *The Anguish of the Jews: Twenty-Three Centuries of Anti-Semitism* (Mahwah: Paulist Press, 2004), 67. Edward H. Flannery (1912-1998) was a Roman Catholic priest. This book was first published in 1965.

[72]The Editors of Encyclopædia Britannica, "Migration Period," *Encyclopedia Britannica Online*. 18 May 2016 last update. Web. 26 July 2016. According to this source, that period of time had several names. " 'Migration Period,' also called the 'Dark Ages' or the 'Early Middle Ages," the early medieval period of western European history—specifically, the time (476–800 C.E.) when there was no Roman (or Holy Roman) emperor in the West or, more generally, the period between about 500 and 1000." AUTHOR'S NOTE: Opinions vary on the time span, but it averages out to being from the late fifth century to around the thirteenth to sixteenth centuries.

CHAPTER 3
THE DARK AGES

Because of Apostate Christian Doctrine, the Dark Ages of Christendom Were Even Darker for the Jews
(Late Fifth through the Thirteenth Centuries A.D.)

Verily [truly] I say unto you, inasmuch as ye have done it unto one of the least of these My brethren [Jesus was born a Jew; therefore, His brethren are Jews], ye have done it unto Me (Matthew 25:40).

SIXTH CENTURY

The Jews Fared No Better in the Sixth Century

With the dawn of the sixth century, not much had changed from the previous centuries. In the city of Daphne, Spain, in 506 A.D., there was another Jewish Synagogue torched by a Christian mob in celebration of a chariot race along with the murder of its entire congregation.[73] The torching of Jewish places of worship continued in 519 A.D. in the city of Ravenna, Italy, and by 528, Emperor Justinian (527-564 A.D.) passed what is known as the "Justinian Code," which banned Jews from building any Synagogues or reading the Bible in Hebrew. Under the Justinian Code, Jews were not allowed to assemble in

---

[73]Heinrich Hirsh Graetz, *History of the Jews, vol. III* (Philadelphia: The Jewish Publication Society of America, 1898), 10-11.

public places, nor were they allowed to celebrate the Passover before Easter. Jews were also forbidden to testify in court against any Christian.[74]

By 535 A.D., the *Synod of Clermont* created a statute that Jews could not hold public office or have authority over Christians.[75] Nineteen years later, in 554 A.D., the Diocese of Clement, France, expelled all the Jews living there, and by 561 A.D., the Catholic Bishop of Uzes,[76] France, had enough of the Jewish *problem* and expelled all of them from his diocese. The Jews, who were living in Merovingian (a part of the Frankish Empire), were forced to convert to Christianity in 582 or have their eyes ripped from their sockets or be slaughtered.[77]

SEVENTH CENTURY

By 612 A.D., all Jews in Visigothic, Spain, were banished, while in other places around Europe, the persecution of the Jews continued. In some European countries, the Jews were not allowed to farm, own land, or work in many of the trades.

The Seventh Century Brought a New Threat to the Jews in Arabia: The Sword of Islam

We pause at this point to redirect our attention from the trouble the Jews were having with their Christian antagonizers and focus on a new threat. A new religion had appeared on the world stage around that time, led by a warlord in the Arabian Peninsula. The warlord's name was Muhammad, and the religion was Islam. At first, Muhammad sought to convert the Jews and Christians to his new faith, which was devoted to his repurposed tribal Moon god,[78] Allah, who was originally one of the 360 gods of the

---

[74]Graetz, *History of the Jews, vol. III*, 12-16.

[75]Ernest L. Abel. *The Roots of Anti-Semitism* (Cranberry: Associated University Press, Inc, 1975), 239.

[76]Dagobert Runes, *The War Against the Jews* (New York: Philosophical Library, 1968), 72.

[77]Runes, *The War Against the Jews*, 105.

[78]This is a very controversial subject with Muslim theologians saying that Allah as a moon god is the invention of Hugo Winckler in 1901. We will go by what we see

Arabian pantheon. Muhammad took a page from the Christians and Jews and not only claimed Allah as the one and only true god, but to make his new religion even more credible, he claimed that Allah was the same god as the God of the Christians and Jews.

Muhammad believed that it would be a simple transition for the Christians and Jews to accept Allah as the same God as theirs. To help make his new religion even more appealing to them, Muhammad incorporated some biblical stories into the new "holy book" called the "Koran" (Qur'an); yet neither Christians nor Jews were buying any part of it. There were too many contradictions between the Koran's version of the biblical accounts and the original (Old and New Testament) versions of the Bible to begin with, not to mention the other koranic revelations Muhammad received from an angel calling himself "Gabriel."

Because it was forbidden to make images of people and animals during Muhammad's lifetime, there are not any historical depictions of the Prophet warrior; or his militant associates. Even today, people are killed for drawing an image of Muhammad; however, the farther away from the 7th century we are, the easier it is to find Muslim art. The picture above is part of a 14th century manuscript titled, "The History of the Tartars," depicting the "Battle of Wadi al-Khazandar" painted in 1299 A.D. and showing the Muslim, Mamluk Army and Mongol Archers.

---

historically as the symbol of Islam (Z) on most mosques and many flags, including the one in the above 1299 A.D. painting and let you decide.

When things got too hot for Muhammad in Mecca, he sought refuge in the Arabian town of Yathrib (Medina). At first, he was well received and even appointed as a judge, but as Muhammad gained military strength, there was a falling away—the honeymoon was over. Because the Jews mocked his new religion, the Prophet of Islam dealt harshly with the Jews of Yathrib. Muhammad first expelled the Banu Qaynuqa (a Jewish tribe) from Medina, Arabia, in 624 A.D. and Nadir, Arabia, in 625. There was no love for the Jews in Muhammad's heart, so on another occasion in 627, he declared war on the other remaining Jewish tribe in Medina, known as the "Banu Qurayza." There was no contest, and sadly, the Jews were soundly defeated. It has been reported by some Muslim historians that Muhammad personally beheaded 600 (some historians put the figure at 900[79]) Jewish men and pubescent boys in Medina. It has also been reported that he did this bloody work all day and into the evening.[80] As for the women, Muhammad forced women and girls into slavery and concubinage. He persecuted the Jews with a vengeance. Apparently, Allah must have shared Muhammad's hatred for the Jews since the Prophet of Islam encapsulated Allah's hatred for them in the Koran

> So when they [Jews] took pride in that which they had been forbidden, We said unto them: *Be ye apes* despised and loathed! (Sûrah 7:166, bracketed clarification mine, emphasis added).

> And you know of those of you [Jews] who broke the Sabbath, how We said unto them: *Be you apes, despised and hated!* (Sûrah 2:65, bracketed clarification mine, emphasis added).

> Shall I tell thee of a worse (case) than theirs [people of the Book] for retribution with Allah? Worse (is the case of him) Whom Allah has cursed, him on whom His wrath has fallen and of whose sort Allah has *turned some to apes and swine* [pigs], and who serves idols. Such are in worse plight and further astray from the plain road (Sûrah 5:60, bracketed clarification mine, emphasis added).

---

[79]W. Montgomery Watt, *Muhammad at Medina* (Oxford: Clarendon Press, 1956), 15-16.

[80]Ibn Ishaq, Sirat Rasul Allah, *The Life of Muhammad,* trans. A. Guillaume (New York: Oxford University Press, 1980), 464.

The carnage did not stop with the Jews. Through the establishment and growth of Islam, the aggression was also aimed at Christians in the Middle East and Europe, who also rejected the new religion.

Since we are dealing with the Church's heresy of replacement theology, we will not go into great detail regarding all the atrocities performed by the Muslims against the Jews, but we want to share a few to show how those brethren of Jesus were unfairly forced to suffer down through the ages. It should suffice to say that we still see just as many of the same, disgraceful atrocities going on against Jews around the world today and against the re-established nation of Israel—in the name of Islam.

Unfortunately, Europe and even America seem to be falling in line with Israel's antagonists, as we can see in these prophetic words in the Bible: " 'Come,' they say, 'let us destroy them as a nation, so that Israel's name is remembered no more' " (Psalm 83:4). Appallingly, some things never change.

More Dark Ages for the Jews

During the Dark Ages in European Christendom (628 A.D.), the Jews who were living in Byzantium were forced to convert to Christianity. A year later, in 629, the Merovingian Jews (those ruled by the Merovingian Dynasty in France and surrounding European countries) were also forced to convert—which, in turn, was followed by the forced conversion to Christianity of Jews living in Toledo, Spain, during 633. Jewish conversion to Christianity was not sufficient for those in power, so just five years later, the Jews in Toledo were hunted down and savagely burned at the stake.

When 642 A.D. arrived, all the Jews living in the Visigoth Hispanic Empire (Portugal, Spain, and a part of Southeastern France) were financially crushed by being expelled from their borders with no compensation. Then again, in 653, the Jews who managed to survive the carnage in Toledo were banished. Eventually, in 681, Spain ousted all the Jews from the kingdom, including all the Jews throughout Spain, who were compelled to convert to Christianity under pain of death.

In 693 A.D., in Toledo, the Spanish took a page from Islamic Sharia Law where non-Muslims—or "Dhimmis" as they are referred to in Islam—were subjected to harsh treatment, including taxation and given second-class status. It was declared that any Jew who had not converted to Christianity would be made a slave!

With the concluding years of the seventh century in 694 A.D., the engine of anti-Semitism in the Church was operating at full speed as we read from Cannon II of the *Quinisext Council*:

> Let no one in the priestly order nor any layman eat the unleavened bread of the Jews, nor have any familiar [friendly] intercourse [interaction] with them, nor summon them [Jewish Doctors] in illness, nor receive medicines from them, nor bathe with them; but if anyone shall take in hand to do so, if he is a cleric, let him be deposed [removed from the clergy], but if a layman, let him be cut off [excommunicated] (bracketed clarifications mine).

EIGHTH CENTURY

First Came Carnage; Then Some Relief for the Jews

About a quarter of the way through the eighth century, in 722 A.D., Pope Leo III banned Judaism altogether. Jews were rounded up and forced into Christian baptisms against their will[81]—as if that was the method to become a Christian.[82] Understandably, some of the Jews sought refuge in their synagogues, which were then torched. As a result, the Jews who

---

[81]Cecil Roth, "Encyclopedia Judaica: Forced Baptism," *Forced Baptism*, n.p. Web. 25 April 2016.

[82]Paul said in 1 Corinthians 1:17, "For Christ sent me not to baptize, but to preach the gospel..." This is not to say that baptism is not an outward expression of accepting Jesus as Lord because it is (Matthew 28:19), but baptism is also "a work." The Bible makes it clear that Christians are not saved by works. Consider: If we believers can do something good enough to impress God and participate in our own salvation—aside from what Jesus did for us—then that would give a person something to brag about, which is the very reason the Bible rejects a works-based salvation (Ephesians 2:8-9).

refused to convert were burned to death.[83] Despite the continued horrid offenses against the Jews, the eighth century was relatively calm and more tolerable.

Ten years later, in 732 A.D., on the European-Muslim front, Islamic troops moved toward Tours, France, and were met by bad weather and clever deception. Through the leadership of Charles Martel, during what became known as the *Battle of Tours*, the Muslim troops (Spanish Moors) were defeated, which halted their advance into Western Europe.

In 764 A.D. (some reports say 762/766 A.D.), Caliph al-Mansur founded the city of Baghdad when he relocated the Muslim Caliphate. In doing so, Caliph al-Mansur established a learning center, which he had formally instituted under his son, al-Ma'mun. He called it the "House of Wisdom" and made it accessible to all distinguished scholars, including Jews and Christians, to meet and discuss science, culture, and exchange ideas. In the palace, the caliph had a large library constructed, which housed a collection of many books from around the world, including books from Greece, China, India, Persia, Syria, and other places, which he had translated into Arabic.[84] With that "enlightened" attitude, the Golden Age of Islam had begun and has continued to flourish.

759 A.D. saw the end of the Muslim European conquests throughout France, with Islamic hordes turned away by Pippin (Pépin III, the king of the Franks) in the city of Narbonne, which was the farthest point the Muslims had penetrated into France.

With the Muslims turned away in France and the dawning of 768 A.D., Pepin's son, Charlemagne (Charles I), also known as "Charles the Great," became King of the Franks and shortly after that in 774, he also became the king of Italy. Because of that and more, Charlemagne was instrumental in making life better for the Jews through his example of tolerance toward them and admired for uniting most of Western Europe.

---

[83]Will J. Durant. *The Age of Faith* (New York: Simon & Schuster, 1950), 389.
[84]'House of Wisdom, in *Wikipedia, The Free Encyclopedia*, n.p. Web. 24 April 2016.

THE SECOND BLOOD MOON TETRAD OF
THE CHRISTIAN ERA (795-796 A.D.)

In 795-796 A.D., there was a biblical Tetrad during the Hebrew holidays of Passover and Yom Kippur (Day of Atonement). Shortly after Yom Kippur, on Christmas day in 795, Pope Adrian I (Hadrian) died. The next day, Leo III was elected pope, and on the following day (December 27), Pope Leo III was consecrated and officially ascended the papal throne.

The Lord does seem to work in mysterious ways. To set events in motion that would allow the Jews some relief, Pope Leo III would have to suffer some adversity. In 799, just four short years after his inauguration, Pope Leo III was attacked by some of his enemies, which caused him injuries and forced him to seek sanctuary with King Charlemagne, who was also known for having tolerance toward the Jews.

NINTH CENTURY

To show his appreciation to the Frankish King for giving him sanctuary—perhaps with a little royal encouragement by Charlemagne—on Christmas day in 800 A.D., Pope Leo III established and crowned Charlemagne as Emperor of the Holy Roman Empire. It would be an empire that would last, in one form or another, for over a thousand years. Unfortunately, for the Jews, the next blood moon Tetrad—just 43 years later—would end their much-needed reprieve.

Algebra Was Rediscovered by
Muhammad Al-Khwariaimi in 820 A.D.

As we saw in the last century, during 764 A.D., the Muslim caliph, al-Mansur, moved the Caliphate to Baghdad, where he collected many books about philosophy, medicine, and science to establish a research center known as the "House of Wisdom." One of the first scholars to take advantage of that was the Persian mathematician, astronomer, and geographer, Muhammad ibn Musa al-Khwarizmi, who researched the mathematical discoveries of the Greeks, Hebrews, and Hindus, which were based on earlier arithmetic developed by the Babylonians. In 820 A.D., al-Khwarizmi formulated his research into a thesis, known in English as, *The Compendious Book on Calculation by Completion and Balancing* (in Arabic as, *al-Kitab al-mukhtasar fi hisab **al-jabr** wa'l-muqabala*) (bolded emphasis added). Notice the word *al-jabr* (in English, it means "restoring") in the Arabic title. The Latinizing of that word is from where the word "algebra" derives. While many give credits to the Arabs for inventing this mathematical discipline, the truth is that it was *restored*— not invented—by al-Khwarizmi.

A few years after the first quarter of the ninth century had passed, in June of 827 A.D., Muslims continued their onslaught against Italy by capturing the city of Messina, Sicily.

THE THIRD BLOOD MOON TETRAD
OF THE CHRISTIAN ERA (842-843 A.D.):
AN OMINOUS SIGN FOR CHRISTENDOM

During the first year of that biblical Tetrad, the Greek Orthodox Church reinstated the use of religious icons, which had been banned twice before; the last time was 28 years earlier in 814 A.D.

The second half of the blood moon Tetrad events of 843 A.D. proved to be a bad omen for the Jews when the *Treaty of Verdun* divided the Holy Roman Empire in three ways. With that division, the Jews—who had benefited to some degree from the tolerance extended to them by the French—no longer had that leniency granted to them.

There were other casualties of the blood moon harbinger besides the Jews. Within months of the last blood moon[85] and the signing of the *Treaty of Verdun,* there were two different popes.

First, Pope Gregory IV (827-844)—who approved of the *Treaty of Verdun*—died in January of 844, just months after he signed that terrible treaty. Then Pope Sergius II (844-847) became pope—just three and a half months after that same blood moon (September 12, 843). He replaced Gregory in January of 844, but it seemed that God was not finished with the perpetrators of the *Treaty of Verdun* yet.

---

[85]September to December 843 A.D. = 4 months. Next is 844-846 A.D. = 3 years. Finally, January 847 A.D. = 1 month for a total of 3 years and 5 months.

On the heels of that treaty, during 846 A.D., Rome was attacked and even temporarily captured by Muslim hordes who looted all the Vatican's treasures.

On January 27, 847, Pope Sergius II also died. On April 10, Pope Leo IV (847-855) was consecrated and took office. He was the pope who set the stage for the unbiblical concept of a Christian warrior class (as we will discuss), which was in response to the Muslims sacking the Vatican under Sergius II and also to regain the Vatican's wealth and reassert its influence once again throughout Europe. It was that unbiblical warrior class who became known as the "Crusaders" under Pope Urban II. They would become responsible for some of the worst atrocities and carnage ever perpetrated against the Jews for many centuries that followed.

A Quick Review

In the shadow of the blood moon's far-reaching events of 843 A.D., we saw the termination of the *Treaty of Verdun,* which divided the Holy Roman Empire three ways and brought an end to a peaceful period of time for the Jews. That was abruptly followed by three successive popes in a manner of just a few years, accompanied by a Muslim invasion of Rome. To a natural onlooker, it must have appeared that God remembered His promise to Abraham and Sarah's descendants: "I will bless them who bless you and curse them who curse you" (Genesis 12:3), and once again manifested His displeasure with Europe's treatment of the Jews during the middle of that century's two blood moon Tetrad events.

Because God is not mocked, when Europe renewed their carnage against the Jews after ending the *Treaty of Verdun*, not only did the Muslims sack Rome and the Vatican, but within a generation, hordes of murderous Viking raiders were unleashed against northern Europe, and in June of 879, the bloody Age of the Vikings was born.

In the Scandinavian region of Europe, the Danish Vikings sailed to England and sacked the city of London, then turned their attention toward Canterbury and were only stopped by the heroic efforts of King Cynric (Cerdic I) of Wessex at Ockley.

Meanwhile, the rest of Europe still had to deal with the Muslim hordes coming from the south and southeast.

The Birth of What Eventually Became the Unbiblical Christian Warrior Class Known as the "Crusaders"

As the Muslim hordes spread throughout the ninth century Mediterranean, Pope Leo IV could not help but notice their suicidal devotion to Islam. Pope Leo realized that he needed a way to encourage Christians to fight like the Muslims who fearlessly seemed to welcome death. However, to do so, he had to ignore the biblical teaching: "For by grace are you saved through faith; and that not of yourselves. It is the gift of God: not of works, lest any man should boast"[86] and replace it with the koranic teaching, which promised the Muslim Jihadists, "And if you are slain in the way of Allah (the pope substituted the Christian God in place of Allah for his warriors) or you die, certainly forgiveness from Allah and mercy is better than what they (the enemy) amass (i.e., earn for themselves)."[87] The Koran also promises:

> Let those fight in the cause of Allah Who sell the life of this world for the other [paradise]. Whoso fights in the way of Allah, be he slain or be he victorious, on him We shall bestow a vast reward (Sûrah 4:74, bracketed clarification mine)

> Look! Allah has bought from the believers their lives and their wealth because the Garden [Paradise]will be theirs: (in return) is the garden (of Paradise): they shall fight in the way of Allah and shall slay and be slain. It is a promise which is binding on Him in the Tora and the Gospel and the Qur'an. Who fulfills His covenant better than Allah? Rejoice then in your bargain that you have made, for that is the supreme triumph [earning admittance into Heaven] (Sûrah 9:111, bracketed clarifications mine).

Consequently, we can see how Pope Leo IV adapted those unbiblical heresies from the Koran when he assured the Frankish Army of the

---

[86]The Bible, Ephesians 2:8-9.
[87]The Koran, Sûrah 3:157, translated by Mohammad Habib Shakir.

eternal rewards they would receive if they died defending their Christian homeland:

> Now we hope that none of you will be slain, but we wish you to know that the kingdom of Heaven will be given as a reward to those who shall be killed in this war. For the Omnipotent knows that they lost their lives fighting for the truth of the faith, for the preservation of their country, and the defense of Christians. And therefore God will give them the reward, which we have named.[88]

> **NOTE:** Although Allah assigns this type of behavior as sanctioned in the Law of Moses and in the Gospel, it is not a concept found anywhere in

Thus, it was Pope Leo IV, who began an Islamic type of non-biblical and even bloodier relationship between the Church and the Jews.[89]

In 855 A.D., Louis II outlawed Judaism in Italy and once again—in the very heartland of Christendom—all Jewish citizens were unceremoniously exiled from Italy's shores and forced to leave their homes, friends, businesses, and belongings.[90]

During that time, the bishops of Beziers, France, initiated a tradition of Easter sermons inspiring the Christian townspeople to stone Jews for their hand in the killing of Jesus, sad and ignorant events, which lasted centuries.

THE FOURTH BLOOD MOON TETRAD OF
THE CHRISTIAN ERA (860-861 A.D.)

For the second time that century, there was another biblical Tetrad during 860-861 A.D., which once again fell on Passover and the Day of Atonement. In Egypt, during the last year of the Tetrad,

---

[88]Oliver J. Thatcher, and Edgar Holmes McNeal, eds., *A Source Book for Medieval History* (New York: Scribners, 1905), 511-12; also Migne, *The Patrologia Latina*, 115: 656-657 and 161:720, circa 850.

[89]According to the Koran, Jihad is the only way of obtaining eternal security: "And if you are slain, or die in the way of Allah, forgiveness and mercy from Allah are far better than all they could amass ..." (Koran, Sûrah 3:157).

[90]Graetz, *History of the Jews,* vol. III, 174.

Muhammad al-Mudabbir tripled the *jizya* (i.e., tax) on Jews and Christians. Since few could afford such a financial burden, they went to prison. He also deprived the Christian clergy of their tax-exempt status and exemptions.[91] Even the Coptic patriarch himself was unable to pay that burdensome tax. As a result, al-Mudabbir confiscated all the assets of the Churches, which in turn forced the remaining Christians and Jews to flee.

During the last year of that blood moon Tetrad, King Erwig of Spain, not only redoubled the efforts to enforce existing depraved laws against his already suffering Jewish subjects, but the king also piled on even more restrictions that would turn the proverbial screws against the poor Jews even more! In an unthinkable move, King Erwig allowed Christian converts to be exempt from taxes and made up for the shortfall by doubling down on taxing the already overburdened Jews. As if that were not bad enough, the *Twelfth Session of the Council of Trent* validated King Erwig's malicious laws against the Jews.[92]

Also, in 861 A.D., during the Tetrad event, Russia sent 200 ships to attack the Eastern Roman Church in Constantinople. It was only after the Pagan, Russian troops captured the Virgin Mary's alleged robe that they withdrew—but first, they marched around the walls of Constantinople carrying the Virgin's robe. It is not clear why the Russians wanted the holy icon, but it did have a morally chilling effect on the Byzantines.

Shortly after the last blood moon, the Byzantines defeated the Muslims at the *Battle of Lalakaon* in Turkey, which halted the Islamic invasions of Eastern Europe.

Around that same time, Russia and Constantinople formed diplomatic ties, and the first ambassador to Constantinople converted to Christianity. Eventually, all of Russia would follow and become a Christian nation.

During 863 A.D., a year or so after the end of the Tetrad, St. Methodius and St. Cyril embarked on translating the Bible into the Slavonic language,

---

[91]H.L. Gottschalk, *The Encyclopedia of Islam,* New Edition: H-Iram ed., vol. III (New York: Brill, 1986), 879-890.

[92]Flannery, *The Anguish of the Jews,* 75.

which the Russians spoke. For the Russian people to have been able to read the Bible in their language, which exposed even more Russians to Christianity, was a God-send; however, it had no benefit for the Russian Jews, as the future would show.

In an unrelated event in Scandinavia during 872 A.D., King Harold I removed many of Scandinavia's troublesome tribal chiefs. He thus unified his country and paved the way for what became modern Norway.

Four years later, during 876 A.D. in Sens, France, the town's Jews became destitute when Archbishop Ansegis banished them after he confiscated everything they owned. Reluctantly, they packed up a few personal things and left. Toward the end of the century, during 897 in Narbonne (the first Roman city in France, and later a Visigoth capital), Charles III stole all the land and vineyards the Jews had worked so hard to develop and gifted them to the Church while leaving the Jews in financial ruin.[93]

TENTH CENTURY

A Century of Relative Calm for the Jews

That period is sometimes referred to as the "Golden Age" for Jews in Europe, but there were still unpleasantries. In 945 A.D., the Republic of Venice (which later became part of Italy) declared a ban on all Jews who wanted to travel by sea.[94] In other places, we also saw the occasional outbreak of anti-Semitism, but it was a peaceful period for the most part.

It was also during that period when Rabbenu Gershom ben Judah (960-1028 A.D.), who was known as "the light of the exile," began what would become the most important intellectual movement throughout Europe—the establishment of a yeshiva (i.e., Jewish academy of Talmudic[95] learning) in the German town of Mainz. (Mainz would later

---

[93]Flannery, *The Anguish of the Jews,* 81.

[94]Roth, "Encyclopedia Judaica" 8.

[95]"Rabbenu Gershom Ben Yehuda (C.960 - 1028)." *Rabbenu Gershom Ben Yehuda*, American-Israeli Cooperative Enterprise. Web. 15 November 2019. The

become the home of the first movable type printing press invented by Johannes Gutenberg in the early 1400s. Gutenberg was a blacksmith, goldsmith, inventor, and publisher.) Because of the incredible intellect of Rabbenu ben Judah, the school drew Jews from all over Europe, most notably Rabbi Shlomo Yitzchaki, also known as "Rashi." When Rashi was 25, he founded an academy in France. He believed every word in the Bible needed an explanation for his students, so he wrote unique commentaries—unique from the standpoint that he used the least amount of words possible to do it.

ELEVENTH CENTURY

The Rapture That Did Not Happen

As the eleventh century approached, many in the Church believed that Christ's return would happen in 1000 A.D. That belief was due, in part, to the anguish and tribulation caused by the hordes of Muslim invaders; it was also due to the fact that Jesus Himself had been gone for a thousand years, which gave people hope that the next millennium would usher in the Apocalyptic return of Christ and His millennium reign spoken of in Revelation 20:6.

Around 1000 A.D., the Christians who expected Christ's return was imminent, believed it was their duty to conduct wars against the Pagan, northern European countries in an attempt to convert as many Pagans as they could before Jesus' anticipated return. Many Christians sold what they had and donated their money to the Church in preparation for the long-awaited Divine event. Even though Christ failed to return, the Church refused to return what was donated, which did not sit well with the people and—understandably—resulted in severe criticism of the Church. Because of the rising criticism and anger directed toward the Church and its clergy, the Church began rounding up many of the dissenting leaders in the various communities. They even went so far as to declare those who demanded their charitable gifts back as heretics and began sentencing them to death to silence the others.

Talmud was developed through arguments presented at an early Jewish learning center in Babylonia from 220 A.D. to the 10th century

You might wonder if the early Church Fathers of the first century also believed Christ would return after the next thousand years. Based on Scripture, most of the disciples believed that Jesus was only going to be away with the Father for a short time and that He would return in their lifetime. At least that was their hope (1 Peter 4:7; Revelation 22:12-14).

With the turn of the second century, some early Church Fathers began to believe that Jesus might not return until around the beginning of the seventh millennium. Because the Bible taught that a millennium (a thousand years) on earth is a but a day in Heaven (Psalm 90:4; 2 Peter 3:8), and because God rested on the seventh day (which we know as Saturday, Genesis 2:2) and made it holy (Genesis 2:3), they reasoned that it made perfect sense for Jesus to return from Heaven for His millennial reign at the beginning of the seventh day from earth's creation, which would be the seventh (or Sabbath/holy; Heb. *Sabbat*) millennium here on earth.

Many today believe that we are now entering that Sabbath millennium; however, because of the change in 325 A.D. from the Hebrew lunar calendar to the Roman solar calendar and also because the Jews began counting their calendar from around 3760 B.C.—and not from the time Adam was created—the Hebrew calendar could be off from our calendar by as much as some 1,250 years. Our solar calendar could very likely be off, as well. Only God knows the time when Jesus will return (Matthew 24:36).

Another equally important factor as to why the congregations of the Middle Ages thought Jesus would return around 1000 A.D. was due to the biblical ignorance of Christian parishioners and the Church. They were unaware of the prophetic signs indicating that Christ could not have possibly returned then. They ignored those passages of Scripture because they were not looking for the prophecies Jesus had given regarding His return *within the context* of Jews living in a nation known as "Israel."

Of course, Jesus did not return in 1000 A.D. because Israel was not back in the land. Jesus had predicted certain things must happen before His return; one of them was the restoration of the Jews to their holy city, "... Jerusalem shall be trodden down of the Gentiles [non-Israeli rulers] until the times of the Gentiles be fulfilled ..." (Luke 21:24b, bracketed clarification mine). After the times of the Gentiles, when the Jews will once again have control of Jerusalem, the Bible tells us that the whole world will come against Jerusalem (Zechariah 12:3). In 1000 A.D., very few Jews were in the land because the times of the Gentiles had not yet been fulfilled!

Consider that even if all things had come together for the return of Jesus, He still would not have returned on the first day of the millennium because, as we already pointed out, the Church was using the Roman solar calendar, not the Hebrew lunar calendar; thus making the years and dates fall differently, a fact which still applies today.

Another factor is that the average Christian during the Middle or Dark Ages was illiterate, and the Catholic Church only allowed the ignorant parishioners to understand the Bible through the prism of the Church in Rome. Because of their biblical ignorance, there was a massive disillusionment among the people when Christ failed to return. This continuation of biblical ignorance by the Church only served to increase the horrendous and barbaric treatment of innocent Jews who were perceived as "Christ-Killers." With the arrival of the new millennium— nothing improved for the Jews; in fact, things got worse.

It was during the early years of the eleventh century when the hatred against the Jews was, once again, fanned into a fevered pitch, which escalated into the most inhuman deprivation that any century, up until that time, had witnessed.

During 1009 A.D. in Orleans, France, Jews were massacred indiscriminately,[96] and as if that were not enough, the deprivation repeated itself in 1012, where Jewish blood flowed freely in the streets of Rouen and Limoges, France.[97] Not to be outdone, the horrors against God's covenant people manifested itself in the Holy City of Rome. As for the French, France was not finished with the Jews either because, in that same year, they were expelled from the city of Mayence—with great

---

[96]Flannery, *The Anguish of the Jews,* 90.
[97]Leon Poliakov, *The History of Anti-Semitism.* Trans. Richard Howard (New York: Vanguard Press, 1965), 36.

personal losses and financial ruin.[98]

In 1021 A.D., the excruciating and terrified screams of Jews could be heard echoing throughout the narrow cobblestone streets and luxurious churchyards as they were herded into a vast pit. Their horrific screams soon became muffled and then fell silent as shovelfuls of dirt were tossed onto the bodies of those defenseless Jews. Many of the townsfolk watched in silence as those desperate families were mercilessly buried alive. Little Jewish children desperately clung to their mother's aprons with eyes wide open and filled with horror as piles of dirt slowly consumed them—in the very heart—in the very center—in the very capital of Christendom—Rome!

Were the murders of the Jews done to appease Jesus? Did they believe that Jesus had not returned in 1000 A.D. because there were still Jews living among them? Could it be, in some perverted way, those ignorant Christians believed that by attacking and killing the Jews, Jesus would somehow be pacified and help usher in His return?

Throughout the illiterate world of the Dark Ages, Jews were not the only casualties. The words of our Lord fell victim as well, like His cautioning found in Matthew 25:40:

> Verily I say unto you, "Inasmuch as you have done it unto one of the least of these My brethren you have done it unto Me."

His words fell silent in a world where few could read.

With the *Synod of Narbonne* (1050 A.D.), Christians were forbidden to live in Jewish homes, and Pope Gregory VII decreed that Jews were forbidden from holding political office or holding any office that would place them in a superior position over Christians.

In Spain, during 1063 A.D., terrified Jews screamed in panic when they were pulled out of their homes, and dragged along the roughly-surfaced streets. In the countryside, Jews were also herded like animals in the same manner throughout the land. Finally, they were assembled and

---

[98]Graetz, *History of the Jews,* vol. III, 254-256.

forced to huddle together in trembling fear before the citizens of Spain, who proceeded to slaughter their Jewish neighbors, right down to the very last man, woman, and innocent little child!

In 1065 A.D., Jews were slaughtered in Lorraine, France, only to see Jewish blood running in the streets of Metz, France, as well as in the nation of Hungary a year later. The eleventh century saw many Jews murdered—all because people falsely believed God hated the Jews, and that the Church had replaced them.

During that same year in England, the Anglo-Saxons were having problems of their own when the Norman warrior, "Billy the Bastard," crossed the channel and attacked them. After defeating the Englanders in 1066 at the *Battle of Hastings,* "Billy the Bastard" became known as "William the Conqueror."[99]

Twelve years later, in 1078 A.D., the *Synod of Gerona* (another Church council) decreed that although Jews were not Catholics, they still had to help support the Church through a special tax forced on them.

---

[99]*William I "The Conqueror" (r. 1066-1087).* The Official Website of the British Monarchy, n.p. Web. 25 January 2016: "Born around 1028, William was the illegitimate son of Duke Robert I of Normandy and Herleva Arlette (also known as Herleva of de Falaise), daughter of a tanner in Falaise in Normandy. She was 16 years old when she gave birth. Known as 'William the Bastard' to his contemporaries, his illegitimacy shaped his career when he was young." The Royal Household © Copyright 2008/09, the Royal Household © *Crown* Copyright.

THE CRUSADES

At the end of the eleventh century, when Pope Urban II initiated the First Crusade, two goals were in mind: (1) To defend Europe from the Muslim hordes invading it, and (2) free the holy city of Jerusalem from the Muslims' control.

As noble as those goals might have sounded, the truth is that the first causalities of the Crusades were not the Islamic warriors, but the peace-loving, God-fearing, European Jews!

The Crusades began in 1095 A.D. at the *Council of Clermont* in France when Pope Urban II called for war against the Muslims:

"Christians, hasten to help your brothers in the East, for they are being attacked. Arm for the rescue of Jerusalem under your captain Christ. Wear His cross as your badge. If you are killed, your sins will be pardoned."

With that statement, Urban II echoed the unbiblical and Islamic legacy adopted by his predecessor, Pope Leo IV: "... If you are killed, your sins will be pardoned;" never mind that the Bible teaches a person can do nothing to earn or buy salvation because it is an undeserved gift from God through His Son, Jesus, the Jew (Titus 3:5).

Pope Urban II at the Council of Clermount Preparing for the First Crusade

It was then when Pope Urban II began the First Crusade. During that time, we saw a ghastly display of the era's anti-Semitism manifested in the words of Godfrey of Bouillon. He swore, "to go on this journey (First Crusade)—but only after avenging the blood of the crucified One (Jesus) by shedding Jewish blood and completely eradicating any trace of those bearing the name 'Jew;' thus assuaging (appeasing) his own burning wrath."[100]

It appears that the First Crusade was more about attacking the defenseless Jews of Europe—killing, torturing, and stripping them of what wealth they had—rather than attacking the Muslim hordes on their turf in the Middle East.

Edward Flannery also documented the persecution of the Jews in the name of Christ:

> The First Crusade began in 1095. Guibert of Nogent (1053-1124) reported that the Crusaders of Rouen said: "We desire to combat the enemies of God in the East; but we have under our eyes the Jews, a race more inimical [hostile] to God than all the others ...."

> The Crusaders in Rouen and elsewhere in Lorraine massacred Jews who refused baptism. That was not the first instance of forced conversions. It is estimated that upwards of 10,000 Jews [some historians dispute that figure] were murdered in Europe during the First Crusade, constituting a third to a quarter of the Jewish population[101] (bracketed clarification mine).

This instruction of "convert or die" is again the sadistic influence of Islam's teachings as we read:

> And fight them until persecution is no more, and [the] religion is for Allah. But if they desist, then let there be no hostility except against wrongdoers (Koran, Sûrah 2:193).

---

[100]Patrick J. Geary, ed, *Readings in Medieval History* (Toronto: Broadview Press, 2003), 119.

[101]Edward Flannery, *The Anguish of the Jews*. 93-94.

Thus, the hapless Muslim initiate (i.e., intended convert) was offered life if he accepted Islam—or death if he refused.[102] What a contrast to the teachings of Christ, as we have seen regarding those who refuse His salvation.

> And whosoever shall not receive you, nor hear your words, when you depart out of that house or city, shake off the dust of your feet (Matthew 10:14).

In other words, do not harm or kill them; instead, move on!

Persecution of the Jews in Europe by knights of the Crusade

The original purpose of this crusade was to liberate Jerusalem from the Muslims, but the reality was that the Jews were a second objective. When the soldiers passed through Europe on their march toward Jerusalem and the Holy Land, all the Jews they encountered were confronted with this slogan: "*Christ-killers, embrace the Cross or die!*" In the Rhine Valley alone, 12,000 Jews[103] were massacred in

---

[102](1) "Then when the sacred months have passed, slay the idolaters wherever you find them, and take them (captive), and besiege them, and prepare for them each [an] ambush. But if they repent and establish worship and pay the poor-due [jizya tax], then leave their way free. Lo! Allah is Forgiving, Merciful" (Koran, Sûrah 9:5, bracketed clarification mine).

(2) "Fight against such of those who have been given the Scripture [Jews and Christians] as believe *not* in Allah *nor* the Last Day, and forbid not which Allah has forbidden by His messenger, and follow not the religion of truth [Islam], until they pay the tribute readily, being brought low" (Koran, Sûrah 9:29, bracketed clarification mine, emphases added).

[103]Estimates varied by region due to the nature of how information was gathered during the Dark Ages. Many times, people just focused on their own accounting as an entire total when it was actually only a regional summation, not an accurate overall number. In other words, they gathered information throughout their own regions and applied it as an overall reckoning of the times.

that First Crusade—all in the name of Christ Jesus.

During 1096 A.D., with Jewish blood that flowed once again throughout the gutters and streets of Mainz,[104] an incredible one-third of the entire Jewish population was slaughtered in Northern France and Germany![105]

Armed knights, led by Count Emicho, conducted the slaughter that time, not an unruly mob. A chronicler of Mainz recorded this passage from the Jewish perspective:

> When the enemies came to the rooms, they broke the doors and found the Jews still twitching and rolling in their own blood. They took the Jews' money, stripped them naked, and smote (killed) the remaining ones, not leaving any remnant. This they did in all the rooms that had members of the holy covenant, but there was one room that was strongly (fortified); the enemies fought until evening to (enter) it. When the holy ones saw that the enemies were stronger than they, they stood up, men and women, and slaughtered the children, and then one another; some fell on their swords and died, some were killed by their own swords or knives. The righteous women would toss rocks to the enemies outside the windows so that the enemies would stone them, and they accepted all the stones (thrown back) until their entire flesh and face had become strips. They were abusing and insulting the Crusaders regarding the name of the hung one, the disgraced, disgusting son of adultery: "In whom do you trust, a trodden corpse?" And the Crusaders approached the door to break it.
>
> The Crusaders killed everyone in that room and stripped them naked; the corpses were still twitching and becoming stained in their blood as they were stripping them.

---

[104]Yohanan Aharoni and Shmuel Aḥituv, *The Jewish People: An Illustrated History* (New York: Continuum, 2006), 251.

[105]Contained in the Conclusion of "The First Crusade" (c. 1101) by Ekkehard of Aura (1050?-1125?), a German Abbot of Aura and chronologist who was on the First Crusade, 131. *Mainz Anonymous* or *The Narrative of the Old Persecutions* is an account of the First Crusade of 1096 written soon thereafter by an anonymous Jewish author.

Then they tossed them naked from the room through the windows; hills upon hills, mounds upon mounds, until they became like a tall mountain. Many members of the holy covenant, when they were being tossed, still had a bit of life left in them, and gestured with their fingers, "Give us water, that we may drink" When the Crusaders saw this, they asked them, "Do you want to sully (baptize) yourselves?" But they shook their heads and looked to their Father in Heaven to say, "No," and they pointed to God. The Crusaders then killed them.[106]

As if the carnage in the city of Mainz was not enough, during that same year, on May 18, 1096, the Crusaders, again led by Count Emicho (also known as "Emich"), slaughtered 800 more Jews living in the town of Worms, Germany.

The Crusaders, who eventually made their way to the Holy Land and captured Jerusalem, brought down a holocaust on the Jews that would make the keeper of Hell's flames blush. Those Knights—who proudly wore a red cross blazoned across their chests—rounded up all the poor Jews they could find in the city and then proceeded to imprison them in Jerusalem's central Synagogue.

Initially, everything was relatively quiet in the holy city of Jerusalem; that is until the pitiless Crusaders put a torch to the Jews' holy place of prayer—possibly the very same place where Jesus might have walked or prayed. As the flames took hold, the silence was broken in the city of Jerusalem—the city of peace—as the first faint sounds of people coughing could be heard, followed immediately by choking and gasping, along with terrified and horrendous screams of panic and pain. There was a hellish stench of burning flesh—the flesh of children, Jewish men, women, mothers, fathers, brothers, and sisters—as Christ's brethren were ruthlessly cremated alive in their beloved Synagogue—not by Nazis, but at the hands of those so-called "noble" Christian Knights of the First Christian Crusade. The Jews who tried to escape were forcibly returned and shoved—as they twisted and struggled in vain—into the burning building while the knights proceeded to march proudly around their pitiful victims, all the while piously praising Jesus and singing hymns in His

---

[106]Terry Michael, ed., *Readers Guide to Judaism* (New York: Routledge, 2000).

honor! Such deprivation—such shame.

As word of those atrocities spread—all done in the name of Jesus—Jews began committing suicide rather than be subjected to the death contrived at the hands of the Crusaders, even though in Judaism, taking one's own life is a sin. The Jews call this practice, *Kiddush ha-Shem*. It means "sanctification (of) the (Divine) Name" (or "Holy [is] the Name"). Because even the title of God is considered too holy to mention, the Jews used "the" or "Ha" (Heb. ה) and substituted "Shem" or "name" (Heb. הם), which together means "the Name" (Heb. השם) to be used in place of "God." The historian and author, Simon Schama, cites historical events throughout Jewish history where the only option was suicide:

> Self-killing is expressly forbidden by the Torah [Jewish Written Law], but the wars of the Maccabees, the collective suicide at Masada in the first century narrated in Josephus, and what had passed into memory as the exemplary martyrdoms of Rabbi Akiva and Rabbi Hananiah at the time of the persecutions of Hadrian, had generated a body of rabbinic literature debating whether death, self-slaughter in particular, was preferable to forced transgression …. But if forced to commit iniquities in public, the acceptance of death was the holier option. Such deaths, moreover, were described as victories for God, indeed ordained by Him over the powers of evil and thus an act of glorification: *Kiddush Hashem,* the Sanctification of the Name, uttered in the last extremity. The reward (just as it was promised to Crusaders) was instant admission to Paradise for the [Jewish] slaughtered[107] (bracketed clarifications mine).

It is sad the word "crusader" means "cross-bearer," but Jesus, who bore the cross, did so to save *all* mankind, which includes His kindred—the Jews. Some might say, "But the Jews killed the prophets and Jesus."

Yes, they did, just like the Americans who killed four of their presidents (Lincoln, Garfield, Taft, and Kennedy). Others might argue, "But those were assassins, and not all of them were Americans." That is correct, and

---

[107]Simon Schama, *The Story of the Jews: Finding the Words (1000 BCE—1492)*, vol. 1 (London: The Bodley Head, 2013), 297.

there is no denying that while there are those who committed those crimes, many more Americans might have been in the wings contemplating or approving of the same horrendous deeds. To be fair, not all Americans killed their presidents, nor did all Jews kill their prophets and Jesus. Placing the blame of Jesus' death solely on the backs of *all* the Jews provoked the longest and worst period of inhumane atrocities perpetrated against the Jewish people. The Jews have suffered more than any other ethnic group throughout the entire recorded history of our planet. Shamefully, the hate continues to this day.

TWELFTH CENTURY

With the dawn of the twelfth century (1100 A.D.), the Jews were once again brutishly attacked by vicious crowds, this time in the Ukrainian[108] city of Kiev. [109]

St. Malachy and the Last Pope

Throughout that same century in 1139 A.D., the Irish Archbishop of Armagh went to Rome to report on his diocese to Pope Innocent II. It was during that visit when the future Saint Malachy had a vision in which he saw the next 112 popes, from Celestine II (elected as pope in 1143) and ending with Pope Petrus Romanus. St. Malachy wrote a brief description of each Pope and described the last—or—112th Pope,[110] who he saw as the one ushering in the Apocalypse or Armageddon:

---

[108]Sharon Schwartz, the BLAZE: UKRAINIAN JEWS REPORTEDLY 'FLOODING' ISRAELI CONSULATE TO GET OUT OF COUNTRY, n.p. Web. 9 May 2014. As some things change, they still remain the same as this article by Sharon Swartz tells us: "Since the [2014] unrest began in Ukraine, there have been reports of anti-Jewish incidents, including the firebombing of a Synagogue, the defacement of a Holocaust memorial and the distribution of leaflets ordering Jews to register their religion, their property and to pay a fine, a document that was later characterized as a provocation" (bracketed clarification mine).

[109]Kyiv is the preferred Ukrainian spelling of the city as the spelling "Kiev," is the detested Russian spelling of the name dating back to when the Ukraine was a part of the U.S.S.R. (1922-1991).

[110]From St. Peter until today, there have been a total of 266 popes. In St. Malachy's prophecy, he was counting all the remaining popes from his day until Armageddon. Above paragraph:

In the final persecution of the Holy Roman Church there will reign Petrus Romanus [Peter the Roman], who will feed his flock amid many tribulations, after which the seven-hilled city will be destroyed and the dreadful Judge will judge the people. The End. (Bracketed clarification mine.)

As of the writing of this book, that time is now. On March 13, 2012, we saw the 112th and possibly last pope (who is also referred to as the false prophet in the book of Revelation), predicted by St. Malachy, has finally ascended to the office of Pope. In Chapter 7, we take a closer look at the curious events surrounding this—the current and 112th pope—of the Catholic Church.

Years later, St. Malachy also prophesied his death by claiming that he would die on November 2, 1148.

During 1140 A.D., the seemingly endless persecution of Jews continued. In the streets of Germany, Jews were routinely and openly murdered. Six years later, in 1146, in the scenic and tranquil Rhine Valley, history repeated itself as the beauty of the countryside was, once again, marred by the wholesale massacre of the *forsaken folk* whose only crime was that they were descendants from the same family as Christ—descendants from the tribe of Judah. Sadly, in that same year, a similar fate also awaited them in the southern German city of Wurzburg. Again, during that same year, Jews were exiled from Flanders, a city which is now the Dutch-speaking part of northern Belgium.

When the Second Crusade began in 1146 A.D., the French Monk, who was known as "Rudolf," already had a six-year history of calling for a new crusade and the killing of Jews.[111] In the following year of 1147, the horrendous sound of shrill screams could be heard, accompanied by the stench of burning flesh as the townspeople of Belitz, Germany, threw guiltless, terrified Jews into the hellish flames prepared for them. The Germans were not the only ones participating in those grizzly actions; the citizens of the French towns of Carentan, Ramenu, and Sully carried out

---

[111]Steven Runciman, *A History of the Crusades*, vol. II: *The Kingdom of Jerusalem* (London: Cambridge University Press, 1957), 92-94.

their bloody massacres against helpless Jewish children, fathers, and mothers desperately clutching their innocent, small babies. One hundred and fifty Jews in Bohemia were also murdered by Crusaders.[112]

Not all incidents of anti-Semitism happened around mass rioting or government edicts; some were isolated incidents, but just as horrendous.

Consider this brief snapshot in time regarding a lovely, young, Jewish woman and her two precious daughters:

> Such beautiful names, such terrible ends. Doulcea,[113] the sweet one, cut to pieces on the streets of Worms in 1196, trying to summon help while her daughters, Hannah and Bellette, lie dying inside the house.[114]

It is unclear by what means she and her daughters were killed, but we do know they were three young, lovely, and defenseless Jews—living and dying—in Worms, Germany, during the twelfth century A.D.

When we read about history and all the battles, injustices and overwhelming carnage, which seems to have never ended, sometimes we become indifferent and numb, not fully realizing those were real people— real people who loved their children and wanted the best for their families—a young girl whose heart would beat fast whenever she saw the young man of her dreams—babies who giggled with delight while being bounced on their daddy's knee, and the daddy who looked down and smiled at his precious child with pride. They were real people who looked forward to worshipping G-d and serving their communities—real people who had real names like "Doulcea." Up until now—before we were introduced to her—we would never have given her a thought. The screams and pleas for mercy, which Doulcea uttered in her panic while she was all alone and terrified on that fateful day, never reached our ears, but hopefully, it will now reach our hearts.

---

[112]Graetz, *History of the Jews,* vol. III, 354-356.

[113]Doulcea is derived from the Latin adjective *"dulcis"* and means "agreeable," "pleasant," and "kind."

[114]Schama, *The Story of the Jews: Finding the Words (1000 BCE—1492),* 290.

The First of Many Blood Libels against the Jews Began

First, we need to understand what a blood libel is. According to the *Encyclopedia Judaica,* a blood libel proposes:

> ...the allegation that Jews murdered non-Jews, especially Christian children, in order to obtain blood for the Passover or other rituals: most blood libels occurred close to Passover, bringing basically another form of the belief that Jews had been and still were responsible for the passion and crucifixion of Jesus Christ.

Jesus observed the Passover and NEVER would have participated in such a bloody ritual. This might be a perversion of when Jesus told His disciples, whenever they drank the Passover wine—from that time forward—it should be remembered as His blood, which He would soon be shedding on the cross (Matthew 26:28; Mark 14:24). Jesus was symbolically referring to the wine as representing His blood and not that of anyone else, a point overlooked by the later Church. Think about this: For a Gentile Church, which allegorized almost everything in the Bible to make it fit its own agenda, it seems unbelievable that they did not pick up on the allegorical symbolism given by Jesus.

For Jews to kill innocent children or anyone for that matter, is pure nonsense because that would be murder—something the Jews take very seriously—especially during the Passover—and a practicing Jew would never willingly break any of the Ten Commandants. The seventh commandment states, "Thou shalt not kill," or as it is stated in Hebrew, "Do not murder" (murder = רצח [*ratsach*] pronounced *raw-tsakh'*, as found in Exodus 20:13). It is also important to know, by law, Jews are forbidden from consuming blood (Leviticus 17:10). Still, when it comes to the Jews throughout history, it seems biblical facts were—and still are—ignored by many in the Church!

During 1171 A.D. in Blois, France, near the city of Orleans, the first false charges of a blood libel against the Jews was established. The story goes that on a Thursday evening, near the time of the Jewish Passover, a Jew by the name of Isaac ben Eleazar rode his horse to the Loire River near the small town of Blois. Around that same time, a resident had also taken his master's horse to drink from the river.

Isaac ben Eleazar was wearing a white-colored, untanned pelt under his coat. When the local stable boy—who was also mentally challenged—brought his master's horse to the river to be watered, the horse became spooked when he caught a glimpse of the white hide under ben Eleazar's coat and refused to go near the river to drink.

Regrettably, the ignorant peasant had heard his parish priest speak on several occasions about the mythical Jewish blood libel! The priest warned his illiterate flock to "keep a watchful eye" to protect the children of the parish. The servant feared the wrath of his master because he could not water his frightened horse, so he seized upon the unfounded folk tales of blood libels.

The peasant knew that his master was at odds with a prominent, Jewish woman who had great influence at the court in their city. Because of her esteemed position, she was instrumental in gaining favors for the Jewish Merchants of Blois. The stable boy reasoned that he could divert and redirect his master's anger away from him and toward her when he had to explain why he did not water his master's horse.

According to Nissan Mindel, the deceitful servant had this to say to his master:

> Hear, my lord, what a certain Jew did. As I rode behind him toward the river in order to give your horse a drink, I saw him throw a little Christian child, whom the Jews have killed, into the water. When I saw this I was horrified and hastened back quickly for fear he might kill me too. Even the horse under me was so frightened by the splash of water, when he threw the child in it, that it would not drink! [the master exclaimed], "Now I can have my vengeance on that woman and the rest of the Jews" (bracketed clarification mine).[115]

The next day the master went to Theobald—the son of the Count of

---

[115]Nissan Mindel, "The Martyrs of Blois—(circa 1171)—Jewish History." *The Martyrs of Blois—(circa 1171)—Jewish History*, Kehot Publication Society; Web. 15 August 2014.

Blois—to present his unsubstantiated accusations. (Count Blois' son was married to the daughter of King Louis VII of France.) When Theobald, the ruler of Blois, heard the charges, he immediately rounded up all the Jews in Blois and put them in prison; however, the influential Jewess, who the servant's master hated, was not arrested because she had married well and bore the title of Dame Pulcelina (a dame is the feminine equivalent of knighthood. In the case of a knight, he would have "Sir" before his first name). The king's daughter, Alix, gave orders for the servants to keep silent on the matter to protect the Jewess, Dame Pulcelina.

Because Theobald did not have anything other than the story given by the half-witted servant to his master, he thought he might have been able to settle the problem—which by now had received the attention of the citizens of Blois—by insisting the Jews pay a huge ransom as punishment to be freed.

Consequently, a Jewish representative was immediately dispatched to several of the surrounding communities to ask the other Jews what they thought would be an appropriate amount of ransom to acquire the freedom of the Jews who were imprisoned. The Jews who remained free suggested forgiving all debts the Christians owed them (a combined total of one hundred eighty pounds), in addition to giving the Christians an additional one hundred pounds. When the imprisoned Jews were told about the offer, they refused to accept it because they believed it would begin a precedent—one that could result in trumped-up lies being waged against other Jews, along with demands for more ransom monies, which would make the imprisonment of Jews very profitable.

Before anything would come of the plan, the local bishop came on the scene and demanded that all the Jews should be killed. For the sake of Christian compassion, the bishop allowed the Jews to be proven innocent through a trial by ordeal. In that instance, the ordeal would be trial by water. The usual way of conducting it was tying the hands and feet of the accused so they could not tread water or swim. They then threw the accused into a large container of water. If they floated, they were innocent; if they sank, they were guilty.

To be fair, they had to begin with the half-witted servant who claimed to have seen the Jew throw the Christian child into the river. To make sure the servant would be "proven truthful," a large tank was filled with water, and the accused servant was prepared specifically to ensure he would not sink; thus, proving his story to be authentic;[116] not so for the hapless Jews of Blois. They all sank to the bottom of the tank—only to be quickly retrieved and condemned to be burned alive—as was the sadistic custom.

The Jews who failed their trial by water were then taken to a wooden building which had been prepared with thorn bushes tied into bundles and dried in the sun. In the now acceptable tradition, learned at the hands of the Muslims, the helpless Jews were offered the opportunity to convert to Catholicism or die. They refused the offer, preferring to be faithful to the God of Abraham, Isaac, and Jacob.[117]

As the flames began to consume them, the godly Jews began to sing the "Aleinu" (עֵלֵינוּ) prayer, which expresses the love for the one true God of Israel and the difference between the Jews and the Gentiles.[118] The heresy of replacement theology continued with yet another demonic layer added to it—blood libel. According to Rabbi David Kimchi-RaDak regarding this event:

> The 20th of Sivan[119] is the anniversary of the martyrdom of the Jews of Blois, who were victims of the first ritual murder accusation in France, more than 800 years ago.
>
> Blois is a city in France, on the river Loire, not far from Orleans. It is not a large city (its present population is about 25,000), but it has the "distinction" of being one of the very few cities in France, or for that matter in all of Europe, where there has been no Jewish community for the past 800 years. Jews simply shunned that horrible place, where the Jewish community was so cruelly destroyed as a result of a false ritual murder accusation in 1171.[120]

---

[116]Sometimes the trial by water result would be just the opposite; if you floated you were guilty.

[117]Mindel, "The Martyrs of Blois—(circa 1171)—Jewish History."

[118]Michael Freund, "Passover Blood Libels Then and Now," Jerusalem Post, Jan. 2014. Web. 13 August 2014.

[119]Sivan is a Hebrew month which falls sometime between May and June on our Gregorian calendar.

[120]Mindel.

As if the curse of the newly contrived blood libel was not enough, in 1179 A.D.—at the XXVI Canon of the *Third Lateran Council*—it was proclaimed: "... that the evidence [testimony] of Christians is to be accepted [preferred] against Jews in every case since Jews employ their own witnesses against Christians." We also read, "... those who prefer Jews to Christians in this matter are to lie under anathema [damnation] since Jews ought to be subject to Christians and to be supported by them [only] on the grounds of humanity [considerations] alone" (bracketed clarification mine).

The French continued their persecutions and expulsions of Jews in 1181 A.D., while across the channel, the English confiscated all the property owned by the Jews. It was also during that same year when Giovanni di Pietro di Bernardone became better known by his *nickname,* Francisco—a name that would stick when he received sainthood. The name Giovanni di Pietro means "God's gift of Peter," yet he is remembered as St. Francis of Assisi (1181/82—1226 A.D.; canonized July 16, 1228).

Massacre of the Jews during the coronation of Richard I, known as "Richard the Lion-Hearted."

From the beginning of 1184 through 1230 (?) A.D., the Episcopal (Bishops) Inquisitions were established.

In London and York during 1188 A.D., mobs viciously hunted down the Jews in the streets like dogs and mercilessly beat them. On July 20, 1189, Richard I (also known as "Richard the Lion Heart") became the Duke of Normandy. On September 3 of that same year, he was crowned King of England at Westminster Abbey.

It was a happy day for all of his subjects except—that is—the Jews who were sought out, hunted down and ruthlessly attacked in the streets, an incident which resulted in 30 Jews murdered after King Richard's coronation. To his credit, Richard had the perpetrators executed, but the hostilities were not limited to England.

While that was happening, across the channel in France in 1189, King Philip Augustus randomly seized the property of all of his Jewish subjects before he expelled them from his kingdom. Since there was no legal precedent for seizing their property, the clever king was able to increase his wealth and, at the same time, rid the country of Jews—a *win-win* for him as he saw it.

However, in the spirit of "Christian charity," the Jews were permitted to sell all transportable possessions, but not their land and houses; King Philip confiscated those. Nine years later, King Richard the Lion Heart, decided that Philip might be onto something and followed suit by persecuting the Jews and seizing all of their assets and burning most of their homes.

As we just saw, King Richard's protection of his Jewish subjects was short-lived. In 1190 A.D., when he left England seeking recruits for another Crusade, the Crusaders who were still in England took advantage of the king's absence and attacked Richard's Jewish subjects. Once again, the repugnant smell of burned, human flesh drifted on the English breeze as the so-called "civilized Christian" citizens of Norfolk brutally cremated terrified, living Jews.[121] One year later, in Bray, France, the same hellish holocaust awaited the poor Jews there as well.[122] France was far from finished with their Jewish persecution. In 1195, a preacher named Friar Foulques de Neuilly (Eng. Fulk of Neuilly) called for new crusades and the confiscation of all the Jews' ill-gotten money to be given to the poor. This gave mobs in various towns the excuse to attack, rob, and cause injury to the terrified and bewildered Jews. That terrible and false accusation was even ceased on by wealthy barons who confiscated everything they owned, leaving the Jews abandoned and completely destitute.[123]

---

[121]Cecil Roth, *A History of the Jews in England* (Oxford: Clarendon Press, 1965), 21.

[122]Graetz, *History of the Jews,* vol. III, 404. The Jews were given a choice of either baptism or death, and they chose death. One hundred Jews were burned with children, not yet in their teens, spared.

[123]Graetz, 405.

THIRTEENTH CENTURY

With the onset of the thirteenth century, the Fourth Crusade began. King Philip II of France established the University of Paris, and some historians tell us that the seat of the Greek Orthodox Church in Constantinople fell to the Roman Catholic Crusaders during 1204, although Catholic historians would argue differently.

There was a man in the East by the name of *Temüjin,* who was not very well known, but all that would change in 1206 A.D. when he was given the title of "Genghis Kahn" and established his Mongolian capital at Karakorum. His Mongolian Empire would stretch from the Black Sea to the Pacific Ocean, plus he went on to conquer most of northern China and Korea.

Three years later, in 1209, construction of the London Bridge was completed. That same year in the French city of Beziers, while very few Europeans paid attention, Jews were once again rounded up, seized, and brutally murdered, which resulted in yet another blood bath of the innocent fathers, mothers, children, and infants of our Lord's family.[124]
In Spain, during 1212 A.D., there were riots ac-companied by more Jewish blood spilled in Toledo, Spain. Three years later, in 1215 A.D., the *Lateran Council of Rome* decreed that all Jews had to be forced to wear a Badge of Shame through-out Christendom (an idea that was seized upon and repeated in 1939 when the Nazis invaded Poland and again in 1941 Nazi Germany).

Because of that decree, the Jews were denied any employment in the public arena and were forced to suffer extra burdensome taxes—all in the name of replacement theology.

In the city of Toulouse, France, in 1215 A.D., the Jews were arrested en masse. The irony is during that same year in Runnymede, England, on the banks of the River Thames, King John—at the bidding of his barons—was forced to sign the first document ever mandated on a king—a document declaring certain rights for his feudal barons—while at the same time

---

[124]Ibid., 502-503.

limiting his powers as the ruling monarch. That document is known as the *Magna Carta* and is a forerunner, not only of England's constitutional law, but also the Constitution of the United States of America. Ironically, only two years later in 1218, England became the first European country under the *Lateran Council* decree to take away liberties of a small class of its citizens who had no political champions—the Jews—and forced them to wear, what was by then, the established Jewish Badge of Shame.[125]

As the Dark Ages progressed, another problem with unintended and unforeseeable consequences fell to the Jews, which would eventually cause them to be the target of even more hatred. The Church, in its wisdom, did not permit Christians to profit from

This picture, on a medieval manuscript, shows Jews being beaten by the man on the right. Notice the Ten Commandments emblazoned on their chests (they would have been colored yellow).

lending money. Because interest could not be charged or collected by Christians—a financial vacuum was created and, therefore, it fell to the Jewish merchants to handle the job of establishing the concept of banking.[126]

Because the Church's prohibition was not only a very bad business practice, the problem of allowing the flow of money to the crown also became a real issue; however, since the Jews did not fall under the Church's decree, the king was able to allow the Jews to engage in lending

---

[125]David Grossman, *Anti-Semitic Stereotypes without Jews: Images of the Jews in England 1290-1700* (Detroit: Wayne State University Press, 1975), 16.

[126]James Parks, *The Jew in the Medieval Community* (New York: Hermon Press, 1976), 303.

money for profit.[127] Predictably, that created circumstances for the Jews to become very prosperous.[128] Since revenue was needed to manage England, the King saw an opportunity to have the Jews (his non-Christian subjects) taxed.

The king could legally place heavy taxes on Jews, and he could do so without the approval of Parliament. Of course, the Jews passed along that expense by simply raising the interest rates on the money they were loaning to others. Unfortunately, with success comes envy, then hate. The illiterate masses of the day believed that the Jews became wealthy through ill-gotten gain, so they accused the Jews of being "extortionate[129] moneylenders." Needless to say, because of the king's greed, this misdirected resentment by the uneducated masses caused the Jewish moneylenders to become very unpopular.

In other matters, on July 16, 1228, St. Francis of Assisi was canonized, which is to say that the Catholic Church placed him in the canon or on a list of recognized saints. St. Francis is remembered for many things, but this prayer of St. Francis is truly cherished:

> Lord, make me an instrument of Your peace.
>
> Where there is hatred, let me sow love;
>
> Where there is injury, pardon;
> Where there is doubt, faith;
>
> Where there is despair, hope;
>
> Where there is darkness, light;
>
> Where there is sadness, joy.
>
> O, Divine Master, grant that I may not so much seek to be consoled as to console;
>
> To be understood as to understand;

---

[127]Ibid., 306.

[128]Ibid., 307.

[129]Root word "extortion" (i.e., forcing people to pay too high a price for something (unreasonably high interest on money lending) under threats or penalty of law.

To be loved as to love;

For it is in giving that we receive;

it is in pardoning that we are pardoned;

It is in dying that we are born again to eternal life.

What a wonderful example for all of us, which makes it even more ironic that only three years after the canonization of this unassuming and gentle monk, in 1231, the Medieval Papal Inquisition began.

Pope Gregory IX declared his infamous *Papal Bull* (i.e., an official letter or document issued by a pope with a leaded seal attached on the bottom) titled, "Excommunicamus." It established courts of inquiry, which had to answer directly to him. The courts consisted of permanently appointed ecclesiastical (i.e., Church) judges who held the authority of the Roman Church wherever and when-ever it held court sessions. The pope appointed two equally authorized inquisitors who oversaw each tribunal and commanded the support of the local police, notaries, and other counselors as needed. The initial officers were drawn from the *Dominican Order* created by St. Dominic de Guzman in 1216 A.D. The Order was formally recognized by Pope Honorius III on December 22 of that same year. At first, the inquiries avoided the use of torture; nevertheless, during 1236 A.D. in France, the Jews were once again viciously assailed by so-called "Christians" who were using the Muslim practice of forcing their victim to convert to Islam or die, which predictably resulted in the wholesale massacre of Jews.[130]

In the French cities of Angouleme, Anjou, Bordeaux, and Poitou during 1236, the galloping sound of the Crusaders' horses could be heard approaching from the distance on the cobblestone streets. As the people from the Jewish sections of those towns came out to see what all the commotion was about, soon all that could be heard was the muffled cries of the unsuspecting, defenseless Jews being trampled under the horses'

---

[130]"Then when the sacred months have passed, slay the idolaters wherever you find them, and take them (captive), and besiege them, and prepare for them, Each ambush. But if they in repent and establish worship and pay the poor-due [jizya tax], then leave their way free. Lo! Allah is Forgiving, Merciful" (Koran, Sûrah 9:5, bracketed clarification mine).

hooves. That resulted in the muffled and bewildered cries of the brothers of Christ calling out to the God of their Fathers as they were being crushed to death! The Crusaders reached their prey, which consisted of Jewish men, women, and children, as well as pregnant Jewish mothers who were crushed. The carnage was so bad (over 3,000 Jews) that even Pope Gregory IX was appalled and complained to the priests in the cities where the carnage occurred that they were wrong not to have made an effort to prevent it.[131]

Pope Gregory IX must not have been too upset because three years later, in 1239, he ordered all the Jewish Talmuds in England, France, Spain, and Portugal rounded up and placed on trial because they supposedly contained blasphemous and deceitful lies. (The Talmud is a book, which contains the oral traditions of the *Torah* (i.e., Jewish Written Law), with a second section containing commentary about the Hebrew Bible).[132]

Pope Gregory IX ordered all Talmuds confiscated and put on trial for alleged lies (circa 1239). Note the Talmuds being burned in fire pit.

Meanwhile, throughout the rest of the year in the city of London, England, false allegations of a Jewish blood libel circulated again, and Jewish property confiscated yet once more. Around that same time, it was not uncommon to find citizens rioting in the streets, accompanied by the slaying of any Jew unfortunate enough to be seized by the mob.[133]

---

[131]Graetz, *History of the Jews,* vol. III, 110-111.
[132]Yitzhak Baer, *History of the Jews in Spain* trans, Louis Schoffman. (Philadelphia: Jewish Publication Society of America, 196), 150-151.
[133]Roth, *A History of the Jews in England*, 59

In Austria (1240 A.D.), more Jewish property was seized, and the Jews were given the choice of converting to Christianity or going to prison. During that same year, many Jews were forcibly expelled from Austria or burned alive at the stake.

Furthermore, in 1240, the French also followed the example of Pope Gregory IX and confiscated all the Talmuds found in that country.[134]

Meanwhile, across the English Channel in London, Jewish books were also confiscated and gleefully tossed into bonfires.[135] In Spain, the never-ending assault against God's chosen people, the Jews, were once again forced to convert to Christianity or suffer a painful death.[136]

In 1242 A.D., the French Parisians gathered to witness the spectacle of burning every Talmud that could be found. Back in England, throughout the city of Oxford, mobs attacked the Jews in 1244.

As for the established papal Inquisitions of 1252 A.D., under the Catholic Church's new papal leadership, Pope Innocent IV introduced torture as a legal means of inquiry. In the city of Lincoln, England, eleven years later, in 1255, a blood libel was again leveled against the Jews. They were tortured, publicly hung, and burned by unruly mobs, all because of the unfounded accusation against God's helpless people that they were using the blood of innocent Christian children for preparing their Passover ritual.[137] As previously noted, the truth is, the only human blood *ever* shed for the Passover, up until that time, was that of the Messiah, Jesus, which He willingly offered for the sins of humanity (John 10:17-18).

The picture on the next page is from a seventeenth-century fresco on a window in the "cult-Church of Anderl von Rinn." The men in the depiction were Jews, identified by the hats they were forced to wear. The verbiage at the bottom of the picture reads, in German:

---

[134]Graetz, *History of the Jews,* vol. III, 575-576.

[135]Roth, *A History of the Jews in England*, 55.

[136]Baer, *History of the Jews in Spain,* 151-1152.

[137]Blood Libel (2014, May 9), *Wikipedia, the Free Encyclopedia*; Web. May 14, 2014.

"Sie schneiden dem Marterer, die Gurgl ab und nemen alles Blut Von Ihm."[138]

The basic translation of the caption is "they cut the throat of the martyr and take [took] all the blood from him."

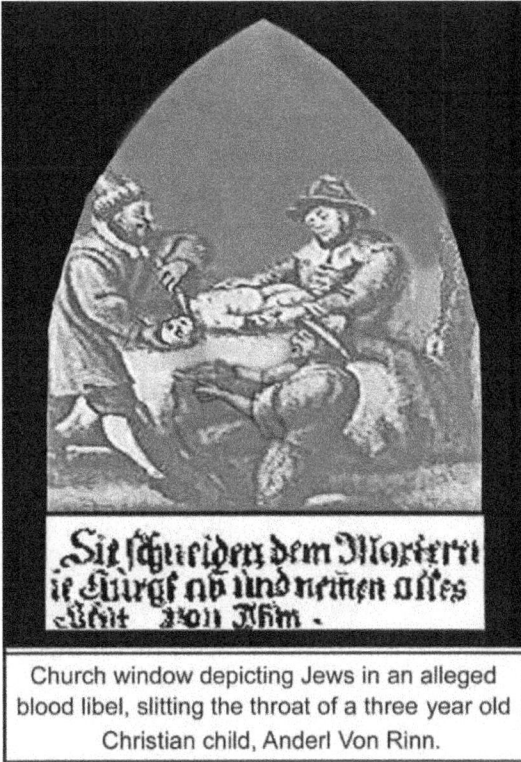

Church window depicting Jews in an alleged blood libel, slitting the throat of a three year old Christian child, Anderl Von Rinn.

Notice the man on the left—his hand is holding a knife at the naked child's throat as he prepares to slit it. That would cause the entire amount of the child's blood to be drained into the container being held by the man kneeling in the center of the picture, while the man on the right is holding down the helpless child.

The priests of that church continued to display this heresy against God's eternally beloved people (Genesis 17:7) until recently (the 1990s), when Bishop Reinhold Stecher, to his credit, removed this slanderous and hateful stained-glass window.

Remember, if God can go back on His promise to Israel, what is to stop Him from turning His back on us? Rest assured; God never goes back on His promises because He cannot lie (Numbers 23:19; 1 Samuel 15:29; Titus 1:2). It is disgraceful that the clergy who were venerating the tradition of Jewish blood libel did not take the time to read the Bible where God specifically instructs both Jews and Christians:

---

[138]Ibid.

135

And whatsoever man there be of the house of Israel, or of the strangers that sojourn among you, that eats any manner of blood; I will even set my face against that soul that eats blood and will cut him off from among his people (Leviticus 17:10).

That you abstain from meats offered to idols, and from blood, and from things strangled, and from fornication: from which if you keep yourselves, you shall do well. Fare ye well (Acts 15:29).

God makes it clear that consuming blood in any form—and that would include mixing blood with matzo—is an abomination to God and for any observant Jew at Passover or any other time for that matter! Do not forget that Jesus and all of His disciples ate the matzo with their Passover meal.

Again, because of Christians' ignorance of the Scriptures, Jesus' brethren were needlessly condemned to suffer great atrocities at the hands of His Church. It is ironic the only real blood that was shed around the Passover during that time was not from Christian children, but the blood of innocent Jews. Perhaps that is the result of what can happen when *Sola Scriptura* (only Scripture/Bible) is replaced by Church tradition, like we have seen—and will continue to see in this dark history of replacement theology—where that particular *Church tradition* is NOT from God, but from the pit of Hell!

In England, the mobs continued to persist against the Jews in Canterbury in 1261 A.D. and also in London in 1262, only to be repeated in London throughout 1264. Sadly, attacking Jews in the cities had become a well-established, Church tradition and shameful blood sport.[139]

During that same year, there was another ruling handed down at the *Council of Vienna* in Germany, where it was declared that each Jew had to wear a pointed dunce cap to make it easier to identify them. The predictable results could be seen throughout the countryside as mobs unrelentingly continued to slaughter thousands of Jews identified as such by their required head attire), who were neighbors of Christians, were slaughtered, all in the name of God. As if the pointed hats were not

---

[139]Roth, *A History of the Jews in England*, 59.

enough, in 1267 A.D., Vienna revisited the hat issue and began forcing all of their Jewish populaces to wear satanically inspired horned hats. In their minds, the Church had taught God was done with the Jews and had turned them over to the devil.[140]

Jewish families being attacked by mobs in the streets of Europe. Notice the funnel-shaped hats the Jewish men were required to wear.

One of the most hideous, demonic, and inhumane events took place in 1270 in the German cities of Weissenberg, Magdeburg, Amstadt, Coblenz, Sinzig, and Erfurt, when Christians rooted out as many Jews as they could and took them to "community graves."[141] After they had thrown the living Jews into the pits, they then proceeded to toss in shovelfuls of rocks, rubble, and dirt. That was bad enough for the adults, but imagine if you were a bewildered, small child—how horrible and terrifying that must have been. Any panicking Jew who tried to climb out was savagely kicked in the face, which broke their nose and jaws and collapsed their facial structure. If they did manage to make it out of the pit, they were beaten and physically forced back into the living grave—until they were overcome by the sheer weight of dirt, rubble, and other bodies thrown on them—resulting in their suffocation—and death.

---

[140]Runes. *The War Against the Jews*, 92.
[141]Graetz, *History of the Jews,* vol. III, 611.

Libel of the Counterfeit Coins

CLIPPED COIN

During 1275 A.D., in England, there was a widespread practice among the people known as "coin-clipping" or "shaving" (removing a small area of a gold/silver coin to pocket for themselves to meltdown later, hoping the clipped coins would go unnoticed). It was a practice indulged in by many British subjects over the years by both Christians and Jews, which eventually devalued the currency and led to a financial crisis. Shortly after King Edward I cracked down on the illegal practice, making coin-clipping punishable by death, suspected culprits' homes and businesses were raided throughout England. [142] When it came to money, sadly, the king blamed the Jews since their business was loaning money for a price (a practice forbidden to Christians). The "Libel of the Counterfeit Coins" edict allowed the king to punish the offenders. Jews received very harsh punishment while the king's actions only put a scare into his other guilty subjects. [143]

Another benefit to the king for singling out the Jews and making them the scapegoat allowed the king, in 1218, to create a statute, which considerably limited the Jews. He mandated all Jews to wear a yellow badge identifying them as Jews, thus following the example of other countries. As a result, the badge regulated where Jews could live.

The king also canceled the ability of Jews to have any dealings with money, but did allow them to engage in "lawful merchandise" or work as a laborer; however, wearing the yellow badge of shame made it very difficult to find a job. After all, the thought at that time was, "Who would want to hire a *crooked* Jew?" While it might have appeared to be charitable when the Jews were permitted to lease plots of land for 15 years to farm, the sad reality is that the real purpose of that act was to deprive Jews of owning land and making a decent living.

1276 A.D. saw Jews in Bavaria, Germany robbed of their homes and

---

[142]Roth, *A History of the Jews in England*, 75.
[143]Roth, *A History of the Jews in England*, 75.

businesses, concluding with all the Jews banished. Meanwhile, back in England, King Edward I was looking for a means to help finance his war against the Welsh, so he levied an exorbitant tax against the Jewish bankers. Sadly, the bankers could not pay the tax, so the king not only rescinded their right to lend money; he also forced them to wear the Jewish patch of shame. As a result, many Jews were arrested and sent to the dreaded Tower of London. Two years later, in Genoa, Spain, bloodthirsty gangs attacked the Jews without any warning, much to the dismayed Jews already experiencing intolerable grief and suffering.

Back in England, during 1278, with the "Libel of the Counterfeit Coins" well underway, 3,000 Jews were arrested. Not surprisingly, it was not only Jewish men who were thrown into prison, but also Jewish women and children too. It was reported in the *Bury Chronicle:* "All Jews in England of whatever condition, age or sex were unexpectedly seized and sent for imprisonment to various castles throughout England. While they were imprisoned, the innermost recesses of their houses were ransacked." Jews were not only held throughout the kingdom, but it was reported a year later, in 1279, that some 700 Jews were being held in the Tower of London, with over 300 of them believed to have been executed there. For every Christian Englishman King Edward I hung for coin clipping, he also hung ten Jews! Within a decade, all Jews were expelled from England and would not be allowed to return for almost 500 years![144]

In Hungary and Poland, during 1279 A.D., the *Council of Offon* convened. They refused the right of Jews to hold any civic office and forced them to wear a Badge of Shame, much like the Nazi's did during the middle of the twentieth century. After all, didn't the Church teach that God had condemned them?

In that horrible century of bloodlust throughout Europe, thousands of Jews were unceremoniously strung up and hung by the neck. That barbaric, wholesale slaughter forced both individuals and families to hang until the strangulation they were forced to endure completed its task— setting these poor souls free from their sadistic torment and allowed

---

[144]*Secrets of Great British Castles: The Tower of London*, season 1, Ep. 2, a Sideline Production/Group M Productions Ltd., 2015.

them—finally—to be at peace.

The mindless bloodlust continued. Jews were attacked and beaten senseless by mobs in the German cities of Mayence and Bacharach in 1283. It seemed like the holocaust against the Jews would never stop. Within just two years, during 1285 in Munich, Jews were again ruthlessly gathered up by their Christian neighbors and brutally burned alive as the horrific screams of their unmanageable pain were ignored.

Two years later as we previously mentioned, in 1290 A.D., King Edward I of England issued another edict to make sure any Jews who managed to escape the exile in 1279 and remained in England were to be banished from his country once and for all with any remaining Jews put to death.[145]

During that same period, it is rumored that many Jews underwent some of the evilest, sadistic, and blasphemous brutality ever used against them when—in the name of the Lord; they were rounded up and forced into a *baptism of death*. It is said that knights (among others) wearing white tunics (the symbol of purity) with a large red cross on their chests, gathered up as many Jews as they could find. Then the knights marched them down to the water's edge and held them underwater until they stopped struggling—all the while declaring they were baptizing the supposed *wretched* Jews in the name of Jesus![146] That behavior continued in force until the end of the Dark Ages. Sadly, it was not an isolated event, and such hostility continued to intensify for the next 200 years. (After 350 years, in 1657, England's Prime Minister, Oliver Cromwell, under the

---

[145]Roth, *A History of the Jews in England*, 85.

[146]While the story of knights holding Jews under water in a forced baptism until they were dead has been repeated many times, it is difficult to certify; nevertheless, there is plenty of documentation of Jews having been forcibly baptized (Roth, *Encyclopedia Judaica: Forced Baptism*). Many Jews would have preferred death than to have renounced the faith of their fathers. Therefore, it is not such a stretch of the imagination to believe that many Jews who underwent forced baptism and then pulled from the water and asked the question, "Do you accept Jesus as your Lord and Savior" would have answered, "No!" As that dunking cycle continued with the woeful Jew struggling against being held under water, the aggravated knight performing that perverted so-called baptism—would likely have decided to just hold the Jew under water to drown many of them—which would give life to such a story.

Cromwellian Protectorate, allowed the Jews back into England but only because he needed their financial expertise.)

One year later, in 1291 A.D., the Jewish refugees who managed to escape from England to France were promptly expelled from that country too. Toward the end of the thirteenth century in 1292, the Jews were forced to convert or be expelled from Italy. In 1298, the Chinese invented the first field gun, referred to as a "cannon." It could deliver large projectiles against hardened walls and castles.

Meanwhile, in Germany, the libel of the "Desecrated Host"[147] was wrongfully blamed against the German Jews. Approximately 150 Jewish communities underwent forced conversions. During that same year in Austria, *Reindfel's Decree* was enforced against the Jews of Franconia and Bavaria. A militia known as the "Jew Slaughterers" (*Judenschächter*) was assembled by a German nobleman known as "Rindfleisch." They set out on their unholy mission by murdering every Jew in their path, which resulted in the massacre of 100,000 Jews and over 140 communities being destroyed.[148]

FOURTEENTH CENTURY:
THE BEGINNING OF THE RENAISSANCE

A Climate Change Event Triggered the *Little Ice Age*

With the beginning of the fourteenth century, temperatures began to drop, which ushered in a worldwide phenomenon—the Little Ice Age. Because of global cooling, places that were once suitable for growing food were no longer able to sustain life. Consequently, Christendom's environment became increasingly more susceptible to the Plague and

---

[147]Ami Isseroff, "Rindfleisch Pogroms," *Rindfleisch Pogroms. Zionism and Israel Encyclopedic Dictionary,* 29 Mar. 2009. Web. 16 Nov. 2011. "The 'desecration of the host' was a medieval superstition which maintained that Jews [somehow] defiled the communion wafer with blood. It is now believed that the wafers were attacked by a brownish-red fungus that looked like blood."

[148]Leon Poliakov, *The History of Anti-Semitism in Germany* (New York: Vanguard Press, 1965), 99-100.

other pestilences. Europe's population was drastically reduced and—like the *miserable conditions* forced on the Chosen People by Christians— Christendom would also have to undergo *miserable conditions* forced on them by Providence.

In 1306 A.D., the French once again began expelling the Jews. In Strasbourg, France, in 1308 A.D., Jews were gruesomely burned alive.[149] In the French cities of Toulouse and Perpignan, in 1320 A.D., many of their Christian citizens descended on their unsuspecting Jewish neighbors to murder every single one. That same year, the French also formed the so-called "Shepherd's Crusade" when they gathered 40,000 shepherds to march from the city of Agen to Toulouse. They killed any Jew who would not convert and be baptized. Five hundred of the Jewish citizens of Verdun took shelter in a tower to commit suicide rather than be baptized. Sadly, there were 120 Jewish communities that underwent slaughter at the hands of those French peasants and shepherds.[150]

As if that were not enough, the sacred Talmuds of the Jews were also consumed in a holocaust of hatred. In Teruel, Spain, during 1321 A.D., Jews were rounded up and paraded about as a spectacle before the jeering citizens of that town. That indignation finally ended when the Jews were publicly executed before the eyes of onlookers. Unfortunately, for the Jews, the carnage against a defenseless people became a routine occurrence.

During 1328 A.D., Europe saw its first sawmill, an invention that greatly aided the building of seagoing ships. Also, in 1328, A.D., Cardinal Hugo de S. Carlo invented a new system for studying the New Testament with the creation of chapters. In the Spanish city of Estella during that same year, over 5,000 of the people who gave us the New Testament—a Jewish publication by Jews about a Jew—were slaughtered.

In October of 1347, a deadly plague known as the "Black Death," was introduced in Europe at a seaport in Sicily. It was not only disastrous for

---

[149]Runes, *The War Against the Jews,* 105.
[150]Graetz, *History of the Jews,* vol. IV, 56.

Europe, but it brought ignorant and unwarranted blame on the Jews because they had fewer infections due to their strict kosher (cleanliness) laws. A kosher home included personal hygienics—a practice that went a long way in preventing the type of filthy environment which drew the vermin (mostly rats). The rats carried infected fleas responsible for the Plague. Still, many of the ignorant European Christian peasants believed that the Jews used witchcraft and were, therefore, responsible for the Plague.

In France and Spain, throughout 1348 A.D., Jews were treated to unthinkable cruelties, as once again, they were rounded up and burned alive.[151] During that same time in Basel, Switzerland, Jews were accused of causing the Black Plague by poisoning the well water. Because of that erroneous belief, the Jews were offered fire and water (i.e., they were offered baptism, and those who refused were cast into a living Hell of fire).

To his credit, during the last half of 1348 A.D., Pope Clement VI issued a proclamation which cleared the Jews of any connection to the Black Plague; nevertheless, on January 9, 1349, in what has become known as the Basel Massacre, nearly every Jew who could be found was captured and burned alive because the citizens ignored the pope's proclamation. Sadly, they never wavered from their belief that the Black Plague was created by the Jews. That carnage continued into 1350 A.D.

With the purging of the Jews, the Christian citizens converted Jewish Synagogues into Churches, while the graveyards of the Jews were desecrated and destroyed.[152]

With the European spring of 1348, after two generations of malnutrition, the Plague spread to England, France, Denmark, and Norway, where a weakened population succumbed to the Plague, and one-third were destined to die.

---

[151]Graetz, *History of the Jews,* vol. IV, 101-102.

[152]Michael Omer-Man, "This Week in History: The Jews of Basel Are Burnt," The Jerusalem Post, 14 January 2011. Web. 7 September 2014.

Meanwhile, over in Germany during 1349, the gagging stench of burning flesh once again permeated the air as more Jewish men, women, boys, and girls were prepared as a living feast for the hungry flames; this time it was in the city of Swabia, Strasbourgon on Sunday, the Christian sabbath, when 2,000 helpless Jews were burned alive at the stake. Those who were not burned were banished for 100 years,[153] while at the same time, over in Openheim in the district of Mayence, 6,000 Jews were slain, with their homes burned to the ground. The village of Erfurt was completely destroyed, leaving 3,000 Jewish souls dead. The same thing happened in the

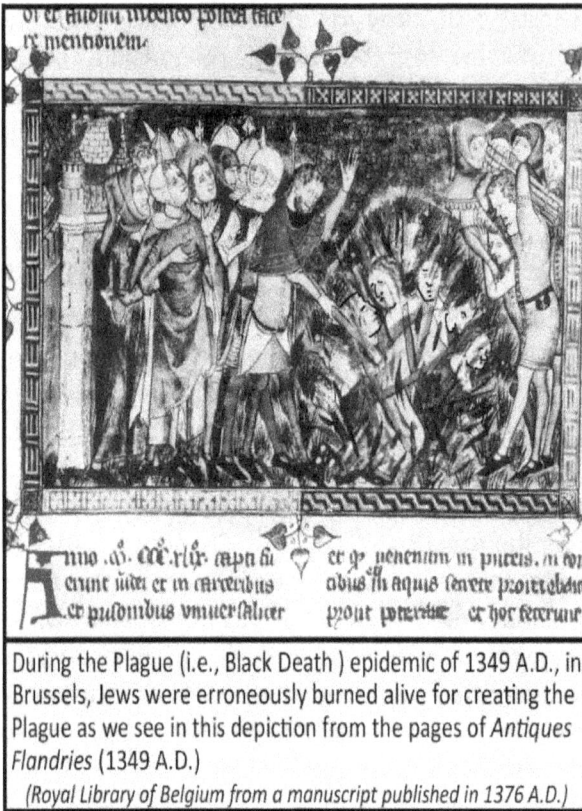

During the Plague (i.e., Black Death) epidemic of 1349 A.D., in Brussels, Jews were erroneously burned alive for creating the Plague as we see in this depiction from the pages of *Antiques Flandries* (1349 A.D.)

(Royal Library of Belgium from a manuscript published in 1376 A.D.)

villages of Breslau, Augsburg, Munich, and Wurzburg, where every single Jewish[154] life was snuffed out.[155] In the beautiful city of Vienna, rather than face a horrible death, the Vienna, Jewish congregation followed the example of their rabbi and committed suicide.[156] The Council of the City of Worms, also ordered all Jews to be burned (400 Jews killed).[157] Sadly, Worms is the city is where Martin Luther would later defend his view that the Bible is the only authority of God, and arguably, where the Protestant reformation was born.

---

[153]Graetz, *History of the Jews,* vol. IV, 108.
[154]Ibid. 109.
[155]Ibid. 110.
[156]Bear, *History of the Jews in Christian Spain.* vol II, 97
[157]Graetz, *History of the Jews,* vol. IV. 108-109.

That did not stop the French from taking their hate and frustrations out on the Jews because, in that same year, *pogroms*[158] were reignited against the Jews. Before the year's end, the violence against the Jews spread to Savoy, Spain, and Germany.

On Valentine's Day, February 14, 1349—a day set aside to celebrate love—the citizens of Strasbourg, France, who had been ravaged by the Plague, made a public spectacle of the Jews; they cremated several hundred of them while they were still alive. As for the Jews who managed to avoid being rounded up and roasted alive, they were later expelled. That massacre of Strasbourg's Jewish population has ramifications to this very day![159]

During that same time, the citizens of Heilbronn, Germany, and the nation of Hungary, expelled all the Jews from their midst without any payment for their homes, businesses, and belongings. In Castile, Spain, during 1354 A.D., over 12,000 Jews were slaughtered like cattle. In Toledo, Spain, in 1368, over 8,000 Jews were killed.[160] That happened during the Spanish Civil War (King Henry of Trastamara vs. King Pedro).[161] King Pedro allowed his Muslim allies to gather up 300 Jewish families in Granada and sell them into slavery.[162] Then in 1370, the Christian citizens of the Mediterranean island of Majorca and its sister cities in Spain, Perignon, and Barcelona violently attacked its unprotected and defenseless Jewish citizens.

With the arrival of 1377 A.D., in the city of Huesca, Spain, mobs attacked and burned the Jews alive. In 1380, Jews in Paris, France, were attacked and badly beaten by mobs. During the year of 1384 A.D, in Nordlingen, Germany, there was a mass murder of Jews. Forty-four years after they were exiled from the city of Strasbourg, the Jews were once again barred from there in 1388.

A year later, in 1389, the citizens of Prague, Czechoslovakia, burned

---

[158]Violent organized persecution and massacre of Jews.

[159]"Strasbourg's Jews Fearful, but Staying Put in France," *Euronews* (European News), 16 Mar. 2015. Web. 14 Feb 2016.

[160]Baer, vol. I, *History of the Jews in Spain*, 367.

[161]Baer, vol. I, *History of the Jews in Spain, 366.*

[162]Ibid.

Jewish writings and conducted a mass slaughter of Jewish families with the belief they were doing God's work. In Spain, during 1391, eighty-

seven years before the Spanish Inquisition, the Church forced Jews to convert or die in the Spanish cities of Castile, Toledo, Madrid, Seville, Cordova, Cuenca, and Barcelona. The Jews not only underwent forced conversion in Spain, but all of their sacred books written in Hebrew were burned, while undeniably, hundreds of Jews who would not embrace Christianity were being murdered.[163]

During that same year in Seville, their Synagogue was totally destroyed; 4,000 Jewish men were killed, and their women and children were sold to Muslims as slaves.[164] In Germany and France, during 1394 A.D., Jews were again expelled. In 1399, the Church—against all biblical reasoning and the teachings of Christ—took countless numbers of Jews and subjected them to a Hell on earth as the peasants gleefully watched their tormented bodies being consumed by the unrelenting flames. Like a

Medieval painting depicting Jews tied to ladders, and then thrown into the fire while still alive.

choir of the damned, those poor souls could be heard crying out in inconceivable pain to the God of their fathers...

"Why?"

---

[163]Graetz, vol. IV, *History of the Jews, 164-165.*
[164]Baer, vol. II. *History of the Jews in Spain*, 97.

FIFTEENTH CENTURY

With the dawning of 1400, God's covenant people were once again ruthlessly burned at the stake in Prague.[165]

London saw a new type of institution emerge in 1407 A.D.—the insane asylum; nevertheless, the insanity was not limited to those institutions as long as the insane treatment of the Jews continued. Mobs in Cracow assaulted helpless Jews because they believed an Easter sermon given by Father Budek, which accused some Jews of killing a defenseless Christian child the previous evening, as well as throwing stones at a priest. The mob was so infuriated that they looted and set fire to homes in the Jewish quarter. Many of the Jews sought shelter in the Tower of St. Anne, which in turn was set on fire by the Easter celebrants.[166] Eight years later, in 1415 in Rome, Talmuds (Jewish oral tradition and commentary) were again confiscated. Any Jew who refused to give them up was killed.[167]

In 1421 A.D. in the small country of Austria, carnage by cremation was the fate of Jewish citizens. Those who managed to escape the Hellish flames were banished from the land. It did not stop there. In Vienna, the same fate awaited 100 or more Jews who were condemned to be purged by fire in a field overlooking the beautiful Danube river.[168] Then in 1424, the Jews were bankrupted when they were expelled from Freiburg, Germany, and Zurich, Switzerland.[169] Jews also faced financial devastation when they were expelled in 1426 from the Holy Roman Empire's sovereign city-state of Cologne, Germany.[170] It was around that time (1429) that Joan of Arc defeated the British at Orleans, only to be burned at the stake soon afterward in 1431 A.D.

---

[165]Graetz, *History of the Jews,* vol. IV, 178.

[166]Simon Dubnow, *History of the Jews in Russia and Poland: From Earliest Times Until the Present Day*, 2 vols. Trans. Russian, by I. Friedlaender (Philadelphia: The Jewish Publication Society of America, 1923; (now known as the Jewish Publication Society), 56-57.

[167]Ibid.

[168]Graetz, *History of the Jews,* vol. IV., 223-224.

[169]Poliakov, *The History of Anti-Semitism in Germany,* 119.

[170]Graetz, *History of the Jews,* vol. IV, 227.

However, in 1431, 19-year-old Joan of Arc was not the only living person to be consumed by fire because during that very same year, in several

Southern German communities, Jews were rounded up like a cattle drive, and then bodily thrown alive into the flames while Christians looked on with what had become an accepted form of perverted entertainment.[171]

With the arrival of 1438, Jews were expelled from the German city of Mainz,[172] followed by the same treatment the following year (1439) in Augsburg, which left them in financial ruin with little or no belongings.[173]

In 1440 A.D., through the inventive mind of the German inventor, Johannes Gutenberg, the printing press was created, which provided the ability to own and read a book. Gutenberg came up with the idea of using small, individual letters that could be moved and used over and over again by adapting an existing apparatus called a "screw press." It worked by placing small, wooden blocks with individually carved letters on one end, arranging them to form words and sentences inside of the lower part of the press. Then ink was applied to the letters, and a print medium such as vellum (an animal skin) cloth or paper was laid across the top. When the press was screwed down with even pressure applied on the vellum,

---

[171]Ibid.

[172]Poliakov, *The History of Anti-Semitism in Germany,* 119.

[173]Graetz, *History of the Jews,* vol. IV, 244.

the ink transferred, and a printed page was produced. That wonderful invention created a relatively inexpensive method of mass-producing books, including the Bible, especially for those who normally could not afford them.[174]

In 1449, in the city of Toledo, Spain, the prominent city fathers publicly tortured and burned the Jews because of the established Church heresy of them being "Christ-killers." The following year, Jews were no longer welcomed in the small country of Bavaria.[175]

With the arrival of 1453 A.D., in the medieval country of Franconia, of which Nuremberg is the largest city (now a part of Germany),[176] the Jews were also banished. The Polish city of Breslau (also known as "Wroclaw") burned one Jew and banished all the rest. During that mayhem, the local rabbi committed suicide. Their crime? They were Jews. In the German city of Passau, false charges were brought against the Jews who allegedly vandalized the host (wafer representing the body of Christ) and were ordered by the local bishop to be killed. That resulted in huge numbers of Jews either burned alive or through the most horrendous form of deadly torture—pinchers were heated in a blacksmith's fiery furnace until they were red hot and then used to grab and burn the defenseless male and female Jews' exposed bodies; other Jews were put to death by the sword. What carnage, what shame![177] Ten years later, in 1463, Jews were attacked by vicious mobs in Cracow, only to be repeated in another ten years (1473), this time in Andalusia, Spain.

The Spanish Inquisition

November 1, 1478, is the date when one of the most reprehensible episodes of Christian history began as their majesties, Ferdinand, and Isabella, requested and received from Pope Sixtus IV, a papal bull (i.e., decree) establishing the Spanish inquisition and with it—for many Jews—Hell on earth.

---

[174]Marshall McLuhan, *The Gutenberg Galaxy: The Making of Typographic Man.*
[175]Baer, vol. II, *History of the Jews in Spain*, 274-280.
[176]Graetz, *History of the Jews,* vol. IV, 259-260
[177]Ibid., 306.

Jews living in the beautiful City of Canals—Venice, Italy—were roasted alive in 1480 A.D.[178] Those who were able fled to the Spanish city of Seville in the following year, only to find another fiery holocaust awaiting them.[179]

In 1486, 750 Jewish conversos (mostly forced Christian converts) were paraded through the streets of Toledo, Spain, and fined one-fifth of their entire wealth, followed in April by 900 more Jews being subjected to the same treatment and then again in June, 750 more Jews paraded throughout the streets of Toledo and subjected to ridicule and obscenities. That shameful treatment culminated in August, with 27 Jews burned[180] while the inquisition burned 23 more Jews alive.[181]

With the advent of 1484 A.D., Pope Innocent VIII condemned the spreading of witchcraft through-out Germany and demanded that condemned witches, along with their cats, be burned.[182] Throughout Spain in 1484, the Jewish holocaust continued in the cities of Ciudad Real, Guadalupe, Zaragoza (Saragossa), and Teruel. Jews were expelled from Vicenza, Italy,[183] during the following year, making them suffer great personal and financial devastation.

Jewish family being burned alive during the Spanish Inquisition as the priest and king look on with approval.

---

[178]Roth, "Encyclopedia Judaica: Forced Baptism," 34.

[179]Baer, vol. II, *History of the Jews in Spain,* 325-327.

[180]Ibid., 343.

[181]Ibid.

[182]L.A. Vocelle, "CATS AND WITCHCRAFT (Part 3-Malleus Maleficarum)." *THE GREAT CAT,* Web 28 Mar. 2016, and Bernard. *The Timetables of History,* 3rd revised edition.

[183]Baer, 336-337; 363.

During the years of 1486 and 1490, in the city of Toledo, Spain, the detestable sport of Christians creating funeral pyres of harmless families of Jews continued.

With the dawning of 1491, the Church-going citizens of Astorga, Spain, participated in the carnival-like spectacle of the unbearable torture and execution of even more Jews.

THE FIFTH BLOOD MOON TETRAD OF
THE CHRISTIAN ERA (1493-1494)

Following the pivotal year of 1492, we saw a cluster of heavenly events from 1493-1494 A.D., which ushered in another biblical Tetrad, only that time, the sign of the blood moons fell on the Jewish holidays of Passover and the Feast of Trumpets.

Accompanying those events, the last Islamic state in Spain—Granada, in the community of Andalusia—was defeated by the Christian forces of King Ferdinand and Queen Isabella, who reunited the Spanish Peninsula after almost 800 years of fighting Muslim occupation.

Beginning with March 31, 1492, one year before the blood moon Tetrad began,[184] the very date when Jews were twice cast out of Jerusalem, they were also cast out of Spain. How ironic it is that date coincided with the same day the two Temples in Jerusalem were destroyed—the first by Babylon on the ninth of *Av* in 587 B.C. and the other by Rome on the ninth of *Av* in 70 A.D. The ninth of *Av Tisha B'Av* (literally the ninth of *Av; Heb.* תשעה באב or ט' באב), is an annual day of fasting in Judaism, which commemorates the anniversary of a number of disasters in Jewish history, primarily—as we just read—the destruction of both the First and Second Temples in Jerusalem.

Once again, on the infamous ninth of *Av* (1492), the Jewish population would be exiled from Spain, but before that dreadful deadline, 200,000 to 250,000 Jews were forced to convert to Catholicism while those who resisted were exiled on that fateful date.

---

[184]Four blood moon Tetrads: April 2, 1493 and September 25, 1493 followed the next year on March 22, 1494, and September 15, 1494.

Christopher Columbus

Of all the Jews who did manage to escape to Morocco, only about 20,000 made it their home—the rest relocated throughout the Islamic Ottoman Empire, but the Jews would eventually find persecution there as well. Traditionally, the Blood moons were a harbinger of major events (good or bad) concerning God's people—the children of Israel—and this time was no exception; however, it was not immediately apparent.

In 1492, on the very eve of the blood moon, events were unfolding that would prove to be a great benefit for the Jews—by a Jew. Many people today are aware that Christopher Columbus was an Italian, but many are unaware that he was also a Jew. Like many Jews who were threatened by the Church, His family thought it prudent to embrace Catholicism to become "Conversos" (Spanish for converts). That was not uncommon among the Jews during that time, and many still secretly practiced their Judaism. The Churches' inquisitors, who brutally tortured tens of thousands of defenseless Jews during the notorious Spanish Inquisition, called the

Christopher Columbus (1451-1506 A.D.)
In a painting by Jose Moria Obreegon

false converts "Marranos" or "pigs." According to historians, Otero Sanchez, Jose Erugo, Nicholas Dias Perez, and Celso Garcia de la Riega—based on recent evidence that had been suppressed for many years—that Columbus himself was a *Marrano*.[185]

Something else, which is rarely revealed by historians, is that Columbus had a burning desire to see Jerusalem liberated from the Muslims. While Columbus would never see that happen, he was able to discover new lands in the Western hemisphere. One specific land would become a

---

[185]Charles Garcia, "Was Columbus Secretly a Jew?" CNN.com. CNN. Cable News Network, 24 May 2012. Web. 1 May 2015.

haven for many of his fellow Jews—the United States of America—the only other country in the history of the world besides Israel—that was founded for the glory of God.

Eventually, the new land discovered by Columbus, on the eve of the biblical and rare blood moon's Tetrad, would provide his fellow Jews sanctuary from around the world and finally allow the Jews to practice their religion in peace.[186] Despite how it might have appeared at the time, God had not turned His back on His people, the Jews; on the contrary, He was still looking out and providing for them during the events just preceding, during, and right after the biblical Tetrad of 1493 and 1494. It would be almost another 500 years before the next miraculous, heavenly phenomenon known as the biblical "blood moon Tetrad" would occur again and with them, another miraculous event would usher in another nation who would provide the Jews with sanctuary and allow them to practice their religion in peace—the name of that country? Israel!

In the years of 1495 and 1497, the Jews—once again—experienced financial ruin because they were expelled from the countries of Lithuania and Portugal, respectively. In between that time, during 1496, the Jews were also banished from Syria in the Middle East.

In Scotland, during 1497 A.D., a law was passed requiring all children to attend school. A year later, in 1498, the toothbrush was introduced in China, and Columbus set sail on his third voyage to the Americas from Spain with six ships. During the last year of that century, Michelangelo completed his famous *Pietà* (the statue of Mary with the lifeless body of Jesus stretched across her lap).

Still, the century could not end without more attacks on the Jews, as witnessed in Germany during 1499, when once more, the Jews were rounded up and ejected from their homes, businesses, and towns.[187]

This is a good time to pause and address some questions: (1) If the Jews had been expelled out of a country, how is it then that more Jews were found years later in that same country, only to be killed or deported again? (2) Do the Jews have a death wish when they sneak back into

---

[186]Ibid.

[187]Graetz, *History of the Jews,* vol. IV, 416.

countries that are hostile to them? The answer is similar to the countries where prosperous, progressive liberals sought to end capitalism and succeeded in doing so. After the socialist agenda eventually failed, they wanted to bring back some of the capitalistic programs to revitalize their economies. Life became easier when prosperity was re-established. The reason socialism returned was that its evils had also faded from their collective memories, and the cycle of rejecting capitalism in favor of returning to their failed socialist agendas was once again initiated. So it was with those hostile countries who kicked out the Jews, only to realize they needed them, which resulted in the Jews being invited back in again, as we will see.

During biblical days, Jews came to realize—after being overthrown and dispersed throughout the world time and time again—skills, which required the possession of land or tools, could be lost or confiscated; a fact not lost on them as the persistent, post-biblical persecution of the Jews continued. In their wisdom, the Jewish people knew the only thing they could take with them across borders, besides the clothes on their backs, was knowledge; therefore, the Jews placed a high premium on education. To their credit, the resourceful Jews developed skills in medicine, accounting, and law. They became very astute in the intellectual arts, while the average European during the Dark Ages knew nothing about banking, medicine, or the law. Because of the prevailing general ignorance and illiteracy of that time, most Europeans during the Dark Ages found it necessary to turn to the Jews for help. Like the countries who rejected capitalism, preferring to embrace the socialist entitlement state (which eventually runs out of money and jobs and in the end—to maintain order—socialism must resort to becoming a totalitarian government), the Europeans of the Dark Ages resented the fact Jews were able to invest and make money. It was because of the Jews' skillful knowledge that the European Monarchs were forced to invite them back into their countries to help their kingdoms prosper again.

Predictably, the commoner did not benefit much from those arrangements. Because of serfdom, the peasants were kept downcast and suffered terrible taxation—as did the Jews, but they were skilled at managing their own money through their knowledge of good accounting methods. Understandably, because the Jews were also heavily taxed on their financial transactions by the king, they were forced to pass those fees along. The masses demanded that the king provide relief; however, the Crown ignored them until the illiterate peasants started rioting. Consequently, the benevolent king deflected and redirected the anger of the peasants toward those "evil," "greedy" Jews who were living better than the peasants were. The monarch's deflection allowed the peasants to take out their frustrations on those "thieving, Christ-killing," Jews by torturing and killing them.

Finally, the king—to the people's delight—expelled all the Jews from the realm, but like the results of socialism, the monarchs soon found themselves in worse shape than before, and so did the rebellious peasants. As a result, the king quietly invited the Jews to return to help with the economy and assist in getting the king's financial house back in order. Then the cycle would start all over again.

The House of Rothschild

Jumping ahead some 268 years into the future,[188] around the 1760s, we

Mayer Amschel Rothschild

discover—not surprisingly—that it was the Jews who finally established the monetary banking system in Europe, built upon Rothschild's brilliant financial knowledge.[189] Mayer Amschel Rothschild was a court factor (i.e., a Jewish financer) to the Landgraves of Hesse-Kassel in the Free City of Frankfurt.

The picture on the left is an artist's rendition of Mayer Rothschild.[190] Ultimately, five lines of the Rothschild family were made Austrian Barons of the Habsburg Empire in 1816, with another line in England made a Baronet (heredity knight) in 1847. That was followed by the English title of Baron in 1885 at the request of Queen Victoria.[191]

---

[188]Rothschild Family, *Wikipedia, the Free Encyclopedia*; May 11, 2014.

[189]Amos Elon, Founder, *Mayer Amschel Rothschild and His Time* (New York: HarperCollins), 1996.

[190]Illustration of Mayer Amschel Rothschild, *The Jewish Encyclopedia*, printed in 1907.

[191]*The House of Rothschild: Money's prophets, 1798–1848*, Vol. 1, Niall Ferguson, 1999, Introduction.

uring the Dark Ages (fifth to thirteenth centuries, also known as the "Middle Ages"), most of the people were illiterate. Because **many were unable to read, illustrated books were produced to indoctrinate** the masses against the Jews. The books contained pictures of Jews desecrating Christian altars and performing blood libels as we can see in the following example:

We have deciphered the words in the picture above for our readers since they are not very legible. Reading horizontally across the above picture:

Top Row
Panels one and two: Jews prepare to steal the Hosts (i.e., communion bread), which represents the body of Christ. Panel three: The Hosts are smuggled out of the Church in a box by Jews. Panel four: The Host/communion bread bleeds as a Jew pierces it. Because the Host literally represents the body of Jesus, the symbolism helped the illiterate

156

congregation understand how the Jews, in that misguided fantasy, continued to harm Jesus by piercing the Host and causing Him to suffer. In this picture, we see the Ten Commandments above the Hosts representing that this desecration is taking place in a Jewish Synagogue.

Middle Row
Panels one and two: It appears that the Jews were found out, and the Hosts are being retrieved, followed by the burning of the Synagogue. Panel three shows the Jews being rounded up and threatened. Panel four shows an executioner about to sever the head from a Jew

Bottom Row
Panel one: Two naked Jews tied in wooden chairs are about to be set on fire. Panel two: We see a fire is set to burn the Jews alive. Panel three: A Jew is being taken away in chains. Panel four: A couple of pious people (left) and a priest (right) are praying.

In medieval Europe, the Jews were forced to wear special clothing, sometimes with a badge shaped like the Ten Commandments or a Star of David. They were also required to wear pointed hats which would identify them as Jews (notice the two Jews on the left).

The picture on the right is from a medieval German manuscript. Also notice Satan (left) preparing to throw a Jew into a boiling pot along with other Jews who are condemned to suffer in Hell for all eternity for the sinful crime of killing Jesus. Notice the Jew's hat and hats of the other Jews. The pot is inscribed with the name "Judet" or "Jew" signifying that it has been specifically prepared just for Jews.

CHAPTER 4

THE PROTESTANT (PROTESTERS) ERA BEGAN
WITH THE SIXTEENTH CENTURY

Most scholars accept the year 1517 as the date the *Protestant Reformation* began—when Martin Luther published his *Ninety-Five Theses*—and put them on the doors of the Castle Church in Wittenberg, Germany; consequently, the first successful break from the Roman Catholic Church began, but with the *Protestant Reformation* came even more confusion and chaos.

In 1502, Columbus set out on his fourth journey to the Caribbean Islands, perhaps still believing those islands were off the coast of India. Two years later, in 1504, Michelangelo finished his statue glorifying—of all things—a Jew—when he unveiled his famous *Statue of David.* At the end of 1504, on November 26, Queen Isabella of Spain died. Eighteen months later, on April 19, 1506, in Lisbon, Portugal, the zealous Christians of that city horrifically slaughtered almost 4,000 Jews; a number equal to the size of a small village was wiped out. In the following month, on May 20, 1506, in Valladolid, Spain, nineteen months after the death of his patron, Queen Isabella, Christopher Columbus died.

In 1509 A.D., Desiderius Erasmus, the celebrated Dutch humanist, published *In Praise of Folly* in which he made the argument the Bible should be translated from Latin into the languages of the people. Erasmus was a devoted Catholic, who was disturbed by how superstitious the average Christian of his day was. He believed they would not be as easily fooled by what he referred to as "absurd superstitions" if they had direct access to the Bible in their own language.[192]

The year of 1517 A.D. triggered events that challenged the traditions of the Catholic Church regarding Luther's criticism of its doctrines, such as buying indulgences (gifts of money to the Church to allow for some sins to be forgiven).[193]

Luther also believed that the *Whore of Babylon* (referred to in Revelation 17:1-18), who sat on the seven hills and clothed in purple and scarlet, was Rome. The purple symbolized the bishops, and the scarlet symbolized the cardinals. Combined, they represented the apostate Church with the last pope being the Antichrist (false prophet). That was more than the Jesuit priest, Luis de Alcasar, could tolerate, so he invented a clever revision of both history and the Bible.

A NEW WORD: *PRETERISM*

End Time Prophecy Revised and
Reallocated Back to the First Century

To (1) counteract Martin Luther's defamation of the Catholic Church by identifying the Whore of Babylon with the End Times pope and (2) how the Catholic Church became apostate, Luis de Alcasar came up with his new scheme called "Preterism" (*preterit* from the Latin word *praetor*, similar to the prefix *pre*, meaning "before;" plus the suffix *ism*: from the Greek, which can be applied to mean "theory or teaching (i.e., doctrine)." In this case, it means a belief in events having already *pre-existed* in the past, and not something looked for in the future). Alcasar developed his argument by writing a commentary on the Book of Revelation titled, *Investigation of the Hidden Sense of the Apocalypse.* In it, he claimed that the Apocalypse (i.e., Revelation) referred to Pagan Rome and the first six centuries of the Christian Church; therefore—the Catholic Church could

---

[192]David Cloud, *The Bible Version Question and Answer* (London: Way of Life Literature, 2006), 5.

[193]Included in Martin Luther's 95 thesis regarding biblical contradictories and the sale of indulgences. Posted on church door in Whittenburg, Germany, October 31, 1517.

not possibly be the "Great Whore" sitting on the seven hills with the religious system of "Mystery Babylon"—spoken of in Revelation 17:5-9. Besides, if that was the case, then naturally, the pope could not be the false prophet of the Antichrist—the one worshiped as the head of the one-world religion.[194] Consequently, it was in response to Martin Luther that it became necessary for the Catholic Church to form a *Counter-Reformation Theology,* and with it, the heresy of Preterism was contrived. According to Alcasar, the millennial reign of Christ began in 70 A.D.; that would mean the millennial reign of Jesus ended 500 years before Alcasar came up with his theory. For those of us living today, it has been a thousand years, so how does that work out? As for the rest of the End Time prophecy found in the first eleven chapters of the Apocalypse (Book of Revelation), Alcasar relegated them to the past in Pagan Rome. He also argued that Revelation 19:20 and Revelation 20:10 speak of the false prophet, and Revelation 13:1, along with Daniel 7, which refers to the first beast (i.e., the Antichrist), was,

REV. PATRIS 13
L V D O V I C I
A B
A L C A S A R
HISPALENSIS,
E SOCIETATE IESV THEOLOGI,
&in Prouincia Bætica facræ Scripturæ Profefforis,
VESTIGATIO ARCANI SENSVS
IN
APOCALYPSI.
Cum opufculo de facris Ponderibus ac Menfuris.

Apud Ioannem Keerbergium.
cIↃ. IↃc. XIV.
Cum Gratia & Priuilegio Regis Hifpaniarum, & Ioua Aufflacum.

This is the title page from:
Vestigatio arcvani sensus in Apocalvpsi
Written by Luis del Alcázar (1554-1613)
Published after his death in 1614 A.D.

in reality, the Roman Emperor Nero (55-68 A.D.). The problem for Alcasar is that the prophies that were given by Daniel and St. John must still be in sometime in the future because Irenaeus showed us that the End Times prophecies in the book of Revelation, were given around 96 A.D.—a quarter of a century *after* the events of 70 A.D., and Nero's death in 68 A.D. was *before* the events of 70 A.D. It is important to notice that the book of Revelation never says those events had already occurred. In light of this, we know Jesus could not have returned 26 years earlier. Another gaping problem is that Paul warned the Church:

---

[194]"And *all that dwell upon the earth shall worship him,* whose names are not written in the book of life of the Lamb slain from the foundation of the world" (Revelation 13:8, emphasis added).

161

not to become easily unsettled or alarmed by the teaching *allegedly* from us—whether by a prophecy or by word of mouth or by letter—asserting that the *day of the Lord has already come*. Don't let anyone deceive you in any way, for that day will not come until the rebellion occurs and the man of lawlessness [also known as "man of perdition" and "son of perdition"] is revealed, the man doomed to destruction (2 Thessalonians 2:2-3, emphasis added NIV).

With Alcasar's history and prophecy revision, he contrived to discredit Luther's charges against the Church, so he doubled down on replacement theology. The effect of Alcasar's revisionist history and perversion of prophecy had a disastrous effect on both the Christians and Jews. First, by perverting Scripture, he gave cover for Pope Francis Petrus de Romanus (Malachy's 112th pope) when he sided with Israel's enemies in the twenty-first century.[195] Second, he helped to bolster the unbiblical concept that God, who cannot lie (Numbers 23:19; Hebrew 6:18), could break His everlasting covenant[196] with Israel, which would allow for Pope Francis Petrus de Romanus to do so as well. After all, the enemy [Muslims] of God's enemy [Jews] is the Church's friend! [197]

Consider: Prophecies, by their very definition, foretell of future events, not events of the past. It is also interesting that Alcasar suggested the false prophet (the second beast in Revelation 13:11) was not just one person, but the whole apostate first-century leadership of Israel. Therefore, Alcasar cleverly deflected attention away from the evil, End Times pope by redirecting attention to the first century with the

---

[195]Francis X. Rocca, Joshua Mitnick: "Vatican to Sign First Treaty With 'State of Palestine,' " Wall Street Journal, n.p. 13 May 2015. Web. 16 May 2015. A nation called "Palestine" does not exist, but an entity called the "Palestinian Liberation Organization," whose charter demands the destruction of Israel, did exist at the date of this signing and was in direct defiance and an affront toward the legally existing State of Israel.

[196]Genesis 17:7, 13, 19; 1 Chronicles 16:17; Psalm 105:10, etc.

[197]"Abu Huraira reported Allah's Messenger as saying: 'The last hour would not come unless the Muslims will fight against the Jews and the Muslims would kill them until the Jews would hide themselves behind a stone or a tree and a stone or a tree would say: 'Muslim, or the servant of Allah, there is a Jew behind me; come and kill him;' but the tree Gharqad (Boxthorn Tree) would not say, 'for it is the tree of the Jews' " (Hadith, Sahih Muslim 41:6985).

possibility that collectively (the Jewish leaders), there hardly could have been just one man, much less a pope.

Still, Alcasar continued building on the already established heresy of replacement theology by explaining how that was possible—something up until then that had never been fully developed. According to Alcasar, all the prophecies found in the Apocalypse, except Chapter 20, verse 4 through Chapter 22, verse 21, were supposedly claimed to have been fulfilled in 70 A.D. The year 70 A.D. was when many of the Jews were dispersed, and Jerusalem was sacked. Alcasar had to ignore the fact it was Rome who came against Jerusalem, and not the whole world as prophesied in Zechariah 12:3; nor were one-third of the people in the world killed (Revelation 9:18), or not one-third of all boats in the sea sunk along with one-third of all the oceans turning to blood, killing one-third of all the fish (Revelation 8:8). When you allegorize—anything becomes possible.

The so-called "abomination" (Matthew 24:15) in the Hebrew Temple never occurred in 70 A.D. because the Temple was destroyed and then replaced with a Roman-built Temple. It was in that newly constructed Pagan temple where the Romans sacrificed abominable things. Caesar (ruler of the Roman Empire) did not go to Jerusalem—as the Antichrist is predicted to do—and stand in the Holy of Holies while declaring himself to be God (Daniel 9:27; Matthew 24:15); neither did the four horsemen of the Apocalypse undertake their catastrophic ride (Revelation 6). It is also important to realize that the times of the Gentiles (Luke 24:21b) began, not ended, with the onset of the Roman destruction of Jerusalem and the Temple in 70 A.D. It would be the events of 70 A.D. that would end the Jewish era, as predicted by Jesus in Luke 21:5-6 and Matthew 24:5-6, but those were not the End Times events He predicted in the Book of Revelation.[198] The Jews would not regain control over Jerusalem for

---

[198]Some Preterists argue that the Apocalypse (Revelation) was written before 70 A.D. because there is no mention of the Temple's destruction. This is a strawman argument because the prophesied Temple destruction by Jesus was recorded around 50 A.D. (See *Islam Exposed, vol. I: A Simple Crash Course on Islam*, J.P. Sloane, Ph.D., pgs. 118-120.) The Apocalypse (Revelation) is not discussing fulfilled prophecy of the past, but *prophecy* dealing with the future. As for the Apocalypse being written before 70 A.D., in this chapter we present evidence by Irenaeus, a disciple of Polycarp who was St. John's disciple, which should dispel Alcasar's theory.

two thousand years—during the seventh blood moon Tetrad of the Christian era—in the twentieth century!

Historically, we know God has used nations to discipline Israel in the past; nevertheless, Nebuchadnezzar and Babylon fared much better than Titus and Rome.

Alcasar mistakenly believed that the destruction of the second Temple in Jerusalem proved that God was finished with the Jews; however, God did not hold Rome and Titus unaccountable for what they did to the Jews. God remembered his promise to Abraham, which was, he would curse those who cursed Israel (Genesis 12:3). What happened to Jerusalem and the Jews in 70 A.D. was definitely a curse.

Titus was honored on his return to Rome the following year in the very heart of Rome, where the Arch of Titus is—the place that flaunted Roman soldiers carrying away Jerusalem's Temple treasures and its menorah back to Rome. That was just the beginning of the story.

What God allowed to happen to Titus and the Roman Empire, is a matter of history. Eight years later, Titus succeeded his father as Emperor in 79 A.D., and only two months into his short reign as Rome's 10th Emperor, there was a devastating eruption of Mount Vesuvius. It was one of the deadliest volcanic eruptions in the history of Europe, completely destroyed the prosperous cities of Pompeii and Herculaneum, as well as several other Roman villages as recorded by Pliny the Younger, a Roman magistrate, and historian. Then on the heels of that disaster, in the following year of 80 A.D., Rome suffered a devastating plague. As if those events were not bad enough for the new Rome and the new Emperor, the following year, Titus died on September 13, 81 A.D. after being Emperor less than three years![199] God remembered the Jews and had His revenge!

Alcasar also insisted that the Church's mission in the new millennium was to Christianize the whole world to make the world ready for Jesus. Of course, as we previously pointed out, that millennium has come and

---

[199]"History - Historic Figures: Titus (39 AD - 81 AD)." *BBC*, The British Broadcasting Corporation, 2014,

gone, preceded by yet another millennium. By suggesting that we must Christianize the world in order to make it perfect for Christ to return, Alcasar had to ignore the biblical fact that the reason for Christ's return would be to *prevent the destruction* of a world gone mad (Matthew 24:22).

Martin Luther

At the beginning of the Reformation of the Church, Martin Luther (1483-1546 A.D.) was pro-Jewish. Unfortunately, that ray of hope for Christendom and the Jews only lasted while Luther tried to convert them to the faith. When that failed—Luther, like Muhammad—turned on the Jewish brethren of Christ.

By this time, however, many Jews had already been tortured, shamed, stolen from, and killed, all in the name of Christ Jesus. For hundreds of years before Luther, as we have already read, many Jews were forced to convert or die under the sign of the cross. It should not have been a surprise that any self-respecting, Torah-observing Jew would refuse to believe the Roman/European Jesus was a loving and benevolent Jewish Savior. When the Jews predictably received the offer to accept Luther's Christian religion, they did so with less than enthusiasm—can we blame them?

In 1521 A.D., at his trial in the German town of Worms, Luther defended himself with these words:

> Unless I am convinced by the testimony of the Scriptures or by clear reason (for I do not trust either in the pope or in councils alone, since it is well known that they have often erred and contradicted themselves), I am bound by the Scriptures I have quoted and my conscience is captive to the Word of God. I cannot and will not recant anything since it is neither safe nor right to go against conscience. May God help me. Amen.[200]

At first, Luther seemed to understand why the Jews were apprehensive

---

[200]Martin Brecht, *Martin Luther,* tran. James L. Schaaf (Philadelphia: Fortress Press, 1985–93), 1:460.

when they were presented with the gospel. In 1523, Luther wrote a thesis stating:

> Were I a Jew and saw what blockheads and windbags rule and guide Christendom, I would rather become a pig than a Christian. For they have treated the Jews more like dogs than men. Yet the Jews are kindred and blood brothers of our Savior. If we are going to boast about the virtues of race, Christ belongs more to them than to us.

It appears Luther got it right at that point in his life; however, as Luther observed, after years of continual persecution in the name of Jesus, the Jews wanted nothing to do with Christianity. As for Luther, he did make an honest effort to come alongside the Jews, but when they refused to accept Jesus as their Messiah, instead of shaking off the dust and moving on as Jesus advised His followers to do (Matthew 10:14), Luther turned on them. It appears that Luther had very thin skin when it came to those who refused his offering of salvation through the gospel message.

By taking it personally, Luther refused to realize they were not rejecting him, but their Messiah. Still—Luther too—turned on the Jews, which reminds us of the old saying, "There is nothing like a lover scorned."

In 1543 A.D., some 20 years later in a scathing and hate-filled book titled, *On the Jews and Their Lies,* Luther attacked God's much-beloved children of Abraham and Sarah when he penned the following:

Title page of Martin Luther's book: *On the Jews and Their Lies (1543 A.D.)*

"What then shall we Christians do with this damned, rejected race of Jews? Since they live among us and we know about their lying and blasphemy and cursing, we cannot tolerate them.... Let me give you my honest advice. First, their Synagogues or Churches should be set on fire...secondly, their homes should likewise be broken down and destroyed...thirdly, they should be deprived of their prayer books and Talmuds...fourthly, their rabbis must be forbidden under threat of death to teach any more...fifthly, you ought not, you cannot, protect them, unless, in the eyes of G-d you want to share all their abomination...sixthly, they ought to be stopped from usury...seventhly, we ought to drive the rascal lazybones out of our system. To sum up, dear princes and nobles who have Jews in your domain, if this advice of mine does not suit you, then find a better one so that you and we may all be free of this devilish burden—the Jews."

Had Luther studied the book of Romans a little closer, he probably would have understood what Paul said God was doing with the Jews when he provided the following explanation:

> I say then, Has God cast away his people? God forbid. For I also am an Israelite, of the seed of Abraham, of the tribe of Benjamin (Romans 11:1).

Paul also wrote:

> I do not want you to be ignorant of this mystery, brothers and sisters, so that you may not be conceited [thinking you have replaced Israel and are better than them in God's sight]: Israel has experienced a hardening in part until the full number of the Gentiles has come in (Romans 11:25, clarification mine).

Paul then explained how it is that Gentiles are grafted into the Tree, which is Israel, and because we receive our nourishment from the Israeli Tree, Christians should not be so foolish as to take an ax to the roots which give us life. Judaism supports Christianity; it is the roots of Judaism from which Christianity receives its nourishment. It is a symbiotic relationship in which the roots feed the branches, and the branches protect their roots.

> If some of the branches have been broken off, and you, though a wild olive shoot, have been grafted in among the others and now share in the nourishing sap from the olive root, do not consider yourself to be superior to those other branches. If you do, consider this: You do not support the root, but the root supports you. You will say then, "Branches were broken off so that I could be grafted in." Granted. But they were broken off because of unbelief, and you stand by faith. *Do*

167

not be arrogant, but tremble. For if God did not spare the natural branches, He will not spare you either (Romans 11:17-21, NIV, emphasis added).

Because Martin Luther turned against the Jews, Johannes Wallmann, a German theologian and Emeritus Professor of Church History at the Ruhr-Universität Bochum, wrote:

> The assertion [argument] that Luther's expressions of anti-Jewish sentiment has been a major and persistent influence in the centuries after the Reformation, and that there exists continuity between Protestant anti-Judaism and modern racially oriented anti-Semitism, is at present wide-spread in literature; since the Second World War it has understandably become the prevailing opinion (bracketed clarification mine).[201]

Sadly, Luther's words condemning the Jews and his hateful attacks against the brothers of Christ continued to resonate down through time, allowing another German to make great use of Luther's rants against the Jews. His name? Adolf Hitler!

The amazing ignorance of those otherwise intelligent giants of the faith is puzzling. Like many Jewish scholars, it is almost as though they prefer to study traditions, writings, and commentaries of fellow theologians rather than pick up the Bible itself and simply read what God has to teach us. Candidly, Luther and many other teachers within the history of the Church were raised under the Church's established, traditional notion that God had turned His back on the "Christ-killing" Jews. Most of the commoners could not read, so as a matter of faith, they had to take replacement theology as being from God. Others, such as Origen, Augustine, Calvin, and Luther, had been so entrenched in that theological environment that they did not even consider the possibility of replacement theology as *not* being Scriptural. Catholicism teaches that Church tradition *can* replace

---

[201]Johannes Wallmann, "*The Reception of Luther's Writings on the Jews from the Reformation to the End of the 19th Century,*" *Lutheran Quarterly*, n.s. 1 (Spring 1987), 1:72-97.

biblical doctrine,[202] despite the warning found in the Bible when Jesus told us:

> [Nevertheless, it is] in vain do they worship Me, *teaching for doctrines the commandments of men*. For laying aside the commandment of God, *you hold the tradition of men*, as the washing of pots and cups: and many other such like things you do. And He [Jesus] said unto them, Full well *you reject the commandment of God, [so] that you may keep your own tradition* (Mark 7:7-9, bracketed clarifications mine, emphases added).

When anti-Semitism is taught to someone from the cradle, then the hatred and mistreatment of the Jewish people are what we would expect to happen. History repeats itself—over and over again; however, it was Martin Luther who returned to the belief that tradition is fine until it conflicts with the Bible,[203] in which case, God's Word—the Bible—is the tie-breaker rather than the traditions of men. While the theological commitment to *sola Scriptura* (Latin phrase meaning "only Scripture") was reinstated in some of the Protestant Churches during the sixteenth century, the biblically unfounded tradition of replacement theology continues to have a strong influence today in mainline denominations and with the World Council of Churches.

---

[202]*The Catholic Encyclopedia* quotes from the *Council of Trent,* which occurred during the sixteenth century with this statement: "The Council, as is evident, held that there are Divine traditions not contained in Holy Scripture, revelations made to the Apostles either orally by Jesus Christ or by the inspiration of the Holy Ghost and transmitted by the Apostles to the Church. Holy Scripture is therefore not the only theological source of the Revelation made by God to His Church. Side by side with Scripture there is tradition, side by side with the written revelation there is the oral revelation. This granted, it is impossible to be satisfied with the Bible alone for the solution of all dogmatic questions" (J. Bainvel, transcribed by Tomas Hancil. *Tradition and Living Magisterium).* The Catholic Encyclopedia, vol. XV, 1912 by Robert Appleton Co. Online Edition K. Knight Nihil. Obstat, October 1, 1912. Remy Lafort, S.T.D., Censor Imprimatur +John Cardinal Farley, Archbishop of New York.

[203]The Church reinforced the doctrine of Church tradition taking precedence over the Bible during Vatican II: "Sacred Scripture and Sacred Tradition" (Dogmatic Constitution on Divine Revelation, *Dei Verbum* #9, *Vatican Council II*) as quoted in Birch D.A. *Trial, Tribulation & Triump*h (Queenship Publishing Co, 1996), 5.

Unfortunately, with the dawn of the sixteenth century, the forlorn Jews received even more of the same cruelty and degradation at the hands of their biblical brothers, the Christians, who had received eternal salvation by the grace of God's blessings through the Jewish Messiah, Yeshua (Jesus).

The events of the sixteenth century in 1506 A.D. continued as the mob mentality still ruled. Jews were viciously attacked in Lisbon, Portugal. Then in 1510, Jews were publicly humiliated, tortured, and then finally—all of them—were executed in Berlin, Germany. Two years later, in 1512, Michelangelo finished his magnificent work on the ceiling of the Sistine Chapel; however, with the onset of 1514, the brethren of Christ were expelled from Strasbourg, France. In 1519, Jews were banished not only from Regensburg, Germany, but also from the entire country of Bavaria. Remember, every time Jews were exiled, the financial cost to them alone was devastating.

In an unrelated matter, in 1535 A.D., Sir Thomas Moore—*A Man for All Seasons* and the author of the classic book, *Utopia*—as well as the former Prime Minister of England under King Henry VIII, was beheaded by King Henry for not renouncing the Catholic Church and submitting himself to the authority of the Church of England, which Henry had created.

Meanwhile, returning to the never-ending plight of the poor Jews, Jewish families were once again inhumanely treated in Cracow, Poland, and in the country of Portugal during 1539 when Jewish families were rounded up, bound, and burned at the stake. Their pleas to Almighty God were masked by the loud crackling of the flames and the coughing coming from their smoke-filled lungs!

Jews were expelled from Naples, Italy, twice: First, in 1533 and second, in 1541 A.D. In between those years, in England, during 1536, King Henry VIII prepared to marry his third wife by beheading his second wife, Anne Boleyn, after charging her with adultery. Her Lady-in-Waiting, Jane Seymour, was a woman waiting patiently until her mistress was out of the way, and then assumed the role of the queen by marrying Boleyn's then widowed husband, King Henry.

While these English Court intrigues took place, the Jews did not fare much better than the late Queen of England.

In 1542 A.D., Jews in Prague and Bohemia were herded together and brutally expelled penniless from their homes and property. One can only imagine how it must have been as those poor people of God made their way into exile along a path that was probably lined by onlookers and hecklers throwing various items at them as they slowly moved on. In another unrelated and inhumane incident during that same year, a 12-year-old boy amused himself by dropping squirming dogs from the towering roof of the Kremlin to their deaths on the ground below. What kind of child could gain such savage and an evil pleasure doing such a horrible and demented thing? It was a boy who would become known as "Ivan the Terrible."

Moving closer to the middle of the sixteenth century, in the following year, in 1543, John Calvin established his theocratic government in Geneva, and the seemingly inexhaustible Michelangelo created even more works of art on the altar and walls of the Sistine Chapel. With the dawning of 1547, on the 28th day of January, King Henry VIII passed away.

Three years later, in 1550 A.D., in the city of Genoa, Italy, Jews were banished, followed in 1551 when they were expelled from Bavaria again just like they were 37 years before. In Pesaro, Italy, Jews were displaced in 1555. The following year in 1556, in the city of Sokhachev, Poland, the "carnival of carnage" continued as Jews were publicly tortured and executed for the crime of just being a Jew. A few years later, in 1559, the brethren of Christ were deported from Austria. Shortly after that, in 1561, Jews were exiled from the Czechoslovakian city of Prague. Jews were also forced to leave Würzburg, Germany, during 1567, and two years after that, during 1569 A.D., they were once again expelled from the Papal States. During 1571 A.D., Jews were removed from Brandenburg, Germany, and a year later, in 1582, they were barred from the Netherlands. Then in 1593, Jews were also banished from Brunswick, Germany. With the onset of 1597, Jews were heartlessly removed from their homes and businesses in the Italian cities of Cremona, Pavia, and Lodi in the never-ending saga of brutality toward the Jews.

CHAPTER 5

THE AGE OF ENLIGHTENMENT,
ALSO KNOWN AS THE "AGE OF REASON"—
EXCEPT TOWARD THE JEWS

SEVENTEENTH CENTURY

With the seventeenth century, England bid farewell to a frail Queen Elizabeth who passed away at the age of 69 in 1603 A.D. A year later, the Presbyterian king of Scotland, James VI, became King James I of England and head of the Anglican Church. Despite his dislike for Puritans, James was persuaded by them to authorize a new translation of the Bible, which would be known as the "Authorized King James Bible." The KJV Bible would eventually take precedence over three other English Bibles—the Geneva Bible, the Great Bible, and the (Anglican) Bishop's Bible, which Queen Elizabeth's father, Henry VIII, authorized when he broke alliance with the Vatican and established the Anglican Church of England.

In the Colonies of 1607, a new settlement in Virginia was established and named after James I as James Towne (now Jamestown), Virginia.

As the European expulsion of Jews continued, Muslims in Spain did not fare any better. In 1609 A.D., King Philip III expelled all the Moriscos—descendants of Spanish Muslims who, a hundred years earlier, had been forced to convert to Christianity. Perhaps King Philip did that because of the prevailing distrust of all things Muslim. Remember, the Muslims conquered Spain in 711 A.D., and they managed to hold on to it for almost a millennium (781 years to be exact).

Some Things Never Change

Jews, on the other hand, never conquered any lands in Christendom, but merely sought refuge among their biblical brethren. Philip was distrustful of the Muslims and their so-called Christian descendants, so he decided to confiscate all of their goods and expel them as well from Spain. He threatened them with death if they did not comply, so the Muslim Moriscos escaped across the Mediterranean to the welcoming arms of the Islamic countries of North Africa. Unlike the Muslims of Spain, the Jews had long since lost a homeland to where they could escape.

Meanwhile, the ongoing Jewish persecution—which far outweighed any other ethnic persecution in history—continued grinding them down in Europe. In 1614 A.D., they were told to leave Frankfurt, Germany. In 1615, the Jews were once again expelled at a great financial loss from the city of Worms, Germany.

Over in the Colonies during 1626, Peter Minuit, a Dutchman, bought Manhattan Island from the Canarsie Indians for 60 Dutch guilders worth of trinkets (an estimated $72.00 in today's money). The Joke might have been on Peter Minuit because, as some have argued, the Canarsie Indians were nomadic and had no concept of land ownership.

Back in Europe in Vilna, the capital of Lithuania, Jews were banished in 1635 A.D. Two years later, in 1637, the people of Cracow found perverted pleasure in watching their defenseless neighbors, the Jews, being publicly taunted, tortured, and then mercilessly executed by those who claimed to follow the teachings of Christ. Never mind that Jesus taught us that the second greatest commandment is to love your neighbor as yourself (Mark 12:30). We know this commandment also had to include the Jews because the audience Jesus was addressing were Jews. Unfortunately, the biblical truth did not matter, and Jews were once again cruelly, and without remorse, burned alive in Lisbon during 1647 A.D. One year later, during the Cossack uprisings, one-third of all Jews were slaughtered in Poland—simply for the unpardonable sin of being members of the family of Christ. With the *Age of Reason and Enlightenment*, the only light shed on the Jews appeared to be from the "Light Bearer"—Lucifer.[204] Sadly,

---

[204]Lucifer means Shining one, "light bearer." Strong's Word 1966

during that emerging period referred to as the "Age of Enlightenment," only darkness continued casting its inhumane and ungodly death shroud over God's Chosen People.

1649 A.D. brought the Jews more pain as they were expelled from the Ukraine and Hamburg. Jews were burned at the stake in Lisbon in 1652. They were also banished in 1654 from *all* of Little Russia and in 1656 from Lithuania. Because of replacement theology—Jews in 1660 A.D. were cold-heartedly burned alive in Seville, Spain—followed three years later with public torture and execution, an event that provided morbid amusement for the city's Christian onlookers. During 1663, a mob in Cracow brutally attacked innocent Jews, a ruthless act that would be repeated the following year (1664) in Lemberg, Ukraine.

In 1665 A.D., England and the Netherlands began the Second Anglo-Dutch War over control of the trade routes and colonies. That quickly spilled over into the American colonies. It did not take long before British soldiers captured New Amsterdam and gave it a new name honoring the British king's brother—the Duke of York—and that is how the city of New Amsterdam became New York.

While the British enjoyed their victory in the colonies, back in London that same year, over two-thirds of the city underwent a forced evacuation because of an outbreak of the Plague. For the almost 70,000 Londoners who did not or were not able to evacuate, death overtook them in just one week. One could almost hear the prophetic echo of God's promise to Abraham, "I will bless them who bless you and curse them who curse you" (Genesis 12:3).

Across the Atlantic Ocean during 1667 in the Colony of Carolina, the Puritans founded Charles Towne (now Charleston) in honor of Charles II of England. Back in Northern Africa—two years later, in 1669—Jews were exiled from Oran, an important coastal town northwest of Algeria, where they probably sought refuge after being expelled from Spain.

A year later, in Europe, in 1670, Vienna and Austria were enjoying their golden age of music and art, but there was nothing golden for the Jews who were callously run out of Vienna. During 1671, Vicious Gangs attacked Jews in Minsk (then part of the Polish-Lithuanian Commonwealth, and now a part of Russia). Ten years later, in 1681, in an unrelated, isolated event, an uppity woman was flogged in London because she dared to become politically active; nevertheless, she was not the only casualty of what was considered uncivilized behavior for women. In that same year, in what by then had become a vicious tradition, attacking helpless Jews continued in both Vilna and Lithuania. In the following year, in 1682, the same depravity happened to the Jews in Cracow. Regrettably, that demonic cycle of hatred toward the Jews would continue through even more bloody attacks in Posen, Prussia, during 1687.

Ironically, the "enlightened" British Parliament created a *Bill of Rights* in 1689, along with the *Toleration Act*. British citizens were finally guaranteed freedom of speech, given the right to petition the government, and assured they would be free from cruel and unusual punishment. Citizens of England would no longer be forced to join the Church of England. While old prejudices die hard, at least in England, there was a flicker of hope and the beginning of tolerance toward the Jews, although it would be a long time before it would be realized.

EIGHTEENTH CENTURY

On January 17, 1706, across the pond from England, over in the colonies, Benjamin Franklin was born. The following year, back in Europe on May 1, 1707, Scotland and England united, and Great Britain was born. Unfortunately, things were not so great for the Jews. Even more Jews were expelled in Europe, and their holy books burned. The city of Sandomir, Germany, expelled their Jewish citizens in 1712 A.D., and Russian Jews fared no better in 1727 when they were purged from those lands. Wurttemberg, Germany, witnessed even more Jewish expulsions by the followers of Christ in 1738, as did Little Russia once again in 1740. The city of Bohemia (then Czechoslovakia, now the Czech Republic) and Livonia (Baltic Sea area) also banned Jews from their countries in 1744 A.D., and the following year, Jews were exiled from Moravia, Czechoslovakia. Nine years later, the town of Kovac, Lithuania, also evicted their Jews in 1753.

Jews did not just suffer personal persecution; for many centuries afterward, they were also forced to witness the desecration of their holy books as well. One example took place during 1757 A.D. in the city of Kamenetz, within the province of Lovech, Bulgaria, where they burned all the Jewish Talmuds. Jews were also barred from Bordeaux, France, in 1761.

A year after the Jews were persecuted and forcibly evicted from France, on July 9, 1762, Sophie von Anhalt-Zerbst, also known as "Catherine the Great," ascended the Russian throne. She became the longest-reigning monarch of Russia, yet her reign was anything but great for the Jews who continued to suffer even more abominable treatment when in 1768 A.D., 3,000 Jews were slaughtered in Kiev (Kyiv). Still, the persecution did not end as the Jews were systemically rounded up and banished from Mother Russia in 1772 with Warsaw, Poland, following suit in 1775.

The year 1789 A.D. saw local rioters storm the Bastille in Paris, beginning the French Revolution. Unfortunately, that gave many in the Eastern Province of Alsace (northeastern France) the perfect opportunity to let old hatreds boil to the surface as they viciously attacked and drove out most of their unsuspecting and innocent Jewish neighbors.

CHAPTER 6

THE POST ENLIGHTENMENT ERA BROUGHT EVEN MORE ATROCITIES AGAINST THE JEWS

NINETEENTH CENTURY

C ontinuing into the nineteenth century, 1801 A.D. saw roving gangs of thugs throughout Bucharest, Romania, indiscriminately attacking Jews, while Jews were once again—brutally banished—from villages in Russian throughout 1804.

In another separate event, during that same year, Emperor Francis II suffered defeat at the *Battle of Austerlitz* at the hands of General Napoleon Bonaparte. Because of that defeat on August 6, 1806, Emperor Francis II was forced to dissolve the iconic Holy Roman Empire, an institution that had been in existence for over a thousand years.

As for the Jews, they were once again caught up in the endless cycle of hatred. During 1808, Jews were rounded up and banished once more from the Russian countryside. With the arrival of 1815, Jews were displaced from their homes and shops throughout the German towns of Lubeck and Bremen. Five years later, in 1820, Jews were exiled from Brémes, France. With the onset of 1821, Russians witnessed the start of the nineteenth century's largest wave of pogroms[205] against the Jews, first ignited in Odessa, Russia. By 1843, the pogroms spread to Austria and Prussia.

The hideous child of replacement theology—anti-Semitism—extended its slimy tentacles across the Atlantic Ocean where—eleven years before the

---

[205]A pogrom is a government or other officially sanctioned agency, such as a ruling Church or religious organization, which authorizes the persecution and/or murder of another religious group, traditionally the Jews.

American Civil War (1850)—New York City police officers led 500 people on an attack against its Jewish citizens. It climaxed with the destruction of a Jewish Synagogue. In 1862 A.D., after the start of the American Civil War, the future United States President, General Ulysses S. Grant, decided that Jews were not needed as far as he was concerned, so he gave an order banishing all Jews from his military jurisdiction.

A "Global Warming" Event Triggered
the End of the *Little Ice Age*

By 1850, we saw another "climate change," only that time it was "global warming," which brought about an end to the *Little Ice Age*. That began 400 years earlier during a different "climate change" event, which had taken place in the fourteenth century.[206]

In 1861, the United States of America entered the War Between the States, also known as the "Civil War," which lasted until 1865 when General Robert E. Lee, the step-great-grandson of America's first president, George Washington,[207] and Commander of the Confederate army, surrendered to General Ulysses S. Grant, Commander of the Union forces, at the courthouse in Appomattox, Virginia. With the end of the Civil War, slavery ended. A fact most people are unaware of is that not all black Africans descended from slaves, but all ethnic Jews are![208] For America, the Civil War had ended, but the war on the Jews continued.

After America's Civil War ended in 1866, Europe continued its well-established, anti-Semitic routine of expelling the Jews, this time from the

---

[206]Working Group I to the Fourth Assessment Report of the Intergovernmental Panel on Climate Change [Solomon. *What Caused the Ice Ages and Other Important Climate Changes Before the Industrial Era?* (n.p.): National Oceanic and Atmospheric Administration. Web. 26 Apr. 2016. There have been at least five major *Ice Ages* with regularity (cycles) accompanied by five "global warmings."

[207]Lee married Mary Anna Randolph Custis (1808–1873), who was the great-grand-daughter of Martha Washington by her first husband, Daniel Parke Custis, and step-great-granddaughter of George Washington, the first president of the United States, which made Lee the step-great-grandson in-law of Washington through marriage.

[208]Not every person of African descent is descended from a slave, something Jews cannot claim because every person of Hebrew descent is descended from a slave (Genesis 15:12; Exodus 1:8-11).

major Romanian seaport city of Galatz, which was soon followed by the rest of Romania. In 1871, it heated up even more for the Jews as unruly mobs sought out and attacked whole families of defenseless—men, women, and children—in Odena and Barcelona, Spain. The violence poured over into Slovakia (1887), part of the Hungarian dual Monarchy, and then spilled over into Kantakuzenka, Russia, during 1897. In 1898, Jews were hunted down like animals and run out of Rennes, France. That bloody century did not end until the Jews were brutally attacked by unruly mobs in the Ukrainian city of Nikolaev (also known as Nikolayev, or Mykolaiv) in 1899.

During that same year, the famous author, Mark Twain, made this observation regarding the Jew:

>...If statistics are right, the Jews constitute but one percent of the human race. It suggests a nebulous dim puff of stardust lost in the blaze of the Milky Way. Properly, the Jew ought hardly to be heard of, but he is heard of, has always been heard of. He is as prominent on the planet as any other people, and his commercial importance is extravagantly out of proportion to the smallness of his bulk. His contributions to the world's list of great names in literature, science, art, music, finance, medicine, and abstruse learning are also way out of proportion to the weakness of his numbers. He has made a marvelous fight in this world, in all the ages; and had done it with his hands tied behind him. He could be vain of himself and be excused for it.

>The Egyptian, the Babylonian, and the Persian rose filled the planet with sound and splendor, then faded to dream-stuff and passed away. The Greek and the Roman followed and made a vast noise, and they are gone. Other people have sprung up and held their torch high for a time, but it burned out, and they sit in twilight now or have vanished. The Jew saw them all, beat them all, and is now what he always was, exhibiting no decadence, no infirmities of age, no weakening of his parts, no slowing of his energies, no dulling of his alert and aggressive mind. All things are mortal but the Jew; all other forces pass, but he remains. What is the secret of his immortality?[209]

---

[209]Mark Twain, "Concerning The Jews," *Harper's Magazine*, 1899.

During the last decade of the nineteenth century, one of the most infamous political scandals of treason was brought against a person of Jewish descent in France—a scandal that divided the entire country. It has become known as the *Dreyfus Affair.* Over a dozen movies and documentaries have been made about it, including three from the silent era (1899, 1902, and 1908) and some as recently as 2002, 2003, 2007, and 2014). As we can see in the picture of the "courtroom," the reason this injustice took place is still a topic of interest.

Le capitaine Dreyfus devant le conseil de guerre

The caption on the picture translates in English as: " Captain Dreyfus in front of the Council of War."

The whole scandal was very contrived and complex. It was centered on a young French artillery officer, Captain Alfred Dreyfus—who just happened to be Jewish—which made him the perfect scapegoat. Once the allegations had been initiated, it did not take long for his enemies to accuse him of compromising military secrets through the German Embassy in Paris. Dreyfus' secret and brief trial ended with him receiving a life sentence for treason. The scandal began on November 1, 1894, and rushed to trial two months later. It ended on January 5, 1895 A.D., but the saga of anti-Semitism and intrigue did not end there. After his initial trial, Dreyfus was sentenced to imprisonment for life on the notorious Devil's Island.

Eventually, a series of events took place which vindicated him, and he was finally set free. It began in 1896 A.D. when new evidence was discovered—which proved Dreyfus was innocent. The newly revealed evidence pointed to a French Army major named Ferdinand Walsin Esterhazy. When Major Esterhazy was brought before the high-ranking military court, his fellow officers suppressed the new evidence, and Major Esterhazy was unanimously acquitted after only two days of trial. To further the military cover-up, they then erroneously accused Dreyfus of using false documents to gain his freedom.

In 1897, Dreyfus' brother, Matthieu, discovered some more incriminating documentation regarding Major Esterhazy, which proved his erroneously imprisoned brother was innocent. Mathieu found that the original evidence used to convict his brother was written by Major Esterhazy himself.

On hearing about this documentation and the forged papers by the hand of Major Esterhazy—the military hierarchy, in an effort to further protect the major against this Jew—Dreyfus—decided to bring young Dreyfus back to France in 1899 to face more trumped-up charges. The legal fiasco ended predictably with Dreyfus, the Jew, once again found guilty of the false charges and sentenced to term more years of hard labor on top of the *life sentence* that he was already serving.

Thus, the modern era began with mobs attacking Jews in Konitz, Prussia. Then in 1902, there were even more bloody massacres in Poland, followed in 1904 A.D. by massacres as far as northeast Asia. In Russian Kiev and Volhynia (romanized *Wołyń*),[210] more Jewish blood flowed in the streets. Gangs of hoodlums preyed on defenseless Jews in Zhytomyr, Ukraine, during 1905.

TWENTIETH CENTURY

The Post-Enlightenment Era Almost Became the Post-Jewish Era

The twentieth century would see the advance of civilization with scientific and intellectual breakthroughs ever witnessed on the planet earth. It was to be the century of unimagined blessings, while at the same time, it would also become the century of unimaginable brutality, suffering, and

---

[210]Volhynia: *Wołyń* is the Russian spelling and *Wolyå* is the Ukraine spelling. It is located in the northwest corner of Ukraine and was under Tsarist rule during that time.

pain. Brilliant men of science like Albert Einstein, Nickola Tesla, and Thomas Edison, just to name a few, brought what was once science fiction to become science fact. On the other hand, men like Pol Pot, Stalin, Mao Tse Tung, and Adolph Hitler murdered millions and millions of their own people that far surpassed all the carnage of the past! New advancements in medicine, along with air-conditioning and cellphones in every home, brought the middle-class comforts that only kings and emperors could have hoped for a century before! The incredible twentieth century began with the *horse and carriage* being the predominant means of transportation, and then things began to rapidly change through new technology. Other modern modes of transportation followed that up until then, the world had only dreamed possible.

The Wright Brothers, in 1903, created and flew an actual heavier than air vehicle, and because of that achievement, mankind was then able to join the birds above the earth and commute all over the world in record time!

In 1908, Henry Ford was one of the people who helped the world change as well with the development of mass production and the modern factory. Because of Ford's invention, the average person was able to afford the ownership of one of his new contraptions, known as a "horseless carriage" or auto (self) mobile (moving). We went from Morse code to cell phones, from slide rules to computers and smartwatches, not to mention the atomic bomb and nuclear-powered electrical plants! Surely, with the explosion of mankind's intellectual advancement in the arts, science, and humanities, Jews—who themselves reaped (as we documented in Chapter 8), the lion's share of Nobel Peace Prizes would finally be respected and find peace. Unfortunately, that did not happen.

Regrettably, the modern era of miracles began with mobs attacking Jews in Konitz, Prussia. Then in 1902 A.D., there were even more bloody massacres in Poland, followed by massacres as far as northeast Asia. In the Russian Kiev and Volhynia, more Jewish blood flowed in the streets. Gangs of hoodlums preyed on defenseless and unarmed Jews in Zhytomyr, Ukraine, during 1905.

The Dreyfus Affair Finally Ended

Back in France the following year (1906)—the Dreyfus Affair finally ended. Thanks to the hard work of his family and many supporters—all the accusations against Captain Alfred Dreyfus were demonstrated to be baseless. He was finally acquitted of all charges and freed from prison, at which time he returned to service in the French Army with a promotion to the rank of major. Major Dreyfus served France with honor and fought bravely in the *War to End All Wars*—World War I (1914-1918). He retired with the rank of Lieutenant Colonel—which brought another dark chapter in the prejudicial mistreatment of Jews to an unusually happy ending.

Alfred Dreyfus was exonerated in 1906, but the military waited almost 100 years to publically acknowledge his innocence.

That brings us to the United States during the year 1915, where we meet Leo Frank, a Jewish factory superintendent of the National Pencil Company in Atlanta, Georgia. It seems that Frank had been accused of murdering 13-year-old Mary Phagan, who worked for him at the factory. The trial was a circus on both sides and ended with Frank's conviction and a death sentence.

However, as Dr. Leonard Dinnerstein, Professor Emeritus of History at the University of Arizona pointed out, then-Governor John M. Salton reviewed over 10,000 documents, along with an on-site inspection of the factory where the crime was committed and concluded that Frank was innocent. Governor Salton then commuted his sentence from death to life, believing that after everything calmed down, Frank's innocence would finally be established, and the governor would eventually be able to set him free.

Frank's attorneys filed three appeals with the Georgia Supreme Court and two more appeals with the United States Supreme Court who eventually overturned Frank's conviction on procedural grounds; however, some prominent citizens whipped up a lynch mob and before any justice could be done on Frank's behalf—they abducted and lynched Frank on August 17, 1915. The lynching had the predictable result of over half of the three thousand Jews who lived in Georgia to flee the state. Dr. Dinnerstein observed:

> The degree of anti-Semitism involved in Frank's conviction and subsequent lynching is difficult to assess, but it was enough of a factor to have inspired Jews, and others throughout the country to protest the conviction of an innocent man.

In an interesting footnote to history, Dr. Dinnerstein informs us:

In 1986 the Georgia State Board of Pardons and Paroles pardoned Frank posthumously—however, old prejudices die hard—so the reason given for the acquittal was simply an effort to heal old wounds.[211]

Old wounds 71 years later? Old yes, but who even remembered that event—if anyone from that era were still alive—after almost three-quarters of a century? Could they not have either left it alone or *acquitted* Frank of the charge when they pardoned him? It appears anti-Semitism was still at play.

A simple search on the Internet exposes how much anti-Semitism and hate still surround those events. Personal attacks, as well as assertions directed toward Dr. Dinnerstein, abound. Discussions on various blogs expose the hardline advocates on both sides of the issue; therefore, what we can all agree on—depending on one's view of Jews as a whole—is that their conclusion on the matter is most likely predictable. We have seen strong arguments on both sides, leaving us with the only fact as to what the outcome of the case is—Leo Frank was finally found to be innocent of any crime and was pardoned by Governor Salton. Today it seems apparent—over a hundred years later—feelings of anti-Semitism are

---

[211]Leonard Dinnerstein, Ph.D., "Leo Frank Case," *New Georgia Encyclopedia*, n.p. 14 May 2003.

shamefully as strong as ever.

The Russian Revolution began in 1917 during World War I (1914-1918), which resulted in the Communist Bolshevik's ascension to power led by Vladimir Lenin. On July 16, 1918, Tsar[212] Nicholas II and his family were executed by the Bolsheviks. Four months later, on November 11, 1918, Germany surrendered, which put an end to World War I.

During the following year, in Europe (1919), Jews were expelled from Bavaria, Germany, with mostly just the clothes on their backs. In Prague, the largest city in the Czech Republic, there were additional looting and destruction of Jewish businesses. Sadly, without missing a beat over in Ukraine, there were 493 pogroms resulting in the murder of over 70,000. Helpless Jews. [213]

Across the pond in the United States, in the city of Boston, Massachusetts—the very heart of American democracy—Lawrence Lowell, the President of Harvard University, a school which began training Christian clergymen from its founding in 1816, tried to limit the number of Jews who could enroll by calling for quotas on Jewish students in 1922. However, the dislike of Jews on college campuses was not limited to the United States. There were widespread anti-Semitic riots on campuses throughout Hungary during 1928. Jews were also attacked by mobs in Limburg, Poland, in 1929, and again in Berlin in 1930, as well as in Bucharest, the largest city in Romania during 1933. Throughout the years of 1938 through 1945 in Europe, the world was witness to the most horrific and bloodiest Holocaust ever executed against the Jews—or any people—for that matter.

---

[212]In an interesting side note, "tsar" is the term taken from the Latin, "caesar," with the "t" sound like that of the Hebrew letter *tsade* "צ" (pronounced **tsah**-dee with a silent "t" and the "s" is pronounced with the tongue on the roof of the mouth). The title "tsar" was a popular designation used by the monarchies in some Slavic states in Europe. Its meaning was understood to be "emperor" in reflection of the Roman caesars, which began with Julius Caesar's grandnephew, Octavia, also known as "Augustus Caesar." We can see the connection reflected by its alternate spellings, *czar or csar, both* pronounced "Zar;" or if one were to separate the first letter from the last three letters and pronounce the "c" as it is pronounced in the alphabet, we have "c-zar."

[213]P.E. Grosser & E.G. Halperin, *Anti-Semitism: Causes and Effects* (New York: Philosophical Library, 1978), 248.

After the—*War to End All Wars (1914-1918)*—on September 1, 1939, the world became involved in yet another World War, a war that consumed the lives of most of Europe's Jewry. World War II ended five years after it started—the same month and one day later than it began—September 2, 1945.

Even in the modern and enlightened age of the twentieth century, under cover of World War II, Jews were made scapegoats. As the world watched, millions of innocent Jewish families were brutally murdered in a holocaust created by the genocidal maniac, Adolf Hitler, and his horrific "final solution" for the Jews.

In this picture, we are witnessing a moment, frozen in time, as a young and helpless Jewish mother tries to shield her precious little girl from the horror that, in less than a heartbeat, is about to take both of their lives. To the left of the solider, we see more Nazi rifles. Lying by the Nazi SS executioner's right foot is the body of what appears to have been another defenseless Jewish girl.

CHAPTER 7

WWII: THE HOLOCAUST AND
THE VOYAGE OF THE DAMNED!

The more things change, the more they stay the same!
—Jean-Baptiste Alphonse Carr

In 1938, with the coordinated attacks against Jewish businesses, homes, and institutions—known as *Kristallnacht* or "Night of the Broken Glass"—the world witnessed the beginning of what was to become the Jewish Holocaust perpetrated

Hamburg-American Liner MS St. Louis in her home port of Hamburg, Germany (photo archives, United States Holocaust Memorial Museum).

by the Nazis (National Socialists) in Germany.

The Holocaust was the systematic, bureaucratic annihilation of six million Jews by the Nazi regime and their collaborators as a central act of state during World War II. In 1933, approximately nine million Jews lived in the 21 countries of Europe, which would be occupied by Germany during the war. By 1945, two out of every three European Jews had been killed.[214]

When they realized their peril, the following year, a few Jews throughout

---

[214]The Holocaust Project—Historical Overview, n.p. Web. 6 December, 2011.

Germany managed to make their way to Hamburg to escape on the Hamburg-America Lines' cruise ship, the MS St. Louis, under the command of Captain Gustav Schröder. Captain Schröder had experienced previous encounters with the Gestapo since it was not uncommon for the Nazis to infiltrate some of the passengers and crew of German ships, as well as all aspects of German life and commerce. The Jews—some of whom managed to be released from concentration camps—made their way on board the *MS St. Louis*, had very little to take with them, but some did manage to smuggle incriminating documents—exposing the Nazis— which would be of great interest and concern to the United States government. That was not a holiday cruise—it was a Holocaust escape— a matter of life and death! By the time the ship set sail, there were over 900 Jews seeking sanctuary. The goal was to reach Cuba and freedom, but the influence of the Nazi propaganda machine had a far reach.

Anti-Semitism had preceded the voyage of the persecuted Jews, and by the time they arrived in Havana, they were not permitted to disembark. One can almost imagine—after the Jews were told they were not welcome in Cuba—what it must have been like among the stunned and fearful passengers on that fateful voyage. Perhaps we would have observed something like this:

> *Suddenly, it is all quiet. A confused little child tugs on her shocked mother's skirt. A tear is in the mother's eye, while all that is heard is the soft splashing of the gentle waters on the sides of that crowded ship floating in a sea of fog. The ship proudly bears the name, St. Louis, which it shares with a city in that bastion of freedom, the United States of America.*

> *Now the silence is broken as the child asks her mother, "Mama, why is everyone so quiet when just a while ago they were all laughing and hugging each other?"*

> *"Be silent, my darling," the mother whispers. "It is because they will not let us off the boat; they say we are not welcome in Cuba."*

> *"But mama," the little child whines. "What will happen to us? I'm afraid...why...why won't they help us? We haven't hurt anybody."*

The mother knows how the world hates them and how the Nazi's would love to get a hold of them, but all she can do is squeeze her daughter's little hand as a sign of affection.

Suddenly there is a change in the air when it was reported that the captain was going to set a course for that great neighbor just north of Cuba, the United States. After all, wasn't America the homeland of immigrants whose Statue of Liberty displayed a plaque in its museum proclaiming, "Give me your tired, your poor, your huddled masses yearning to be free"?

Once again, there was a ray of hope.

"Surely," they thought, "we will be safe in America." The little girl makes a big grin, and begins to jump up and down in her happy childish anticipation as she thinks, "At last! We will be able to stop running and hiding. We can stop being afraid of losing people we love who just disappear without a word. We will not have to fear strangers and shadows and scary sounds in the night anymore."

Yet again, the ship's mood changes as if a great weight had just been lifted. The collective sighs of relief among its passengers sounded as if it were a choir sending up collective praises of thanksgiving to God.

Unfortunately, the joy of arriving on America's shore was short-lived. The compassionate hope of human kindness and mercy, which the Statue of Liberty promised, would not be extended to these poor, sea-weary Jews.

Why did that happen? It happened because the celebrated, progressive president of the United States—Franklin Delano Roosevelt—who was the last hope for the Jews, would not allow the 900 doomed Jewish passengers (almost half of whom were women and children) to have sanctuary on American shores.

America's denial of sanctuary for those forlorn people of God—now condemned by the greatest nation on earth—would be returned to

Germany, where a death sentence awaited them. It is difficult to imagine that America, a country founded on Judeo-Christian principles, did not welcome those Jews who were forced to suffer under the most grotesque and horrendous example of man's inhumanity against other humans. "Shamefully, America not only refused their entry but sent several Coast Guard Cutters to shadow and prevent entry into U.S. ports. One Coast Guard Cutter even fired a warning shot across her bow to keep the MS St. Louis away from Florida's shore."[215]

In that modern age of airplanes, automobiles, weapons of massive destruction, radio, and motion picture newsreels, the world was able to see, played out before their very eyes, the Gospel of Luke—"there was no room for them at the inn." The *MS St. Louis* was turned away.[216] So much for American compassion—at least where the Jews were concerned!

Cuba and America were not the only North American countries to deny the Jews safe harbor; Canada blocked them from her shores as well. Still, the merciful German, Captain Schröder, refused to have their blood on his hands, so he conceived an idea, by avoiding sailing back to Hamburg, Germany, preferring instead to change the ship's course for the coast of England. Capitan Schröder planned to set his ship on fire within swimming distance of the British shoreline, which would enable his *cargo of the dammed* to swim for shore. However, before that became necessary, England, Holland, Belgium, and France each agreed to take some of the hopeless passengers and give them sanctuary in their perspective countries.[217] Unfortunately, that turned out to be only a brief reprieve as Hitler invaded France and Belgium in 1940, and the cycle of terror for the poor Jews who took sanctuary there began all over again. Even though some of the Jews on the *MS St. Louis* were able to escape, many of them

[215]Ted Falcon and David Blatner, *Judaism for Dummies* (Indianapolis: Wiley Publishing, Inc., 2001), 80.

[216]Dr. Rafael Medoff, "FDR and the 'Voyage of the Damned,' " *the Jewish Press RSS*. 14 Nov. 2011. Web. 18 August 2014.

[217]Amy Tikkanen. "MS St. Louis," *Encyclopædia Britannica*, Encyclopædia Britannica, Inc., 28 Mar. 2019.

were returned to Nazi concentration camps, where about half of the ships' passengers, who should have found sanctuary, were murdered.[218]

Hitler blamed Germany's problems on the Jews, which allowed them to murder millions of those innocent, non-combatant Jewish civilians. Historically, the Jews were the perfect scapegoats. Not even their children escaped the sadistic torture and death at the hands of Hitler's National Socialist Party, as we can see in the following photographs.

Many Jews were starved, beaten, and forced to undergo unspeakable horrors, including medical experimentation without any anesthesia,

Reduced to living skeletons, Jews were lined up in a Nazi concentration camp as the shameful tradition continued.

antiseptics, or Novocain. One example of the many Nazi medical barbarisms took place in the summer of 1941 in the German concentration camp located in Buchenwald, Germany. The Nazis randomly picked 104 Jewish prisoners and injected them with a hypnotic

---

[218]Sarah A. Ogilvie and Scott Miller, *Refuge Denied: The St. Louis Passengers and the Holocaust* (Madison: U of Wisconsin, 2006), 174-175. "Of the 620 St. Louis passengers who returned to continental Europe, we determined that eighty-seven were able to emigrate before Germany invaded Western Europe on May 10, 1940. Two hundred fifty-four passengers in Belgium, France, and the Netherlands after that date died during the Holocaust. Most of them were murdered in the killing centers at Auschwitz and Sobibór; the rest died in internment camps, while in hiding or when caught attempting to evade the Nazis. Three hundred sixty-five of the 620 passengers who returned to continental Europe survived the war."

barbiturate, which affects one's memory and is sometimes used in surgery. Back in the 1940s, it was an experimental drug given to the prisoners, which resulted in every one of the victim's death.[219]

Sadly—as has always been the case—neither did the 1.5 million innocent Jewish children escape from those unbearable atrocities; yet, for those children who did manage to survive their cruel ordeals, many of them did so only until they were also unceremoniously gassed and cremated.

Some of the children who survived the Auschwitz concentration camp show their tattooed identification numbers.

One of the things the Nazis did to instill total control over their helpless victims was to strip them naked. They had no sympathy at all for the Jews. It did not matter to the Nazis if they were adults or children, as we have seen in many photographs taken by Nazis, where we see embarrassed adults or the small innocent faces of those precious ones who look so helpless and forlorn.

---

[219]The Jewish Black Book Committee, *The Black Book: The Nazi Crime Against the Jewish People* (New York: Suell, Sloan and Pearce, 1946), 253.

The Nazis subjected those poor Jewish children (see the following picture) to the most unspeakable medical experiments in Auschwitz. Although this old photograph is not in good condition, we can still see the dark splotches caused by the Nazi's experimentations on the naked bodies of the children. Despite all that deprivation and hopelessness, the little girl on the left was still trying to have some semblance of modesty.

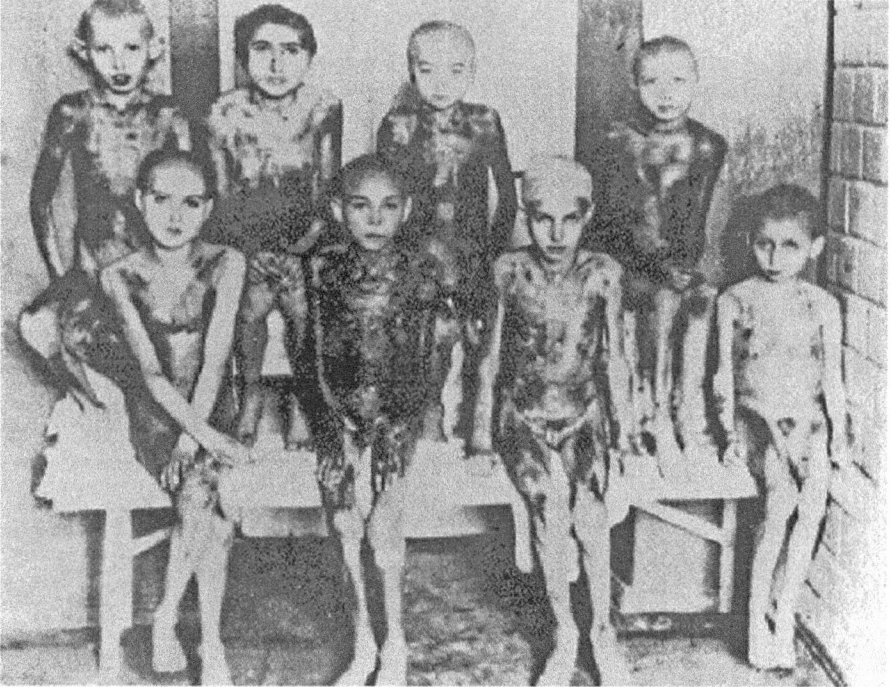

Innocent Jewish children who were victims of Nazi human vivisection (live experimentations)

World War Two also allowed old hatreds to be vented. The teachings of Islam and the Hadiths preach open-ended warfare against the Jews. Muhammad himself warned the faithful:

The last hour would not come unless the Muslims will fight against the Jews and the Muslims would kill them until the Jews would hide themselves behind a stone or a tree and a stone or a tree would say: "Muslim, or the servant of Allah, there is a Jew behind me; come and kill him;" but the tree Gharqad (Boxthorn Tree) would not say, 'for it is the tree of the Jews" (Hadith, Sahih Muslim 41:6985)

195

Haj Amin al-Husseini, the Grand Mufti of Jerusalem, was able to take asylum in Germany, thanks to Adolph Hitler. Together they plotted how best to incorporate Muslims into a Nazi fighting force. After all, who would be a more committed group of fanatical warriors against their common enemies then Muslims?

The Bosnian Elite Nazi Division Comprised of Muslims
A typical Nazi Division consisted of between ten to fifteen thousand men.

Members of the 13th Waffen Mountain Division of the SS Handschar Division at prayer during their training at Neuhammer in November 1943.

Because of the hatred against Jews, which is enshrined in the Koran and Hadith, Muslims found a natural ally during WWII with the Nazis. There was even a special Muslim division of Nazi SS elite troops known as the *13th Waffen Mountain Division.*[220]

---

[220]Chris Bishop. *SS Hitler's Foreign Divisions; Foreign Volunteers in the Waffen-SS, 19400-45* (London: Amber Books Ltd., 2015), 100; 143-144.

The Sailing of the SS Exodus

Shortly after the war in 1947, a tramp steamer called the *USS President Warfield* was renamed the *Exodus* in remembrance of the original biblical Exodus when the Jews made their escape from Egypt pursued by Pharaoh. However, in the 1947 Exodus, the Jews were not escaping from the recently defeated Nazis; this time, they were being pursued by the British!

THE FAILED VOYAGE OF THE SS EXODUS
ARRIVING IN HAIFA HARBOR 1947
PHOTO FROM THE BRITISH ADMIRALITY

The reason the British wanted to stop their exodus was that the Holocaust survivors did not have time to secure legal immigration certificates to permit them to go ashore in Palestine.

More than 4,515 Jewish refugees had been crammed on board the dilapidated old ship when she set sail from Sete, France, on July 11, 1947, toward British Palestine; however, the British Royal Navy had other ideas and intercepted the vessel 40 kilometers off the coast of what is now the Nation of Israel. They offloaded the Jews, divided them up, and placed them on three more seaworthy ships, intending to return them to France, but the French government refused. They said they would allow only passengers into France who wanted, of their own free will, to disembark, but the Jews wanted to return to their ancestral homeland—Israel. Britain, in the act of total depravity, decided to force the ship to set sail for Germany, but when the Jews found out, they went on a hunger strike. Soon, the press and United Nations became involved. As a result, the Jews were redirected to the British-controlled Hamburg, Germany. Of course, the Jews did not want to be on any part of German soil, so they refused to disembark; they were then forcibly carried off the ship. Many were held in detainment camps—not much better than the Nazi concentration camps. That cold-heartedness on the part of the British made no sense at all, especially because it was Britain who championed the Jewish cause when, in "1922, the idea of a Jewish homeland received formal international support. The League of Nations approved the British Mandate of Palestine, thereby entrusting Great Britain with the task of establishing a homeland for the Jewish people in Palestine."[221] It is curious why the British government continued to hold the Jews as prisoners and degrade them. After all, it was the Balfour Declaration of 1917, during WWI, which gave support to the idea of a national home for the Jews—in what was renamed, "Syrio-Palæstina" (i.e., Palestine) by the Romans in 135 A.D.

Before WWII, Great Britain was the largest empire in the world. It was said, "The sun never sets on the British Empire." Britain and its allies won WWII, but after the horrible treatment of the Jews, we could once again see the fulfillment of God's promise to Abraham, "I will bless those who bless thee *and curse them who curse thee*" (Genesis 12:3), and so it was that England went from being the greatest empire on earth to being relegated to a Commonwealth of Nations.

Despite its failed attempt, the sailing of the Exodus was instrumental in bringing the world's attention and sympathy for the plight of the Jews and in doing so, it allowed for the rebirth of the little nation of Israel in 1948 after 2,000 years of having its people scattered all over the world.[222]

On the very same day that Israel declared itself a nation, Harry Truman allowed the United States of America to be the very first nation to acknowledge Israel as a country. He did so over the objections of then-Secretary of State, General George Marshall. Unlike England, who received the curse found in Genesis 12:3, America profited from the blessing found in Genesis 12:3 and replaced Great Britain as the most powerful nation on earth.

In 1960, a motion picture bearing the name of the ship, *Exodus*, was a box office hit, as well as the movie's theme song by the same name. Over the years, the song "Exodus" has been recorded by the likes of Ferrante and

---

[221]HISTORY OF ISRAEL, *League of Nations: Creating a Mandate State*, n.p. Web.

[222]SS Exodus (2014, August 8), *Wikipedia, the Free Encyclopedia*, n.p. Web. 18 August 2014.

Teicher, whose version not only went *Gold,* but it also was #2 on Billboard's Hot 100 list. Many other popular recording artists also recorded it: Mantovani, Peter Nero, Connie Francis, the 1960's British musical group, the Eagles, as well as the Duprees, who sang the theme song to the movie with lyrics written by actor and recording artist, Pat Boone.

In 1921, Haj Amin al-Husseini became the Grand Mufti of Jerusalem with the blessings of the British government. Later in 1941, Hitler allied with al-Husseini (see picture below).

The Islamic Myth Surrounding Jerusalem

A little-known fact of history is that Jerusalem's distinction of being

defined as the "third holiest city in Islam" is not found in the Koran or Hadith. References to Jerusalem only began to appear in the Hadith two hundred years *after* Muhammad's death, as the place where Muhammad left for heaven in a night vision.

There are several versions of Muhammad's "Night Journey" in the Hadith, but we will only address a couple.

There are two versions that mention Muhammad leaving for heaven from Jerusalem, but not by its actual name (Sahih Bukhari, vol. 5, Book 58, No. 227, and Sahih Muslim, 1:309). There are also two other versions in the same two collections where Muhammad left for heaven from his home (not a mosque) in Mecca (Sahih Bukhari vol. 1, Book 8, No. 345, and Sahih Muslim 1:313).

The present-day version of Jerusalem, being Islam's third holiest city, was developed around 1917 by Haj Amin al-Husseini.[223] Its ramifications have contributed to the instability of the Middle East, even to this day. Al-Husseini embellished that fable to maintain control over the Temple Mount, which, in fact, is the holiest site of the Jews. There is no historical or archaeological evidence Muhammad ever set foot in Jerusalem. Ask yourself, "If Jerusalem is the third holiest city in Islam, why was it never the capital of any Muslim province or mentioned even once in the Koran?"

Al-Husseini formed this myth around Sûrah 17 of the Koran, sometimes referred to as, "The Night Journey" (also referred to as "Children of Israel"), which tells the story of a vision Muhammad had in Mecca where he ascended to heaven. In the publication, *Israel My Glory,* we read:

> The Arabs were Germany's natural friends because they had the same enemies as Germany had, namely...the Jews. [This is from a recorded conversation between al-Husseini and Adolf Hitler, November 28, 1941].

> Appointed grand mufti of Jerusalem by Britain in 1921, Nazi-sympathizer al-Husseini was first to designate Jerusalem the "third holiest site in Islam" in 1917. Before then, Islam's holy sites were Mecca and Medina in Saudi Arabia. He also was the first to organize small groups of suicide squads called *fedayeen* to terrorize the Jews in 1929.[224] To avoid punishment for riots he instigated, al-Husseini fled to Germany in 1941. He spent WWII with Hitler, plotting the "final solution" to the Jews in Palestine. His personal protégé was Yasser Arafat (bracketed clarification mine).[225]

To better understand the modern-day tensions between the Jews and Muslims who are surrounding the Temple Mount, we still need to explore

---

[223]"The Moslem Claim to Jerusalem is False," by Dr. Manfred R. Lehmann ALGEMEINER JOURNAL, August 19, 1994.

[224]Some sources put the date at 1921.

[225]Editorial Team, *Israel My Glory,* "Who Are the Refugees?" *Israel My Glory* (2003): 41. Print. This article first appeared in the January/February 2003 issue of *Israel My Glory* magazine, published by the Friends of Israel Gospel Ministry. Copyright 2016 by "Friends of Israel." All rights reserved. Used by permission.

a little more historical background regarding Muhammad and the reason why Muslims so strongly associate the Temple Mount with him. Because everything revolves around a dream Muhammad had, we must start with the Koran's Sûrah 17. It should be pointed out that Sûrah 17 was revealed in Mecca and was actually the 50th sûrah in the order sûrahs were received by Muhammad from Gabriel. The passage in question reads, "Glory to (Allah) Who did take His servant for a Journey by night from the Sacred Mosque [there was no mosque in Mecca until the Ka'aba was converted in 629 A.D., three years before Muhammad's death] to the farthest Mosque..." (Sûrah 17:1a, Yusuf Ali, bracketed clarification mine).

Muhammad began his preaching in 610 A.D. At the time of his *Night Journey* vision (most put it around 621 A.D.), no mosques existed, but eventually, there would be two mosques—the first one was built in Medina after Muhammad escaped from Mecca in 622 A.D., the second was in Mecca when Muhammad converted the Pagan Arab Pantheon, known as the Ka'aba, to a mosque during December of 629 A.D.[226] Marmaduke Pickthall translates that passage from the Koran as "...from the Inviolable Place of Worship to the Far distant place of worship...." Since there is no clarification as to which two buildings are being referenced, some suggest it refers to Solomon's Temple, which is a good suggestion except that Solomon's Temple was destroyed in 586/587 B.C., and Herod's Temple was destroyed in 70 A.D.

Over a half a century after Muhammad died, there was an octagon structure built by the Byzantines on the Temple Mount (one of five so far that have been found throughout Israel) and later converted into an Islamic shrine—but not considered a mosque. It is known as the "Dome of the Rock," but some historians tell us that only the remains of an octagonal foundation were left amid a garbage heap. During that time, the only impressive Inviolable Place of Worship—the basilica *of "Hagia Sophia"* in Constantinople—was the "furthest place" from Mecca, although the Ka'aba had not yet been converted to a mosque so, where the "closest" mosque was is anyone's guess.

---

[226]The dating in Islam varies by sources but the dates we share are the ones on which most historians agree.

It was not until sixty years after Muhammad died when his second successor, Caliph Omar (Umar ibn al-Khattab), went to Jerusalem to receive it's surrender and oversaw the reconstruction of the Dome of the Rock, as an Islamic holy site, which was completed around 691-92 A.D.[227] That was before the Al-Aqsa mosque was completed around 705 A.D. [228] when there were only the two previously mentioned mosques existing during Muhammad's lifetime. To reiterate, it was al-Husseini who created the myth that Jerusalem was the third holiest city in Islam. Ignore the fact that when Muhammad was alive, the Byzantines ruled Jerusalem, and there were no Muslims—much fewer mosques—there, so it is doubtful Muhammad would have gone to heaven from a Christian altar—even in a dream. As previously stated, Jerusalem is not mentioned even once in the Koran, but it is mentioned over 800 times in the Bible (660 times in the Old Testament and 146 times in the New Testament).

When Muhammad was alive, the Arab cities of Mecca and Medina were the only acknowledged Muslim holy cities until the construction of the al-Aqsa Mosque almost a century after Muhammad's death. Why did al-Husseini fabricate such a lie? It was intended to do injury to the Jews—and it worked! Al-Husseini knew that once a lie takes hold, it is almost impossible to reverse it—just like that of replacement theology. After all, Adolf Hitler himself taught about lying in his 1925 book, *Mein Kampf*, when he said that if you are going to lie, use a lie so "colossal" that no one would believe that someone "could have the impudence to distort the truth so infamously."[229]

It appears there was spiritual warfare waged against the Jews and their claim to the land of Israel. With the Temple gone, the Muslims usurped the Jews' claim to their Temple by replacing it with a mosque. Likewise, with the Jews gone, the Gentiles usurped the Jews' blessings by claiming to have replaced the Jews with the Church. There seems to be a pattern here, with one exception—the Jews had started to return to their land, and someday, according to the Bible, the Temple will be rebuilt too.

---

[227]Diane Slavik, *Cities through Time: Daily Life in Ancient and Modern Jerusalem* (Geneva: Runestone Press., 2001), 60.

[228]Rivka Gonen, *Contested Holiness: Jewish, Muslim and Christian Perspectives on the Temple Mount in Jerusalem* (Jersey City: KTAV Publ., 2003), 95.

[229]Adolf Hitler, *Mein Kampf*, Vol. I, Ch. X.

It is important to point out here, unlike Allah of the Muslim faith, Jesus never abrogated [revoked] what He said because "Jesus Christ [is] the same yesterday, and today and forever" (Hebrews 13:8, bracketed clarification mine).

World War II began in September of 1939 and officially ended in September of 1945. If there was any good that came out of that war, it was three years later, on May 14, 1948, after 2,500 years of absence, Israel was restored as a nation to give the Jews who survived the Holocaust a homeland. Nevertheless, old hatreds do not easily die because as soon as Israel became a nation, they were instantly attacked by five Muslim nations. Four of those Muslim nations that bordered Israel—Lebanon, Syria, Transjordan, and Egypt—immediately invaded the Jewish homeland, with support and encouragement from Saudi Arabia. Many of those countries are still technically at war with Israel today and merely observing the—*Treaty of the Prophet*—until they are stronger and believe they are able to strike a death blow against the homeland of the Jews, they so despise.

Today, the goals of these Arab countries are to—once and for all—push Israel into the sea. This is nothing new, but rather a never-ending saga of Arabs vs. Israel as we can see in this ominous prophetic revelation from the Bible:

O God.... See how your enemies growl, how your foes rear their heads. With cunning they conspire against your people (Israel); they plot against those you cherish. *"Come," they say, "let us destroy them as a nation, so that Israel's name is remembered no more."* [All Arab maps show the non-existing state of Palestine, but not the current— and legally existing—Nation of Israel]. With one mind they plot together; they form an alliance against you, the tents of Edom and the Ishmaelites, of Moab and the Hagrites [Edom or Northern Saudi Arabia and the Ishmaelites who are the descendants of Ismael throughout the Islamic Arab world], Byblos, Ammon and Amalek, Jordan, Philistia [Gaza], with the people of Tyre [Lebanon]. Even Assyria has joined them to reinforce Lot's descendants [Lebanon, Syria, Iraq, and Iran] (Psalm 83:1-8, bracketed clarifications mine, emphasis added).

This prophecy reads like something you might see or hear on the front page of any newspaper or television newscasts throughout the world today!

Since the formation of the United Nations, the small country of Israel is condemned regularly. In an article titled, "The Holocaust Project—Historical Overview," by Rabbi Shmuley Boteach, we read about the Jewish perspective of the mindless revulsion against them:

In an article, "The World's Oldest Hatred," by Rabbi Boteach, we read how the world continued to feed the prejudicial, monster content, only to devour the small Jewish nation of Israel. Hatred of Israel is another manifestation of the world's oldest hatred. Why else would British academics currently ban their Israeli counterparts and not—for instance—the Chinese, whose human rights abuses and slaughter of innocent civilians in 1989 at Tiananmen Square took place before the whole world? The Turks bomb Kurdish independence fighters regularly and continue to deny their genocide of more than a million helpless Armenians, yet it is Israel the world condemns.

Consider when Turkey provoked Israel by sending nine ships to run a blockade of Israel's Gaza Strip and forced Israel to board their hostile flotilla on May 31, 2010; it resulted in the killing of 10 men—who were wielding iron bars and knives. It is that hostile act against Israel which gains sympathy and international credibility.

The world ignored how Hugo Chavez brutally dismantled the Venezuelan democracy, imprisoned his political opponents, locked up judges, and persecuted a free press who criticized him. Putting all that aside, on July 4, 2010, when Chavez accused Israel of being a genocidal state, he was lauded by countries throughout the world, and a compliant United Nations censured Israel in its Human Rights Council. If that is not blatant anti-Semitism, then the word has no meaning.[230]

---

[230]Rabbi Shmuley Boteach, "The World's Oldest Hatred," *Levitt Letter* (September, 2010), 13.

THE SIXTH BLOOD MOON TETRAD OF
THE CHRISTIAN ERA (1949-1950 A.D.)

When the blood moons rose again, all signs pointed to the End of the Age and Judgment Day. In 1948, against all the odds, the impossible happened—the State of Israel was reborn, and the caves of the Dead Sea scrolls were discovered!

As the reappearance of the four blood moons was about to begin from 1949-1950, for the first time in almost half a millennium, the Last Days' biblical prophecies began coming together. On the eve of that heavenly event, something happened that has never happened at any other time in the history of the entire planet. Not since the time of Columbus had there been another Tetrad event up until then.

THE SIXTH BLOOD MOON TETRAD USHERED IN THE
MIRACULOUS REBIRTH OF ISRAEL

That particular blood moon sequence is unique in that it appeared 11 months after the rebirth of the State of Israel (May 14, 1948). As soon as Israel was reborn, she was attacked by five Arab nations who did not want Israel to exist. The last war Israel fought on her soil was almost 2,500 years before that, and the last war fought in the Southern Kingdom of Judea was almost 2,000 years ago! [231] Eleven months later, on April 13, 1949, the first blood moon of the sixth blood moon Tetrad sequence of the Christian era began. That happened on May 11, and less than one month later, Israel became the 59th member of the United Nations. The last blood moons of that Tetrad also came in 1950 when they rediscovered the caves at Qumran[232] containing the Dead Sea Scrolls. Both Israel and

---

[231]In 70 A.D., Titus destroyed Jerusalem and the holy Temple and replaced both the name of the city and Temple with a Roman Temple and Latin names. In 135 A.D., Hadrian finished the job and put an end to all things Jewish and dispersed the Jews throughout the Empire. The Roman troops were fighting a Jewish, civilian uprising and not an actual conflict between two standing armies.

[232]Between 1946-47, three Bedouin shepherds stumbled across some caves and found seven scrolls in earthen jars, but had no idea what they had found. They sold the scrolls. Since that time, they changed hands several times. Finally, Dr. John C.

the Dead Sea Scrolls had been missing for 2,000 years! Not only did that affect the Jews, but it was also the start of ominous events to begin unfolding for not only the Children of Israel,[233] but for Christians and the whole world. Israel is the lynchpin for the End of the Age and the long-awaited End Time prophecies to begin.

Why is that a miracle? We touched on it when exploring the events of the fourth century in Chapter 2. In that section, we explained how there had never been a nation that had been re-established after it had been conquered—and remained conquered past the third generation. What we did not tell you was—against all the odds—not only did the Jews (and later lost tribes of Israel) begin returning to the land after innumerable generations, but also Israel was reborn speaking a dead language and using a currency not seen for thousands of years!

As we have shown, one of the contributing factors supporting replacement theology was the absence of the State of Israel. Still, the impossible did happen and the miracle that is the new Nation of Israel—prophesied by God through the prophet Isaiah some 500 years before the birth of Christ—proclaimed an event that would not happen until thousands of years in the future

> Who has ever heard or seen of such things? Can a country be born in a day or a nation be brought forth in a moment? Yet no sooner is Zion in labor than when she gives birth to her children (Isaiah 66:8, NIV).

That is exactly what happened—in one moment—on one day—on May 14, 1948! It is proof God is not finished with the Jews or Israel! "For the gifts of God are irrevocable" (Romans 11:29, NKJV).

Trever, of the American Schools of Oriental Research got a hold of them and began the search to locate the caves from which they were found. The caves were finally rediscovered in 1949

[233]Jonathan Bernis, "A Rabbi Looks at the Lost Tribes of Israel." "*A Rabbi Looks at the Lost Tribes of Israel.*" Jewish Voice, n.p. Web. 27 Apr. 2016. Here we use the term "Children of Israel" instead of "Jews" because the Jews are only one of the twelve tribes and their return to Israel is not exclusive to just the Jews. Just as God predicted, we are able to see Rabbi Bernis' documents regarding how the lost tribes of Israel are being rediscovered throughout the world and repatriated to their ancient homeland of Israel for the first time in over 2,500 thousand years.

After WWII and with it the rebirth of Israel, a phenomenal task was undertaken to honor and remember every single Jew whose life was savagely taken by the hateful Nazi regime. What followed was the establishment of the second most visited museum in all of Israel known as "Yad Vashem—The World Holocaust Remembrance Center"[234] located in Jerusalem on the western slope of the "Mountain of Remembrance," also known as "Mount Herzl." Yad Vashem (Heb. יָד וָשֵׁם); literally, "a monument and a name" is the official authority in Israel for the commemoration of the Holocaust and its victims[235]

Aeriel view of
YAD VASHEM Museum Complex in Jerusalem, Israel

At the Yad Vashem Museum Complex, displays are changed periodically, so there is always something of interest to be seen. One building is home to *The Hall of Remembrance* where special events take place. Among the sites at Yad Vashem, "hollowed out from an underground cavern, is a tribute to the approximately 1.5 million Jewish children [like those in the photographs we have shared with you] who were murdered during the Holocaust. Memorial candles, a customary Jewish tradition to remember the dead, are reflected infinitely in a dark and somber space, creating the impression of millions of stars shining in the firmament. The names of murdered children, their ages and countries of origin can be heard in the background.".[236]

---

[234]Yad Vashem - the World Holocaust Center is a 45-acre campus composed of indoor museums, outdoor monuments, gardens and sculptures.

[235]"Yad Vashem." *Wikipedia*, Wikimedia Foundation, 18 Mar. 2020.

[236]"Children's Memorial." *Yadvashem.org*, www.yadvashem.org/remembrance/commemorative-sites/children-emorial.html.

One of many important missions at Yad Vashem is to seek out and recognize those non-Jews, who either physically or financially, at great personal risk, were able to save some of the Jews from Nazi extinction. Those heroic Gentiles are recognized by the State of Israel in the lovely setting of Yad Vashem's "Garden of the Righteous Among the Nations."

Addressing the Claim: "The Jews Return to Israel Is Not of God; Most of Them Are Secular and Don't Believe in Him!"

Today, many orthodox Jews who are Israeli citizens, as well as some well-known Christian theologians, say the return of Jews to Israel is not a miracle from God. Their rationale is because the Jews who have returned to Israel are either completely secular and do not attend synagogue services, or they only give Him "lip service." Yet, that is precisely how God predicted it would be when He brought them back into their land, as documented in the book of Ezekiel where God foretold us He would return the Jews to their ancient homeland in disbelief:

> I dispersed them among the nations, and they were scattered through the countries; I judged them according to their conduct and their actions. And wherever they went among the nations, they profaned my holy name, for it was said of them, "These are the LORD's people, and yet they had to leave His land." I had concern for My holy name, which the people of Israel profaned among the nations where they had gone.
>
> Therefore say to the Israelites, "This is what the Sovereign LORD says: 'It is not for your sake, people of Israel, that I am going to do these things, but for the sake of My holy name, which you have profaned among the nations where you have gone' " (Ezekiel 36:19-22, NIV).

What is God is going to do for the sake of His holy name? God knew that in the Last Days, His people would be mostly secular, but He still promised He would return them, even though it would be in disbelief, to their land. He will do it, despite those who are godless and blaspheme His name among the nations:

> "And I will sanctify My great name, which was profaned among the heathen, which you have profaned in the midst of them; and the heathen shall know that I am the LORD," says the Lord GOD, "when I

shall be sanctified in you before their eyes. For I will take you from among the heathen, and gather you out of all countries, and will bring you into your own land" (Ezekiel 36:23-24).

That prophecy was also fulfilled by God on May 14, 1948.

Some might argue that this passage in Ezekiel's prophecy, "For I will take you from among the heathen, and gather you out of all countries," could not apply to the Jews living in Europe and the Americas because they are Christian countries, not heathen nations.[237] This passage not only says heathen nations but *all* countries. Claiming that Europe and the Americas are Christian countries and, therefore, not heathen would have been true, but what part of "all countries" is not understood? Nevertheless, European Christendom changed around the middle of the twentieth century after World War II, when the Europeans became weary with two world wars and lost their belief in God. The world we live in today is so radically different from what the countries of Europe and the West used to be, including the United States of America. Today we live in a Pagan, hedonistic society where everything goes, making us look less like Christendom and more like Sodom and Gomorrah.

THE SEVENTH BLOOD MOON TETRAD
OF THE CHRISTIAN ERA (1967-1968 A.D.)

**With the Seventh Blood Moon Tetrad,
the Times of the Gentiles Finally Came to an End!**

Blood moons came rapidly in the twentieth century. After the Blood moons of 1949-1950, which occurred around the re-establishment of the nation of Israel, another biblical Tetrad put an end to the times of the Gentiles in the year of the Jubilee, 1967, as we will read shortly!

As previously stated, replacement theology is not taught in the Bible and has no place in Christianity, but it is taught in the Koran and has its place

---

[237]The Hebrew word used in Ezekiel 36:23-24 is Strong's word #1471, *goy* (יוֹג), which means "Gentile" or "heathen." Some translations, such as the New King James Version and the New International Version, leave out the word heathen.

in Islam (Sûrah 2:106; 16:101). Incredible as it might seem, the entire destiny of the world revolves around the descendants of Israel and their land; yet as recently as World War II, some people believed the terrible Holocaust committed against the Jews—which Hitler referred to as the "final solution"—was the inevitable culmination of God's divine punishment against those "Christ-killers." After all, it had been almost 2,500 years since the nation once was known as "Israel" existed. Again, we ask, "Who could conceive of such a thing as Israel ever becoming a nation again? Can a country be born in a day or a nation be brought forth in a moment (Isaiah 66:8)?" As we read earlier, the answer to our second question is "yes." Israel was reborn in a moment on May 14, 1948, the eve of the biblical Tetrad of 1949-1950.

Jesus also prophesied:

> And they shall fall by the edge of the sword, and shall be led away captive into all nations: and Jerusalem shall be trodden down of the Gentiles, until the times of the Gentiles be fulfilled (Luke 21:24).

> Then up in the Heavens on April 24, 1967, at the time of the Jewish Passover, and the year of the Jubilee, the world witnessed another blood moon, which signaled the beginning of yet another heavenly Tetrad. It foreshadowed the long-awaited event prophesied by Jesus. On June 7, 1967—after almost 2,000 years—the times of the Gentiles were finally fulfilled during the Six-Day War (June 5-10, 1967) when Israeli forces took back all of Jerusalem and the Temple Mount.

Regrettably, since that time, Israel has been regularly at war in almost every decade. As recently as September 19, 2011, Iran's former president, Ahmadinejad, stated that he would "push Israel into the sea,"[238] and eliminate Israel as a nation. Today, the Islamic nations and the Christian denominations who subscribe to replacement theology, plot against Israel, desiring for it not to be a nation anymore (Psalm 83:3-8). The world

---

[238]Jamie Crawford, CNN National Security Producer, "Palestinians seeking statehood: What's at stake—CNN.... President Ahmadinejad of Iran... 'push Israel into the sea.' " [journal on-line]; *NN*. CNN. 16 September 2011. Web. 8 December 2011.

wants to either divide Israel's capital of Jerusalem[239] or take it over completely to make it the capital of a pseudo-Palestinian people. The United Nations, representing 193 sovereign nations[240] of the world, including the Vatican, is allied in such an endeavor.[241] With the sound of war drums beginning to beat, the Bible echoes God's warning:

Israel had been a divided country for hundreds of years by the time Rome had destroyed the Southern Kingdom, but God promised that one day He would restore the Northern Kingdom (Israel) and the Southern Kingdom (Judea, also known as "Judah"), and in doing so, He would restore *them* both at the same time and as one nation (Ezekiel 37:22).

When the lynchpin was pulled, the countdown began, and with it, we saw the signs of the End of the Age begin to be revealed on the front pages of our daily newspapers. One of those signs could only take place in a revived Israel:

> I will gather all nations and bring them down to the Valley of Jehoshaphat[242] There I will put them on trial for what they did to my inheritance, my people Israel, because they scattered my people among the nations and divided up my land (Joel 3:2, NIV, bracketed clarification mine).

Israel has given up 90% of lands they have controlled since 1948, including lands they acquired after being attacked by the same countries over and over again, including its defensive, preemptive Six-Day War. Historically, any land acquired from an enemy is considered "spoils of war" and belongs to the victor, but not where Israel is concerned.

---

[239]"Military," *Jerusalem Must Be Capital of Both Israel and Palestine, Ban Says*, UN NEWS SERVICE, 28 October 2009. Web. 20 October 2014.

[240]World Atlas, "Which Countries Are Not Members of the United Nations? 193 sovereign states are members of the UN." Web. 3 March 2019. 21 October 2019.

[241]UNESCO votes to admit Palestine. NEW YORK—"UNESCO voted Monday to admit Palestine into the organization as its newest member ...." (Peabody: Hendrickson Publ., 2004), December 8, 2011.

[242]Jehoshaphat literally means "God Judges," so this passage could read: "I will gather all nations and bring them down to the Valley of God's judgment!"

One example is the Six-Day War in 1967, when Israel captured the Golan Heights from Syria, the West Bank (Judea and Samaria), East Jerusalem, and the Temple Mount from Jordan, along with the Gaza Strip from Egypt. Israel also conquered the 23,000 square mile Sinai Peninsula, with all its oil-rich desserts from Egypt. Since that time, Israel has divided its land and gifted it to the Arabs who call themselves "Palestinians," which is nothing more than a pseudo-country that has the full backing of the United Nations, although historically, it has never existed.[243] By 1982, Israel returned the Sinai Peninsula to Egypt, and the Gaza was made a gift to the so-called Palestinians in 2005; nonetheless, this land that was given to the Arabs for peace has never resulted in peace for Israel. All this and a division of the actual nation of Israel itself to create, for the first time, a Palestinian nation, a nation whose charter never recognized Israel's right to exist and still doesn't today! On October 18, 2016, during the Jewish holy week of *Sukkot* (Feast of Tabernacles) UNESCO (the United Nations Educational, Scientific and Cultural Organization) ignored over 3,000 years of Jewish history and passed a resolution declaring the Jews have no historical or religious connection to the Temple Mount or Jerusalem; but they said that Muslims do, so the Temple Mount was designated as a Muslim site![244] (Refer to Zechariah 12:3 regarding the Last Days.)

There can never be peace in the Middle-East. From a Muslim's theological point of view, there must always be open warfare against the Jews, which is something that is built into their religion, as we saw in Chapter 7. What we didn't tell you in Chapter 7 was that the Last Days' War against the Jews is mentioned over a half a dozen times in the Islamic Hadith: "The Day of Judgment will not have come until you fight with the Jews and the stones and the trees behind which a Jew will be hiding will say, 'O Muslim! There is a Jew hiding behind me, come and kill him!' " (Hadith: Sahih Muslim, Book 41, Number 6985; see also Sahih Muslim, 41:698; Sahih Muslim, 41:6982; Sahih Muslim, 41:6983; Sahih Muslim, 41:6984; Sahih

---

[243]To prove that a nation calling itself Palestine never existed, see if you can find out why no one can name one Palestinian king, or any historic capital of a nation called Palestine. All countries are noted for something; see if you can find the name of any famous Palestinian national product or the name of Palestine's national currency.

[244]Lela Gilbert, "Jews, Christians and UNESCO's Jerusalem Resolution." *Fox News*. FOX News Network, 21 Oct. 2016. Web. 04 Nov. 2016.

al-Bukhari, 4:52:177, and Sahih al-Bukhari, 4:56:791.)

The *Hadith* is an Islamic collection of the sayings of Muhammad and the second holiest book in Islam. It is an abbreviated version of the full English translated title which is, *The Abridged Collection of Authentic Hadith with Connected Chains Regarding Matters Pertaining to the Prophet, His Practices, and His Times.*

THE DAWNING OF THE TWENTY-FIRST CENTURY

Today, this biblical scenario is being played out right before our very eyes. It seems that the whole world has rapidly been becoming hyper anti-Semitic and right on the heels of WWII and the Nazi Holocaust when the Jews had a short period of reprieve—when the world felt guilty about how the Jews had been treated. That did not last for long. With the long-awaited re-establishment of the Nation of Israel, the world—just as the Bible said it would—is becoming even more intolerant of the Jews.

Consider how several of the United States presidents, as well as the European Union, have been agreeable to dividing or giving Jerusalem—the eternal Jewish capital—to the so-called Palestinian Muslim pretenders as their capital with the whole world gleefully applauding the idea.[245] Why is there such hatred for the Jews? Some claim that Jews are an evil race. In three different verses, the Koran claims that Allah condemned the Jews to be *the sons of apes* (Sûrah 7:166; Sûrah 2:6). As if that were not enough, in Sûrah 5: 60, the Jews are not only called the "sons of apes," but also called the "sons of pigs." We are also told in the Hadith that Jesus will return in the Last Days and break the crosses and "kill the [Jewish] pigs."[246]

---

[245]Rory McCarthy, "East Jerusalem Should Be Palestinian Capital, Says EU Draft Paper," *The Guardian*; Guardian News and Media, 2 December 2009. Web. 3 September 2014.

[246]Hadith: Sahih Bukhari, Vol. 3, Book 43, no. 656 and Sunan Abu Dawud Book 37 N0. 4310.

The World Falsely Accused Israel of Being an Apartheid State

Disdain for the Jews is not limited to Europeans and the Muslim nations. We read in the Bible (I Corinthians) that Satan stood against Israel. Satan has tried to destroy God's people since the very beginning of the world, and just as he used King David (1 Chronicles 21:1a), he also used and continues to use the Church to further that end. At the dawn of the twenty-first century, the Church of England, the Presbyterian Church, the Baptist Church, as well as the Methodist Church—to name a few— became divided over supporting Israel. The World Council of Churches, a liberal/progressive organization, has called for a boycott of Israel along with other religious institutions in the United States, Canada, England, and France. Other countries and many Protestant Churches are calling for a divesting of capital investments in Israel as a means to punish them for being an "Apartheid State." These countries, along with the United Nations, are also falsely accusing Israel of other alleged crimes against the so-called "Palestinian" Arabs. These attacks against Israel happen almost continually, yet deadly rockets are indiscriminately launched periodically, almost every year against innocent Israeli citizens from the Gaza Strip by the so-called "Palestinians."

The World Council of Churches represents over 590 conferences worldwide. While boycotting Israel, they have not once voiced criticism against the Islamic persecution of Christian Arabs. As Italian journalist Giulio Meotti, who writes on Israel and the Middle East, observed, "Today, most of the divestment campaigns against Israel are driven by Christian groups...."

Meotti continued:

> The United Church of Canada recently voted to boycott six companies (Caterpillar, Motorola, Ahava, Veolia, Elbit Systems and Chapters/Indigo), and South African Bishop Desmond Tutu convinced the University of Johannesburg to sever all links with Israeli fellows last year [2010]. The Methodist Church of Britain voted to boycott Israeli-produced goods and services from Judea and Samaria.... At the Rome synod, Archbishop Cyrille Salim Bustros, a cleric chosen by Pope Benedict to draft the synod's 44 final propositions, denied the Jewish people's biblical right to the Promised Land. "We Christians cannot

speak about the Promised Land for the Jewish people. There is no longer a Chosen people," Bustros said, reviving—unbiblical—replacement theology (bracketed clarification mine).[247]

Since the accusation has been raised, it deserves to be addressed. Is Israel an "Apartheid State?" Reverend Dr. Kenneth Meshoe is a member of the South African Parliament, the president of the African Christian Democratic Party, and the Chairman of the South African Israel Allies Caucus, all of whom are part of a group assembling support among lawmakers around the world for an undivided Israel.[248] He is also an indigenous Black African and survivor of former South Africa's state-sponsored apartheid. He says Israel is not an apartheid state. In a May 2013 article in the *San Francisco Examiner*, Dr. Meshoe explained his observances regarding his recent visit to South Africa. He could not help but notice Palestinian posters throughout the city that compared the State of Israel to the former apartheid South African regime where he lived.

That was not an unusual event in the United States since Palestinian activist groups throughout America are also placing similar anti-Israel propaganda signs in various cities and are protesting with demonstrations around the country and on college campuses, shouting down pro-Israel speakers and pro-Israel politicians.[249] In New York City, Palestinian anti-Israel propaganda signs have also appeared in subway stations and on subway trains. One Palestinian poster quotes the celebrated Nobel Prize recipient and Anglican Archbishop, Desmond Tutu, who stated, "I've been very distressed by my visit to the Holy Land; it reminded me so much of what happened to us black people in South Africa. Americans give Israel $3 billion per year. End Apartheid Now! Stop U.S. aid to Israel!" This blatant and unsubstantiated claim so infuriated the South African

---

[247]Giulio Meotti, "Churches Against Israel," *Levitt Letter* (September 2011), 15.

[248]Chris Mitchell, "Christian Broadcasting Network," *Lawmakers Worldwide Mobilize in Defense of Israel*, CBN News Middle East, 18 November 2011. Web. 5 April 2016.

[249]One example would be when a sitting U.S. Congressman, Ted Cruz (R-Texas), was booed off the stage on September 10, 2014, by members of the so-called, "In Defense of Christians" organization (a group of Palestinian and Middle Eastern Christians) at their *IDC Summit 2014* in Washington D.C. They booed him because he spoke in support of Christians and Jews as well as the state of Israel.

Member of Parliament that he made it a point to challenge Bishop Tutu's false claims:

> As a black South African under apartheid, I, among other things, could not vote, nor could I freely travel the landscape of South Africa. No person of color could hold a high government office. The races were strictly segregated at sports arenas, public restrooms, schools, and public transportation. People of color had inferior hospitals, medical care, and education. If a white doctor was willing to take a black patient, he had to examine him or her in a backroom or some other hidden place. *In my numerous visits to Israel, I did not see any of the above.*

Dr. Meshoe also observed:

> If one takes a train or bus in Israel, one will witness Muslims sitting next to Jews and Ethiopian Jews of color sitting next to Jews of European and Middle Eastern origin. On university campuses, in workplaces and restaurants, the same scene can be witnessed. No public bathroom in Israel is segregated by race or religion. Furthermore, there are Arabs serving as university professors, doctors, emergency room heads, soldiers, and even as Knesset members. Arabs in Israel have rights and privileges that a black living under the apartheid regime in South Africa can only dream of.... I believe that it is slanderous and deceptive for Israel's self-defense measures against the terrorists' campaign of suicide bombing, rocket attacks, and other acts of terrorism that have occurred and continue to occur, to be labeled as apartheid. I am shocked by the clzxc71 nm 'aim that the free, diverse, democratic state of Israel practices apartheid. This ridiculous accusation trivializes the word apartheid, minimizing and belittling the magnitude of the racism and suffering endured by South Africans of color.[250]

Sadly, many Christian denominations (Protestants and Catholics) joined a recent Bethlehem Boycott of Israel, claiming that Jews are occupiers of Jerusalem, Judea, and Samaria. Jews? Occupiers of Judea? From where

---

[250]Rachel Avraham, *South African MP: Israel Is Not an Apartheid State*, n.p. Web. 8 May 2014.

do those religious, pseudo intellects think the name Jew came? The tribe of Judah settled in the land God provided for them where Jerusalem is located; consequently, that land took on the name of their tribe. That resulted in those Hebrews being called Jews—derived from the name of their tribe Judah (spelled *Yudah* in Hebrew since there is no "J" in the Hebrew *Aleph-Bet*).

Since WWII, the sympathy for the Jewish people, who experienced the inhumanity of the Holocaust, has slowly reversed itself. Today, hatred of the Jews has grown to the point where some have even denied there ever was a Holocaust. Mahmoud Abbas (President of the pseudo State of Palestine) is among the Holocaust deniers having earned the equivalent of a Ph.D. in Holocaust Denial from a Russian college. (You read correctly—he was awarded an academic doctorate majoring in the study of Holocaust denial!)[251]

The whole world is now politically converging against the small landmass of Jerusalem, a city that has never been the capital of any other nation or province in the world from the time of King David until now, as far as we have researched—aside from Israel. The Arab Palestine Liberation Organization, founded in 1964, and the current Palestine organization (aside from their de facto capital in East Jerusalem) use Ramallah as their provincial capital. Ramallah, which in English translates to "ram" or "mountain" and "Allah," the proper name of the Islamic god (*Ilaha* is the Arabic word for "God"). In other words, the late Yasser Arafat's PLO and the current Palestinian Organization's capital has always been located in a city referred to as "the Mountain of Allah."

The events we are seeing in Israel today were prophesied in Scripture thousands of years ago. As we previously read, the Prophet Zechariah warned that God would make Jerusalem a cup of trembling for the whole world, a time when they would come against Jerusalem (Zechariah 12:2-3). It sure looks as if that time has arrived.

So it begins—now—in our lifetime, the small nation of Israel is the one

---

[251]Vadim Gorelik (Вадим Горелик) "Как товарищи Махмуд Аббас и Евгений Примаков Холокост отрицали" ("Comrades 'Mahmoud Abbas' and Yevgeny Primakov's denial").

country the world has come against and today—through the United Nations and its Muslim neighbors—the world continues its political attacks against the tiny nation of Israel more than any other nation on earth.[252] In the words of Donna Edmunds:

> The UN's Human Rights Council has issued more condemnations of Israel than of all other countries combined, a new report has found, prompting allegations of gross corruption. The Council reserves a special agenda item targeting Israel in every meeting, singling out the country in a way not done for any other.[253]

Why would some Christians also take part in this? Why would Christians join forces with those who want to divide Judea and Samaria from Israel—also called the West Bank[254]—and offer it, along with Jerusalem, as its capital for a people who *never existed* as a nation before in recorded history?[255] It is because of the rebelliousness growing daily against the God of the Bible. It is because evil people in the last days would be "deceiving and [would] be deceived" (2 Timothy 3:13). It is because of the great falling away of traditional, biblical orthodoxy by our so-called

---

[252]Mitchell Bard, "United Nations: The U.N. Relationship with Israel." *The U.N.- Israel Relationship*, American-Israeli Cooperative Enterprise, updated July 2015. Web. 10 February 2016.

[253]Donna Rachel Edmunds, "UN's Human Rights Council Condemns Israel More than Rest of World Combined - Breitbart." *Breitbart News*, n.p. 25 June 2015. Web. 27 April 2016.

[254]Calling this region of Israel, the "West Bank" of the Jordan River is a misnomer. A river's bank is considered to be no further than the farthest area where the river overflows at its flood stage. Jerusalem and much of the so-called "West Bank" is mountainous and the Jordan River flows into to the *lowest* place on earth, the Dead Sea! Surely, the last time the Jordan River was high enough to cover Jerusalem causing it to be part of the Jordan River's West Bank—would only have been during the Noahic flood!

[255]Jerrold L. Sobel. *Articles: There Was Never a Country Called Palestine*. "American Thinker," 12 Feb. 2012. Web. 27 Apr. 2016. "At no time in history has there ever been a nation called 'Palestine.' During the Ottoman Empire, which lasted from 1299-1922 C.E., the land dubbed by the Romans as 'Palestine' was controlled by the Turks; there was never an outcry for a Palestinian State then. During the illegal annexation of Judea and Samaria by the Hashemite Kingdom of Jordan, subsequent to the 1949 Armistice and prior to 1967, there was never talk of 'occupied territory' or a Palestinian State."

mainline, Christian denominations (2 Thessalonians 2:3); therefore, the Most High is allowing the "god" of this age to deceive the world, and only those truly committed to God and His Word have been able to see the truth plainly laid out for them in the Bible (2 Corinthians 4:4, bracketed clarification mine).

The Scriptures tell us why some Christians would not be supportive of Israel's biblical claim.

Consider how there was a plot by the religious leaders to put a stop to Jesus' ministry. To fully understand what was going on during the time of Jesus with the unseemly actions of the Sanhedrin (i.e., council), as well as the similarities between the inappropriate actions of many of today's pastors, we must look at the politics during the first century Judea to make the comparison.

The high priest had held a great deal of power since the time of Moses, but the high priest during Jesus' time, Caiaphas, was also a political animal and, as such, was a pawn of Rome and less a servant of God. During the time of Jesus, there were several Jewish sects, not unlike our Christian denominations today, which consisted of three main branches: Sadducees, Pharisees, and Zealots. The Sadducees were not unlike our liberal pastors and Churches today—in their case, recognizing the value of the Torah—while ignoring or rejecting the rest of the Scriptures. The high priest, Caiaphas, was more inclined toward the Sadducees. The Pharisees had similarities to today's Christians in the sense they believed in angels and the resurrection; they were more closely inclined toward the teachings of Jesus. Zealots were fanatical Jews who wanted to overthrow the Romans and bring about Israeli independence. The Zealots, many of whom also believed in Jesus, expected that the kingdom would soon be set up under Him, and He would lead them to victory by overthrowing the despised Romans. It is because of the Zealots the Temple was destroyed in 70 A.D. (Matthew 24:2; Mark 13:2; Luke 21:5-7) and the final destruction of Judea in 135 A.D. With it, the Jews were dispersed throughout the whole world, as foretold by Jesus in Luke 24:21.

With this background in mind, we are better able to understand the events surrounding the crucifixion of Jesus and how apostasy in the Church today parallels apostasy in Judaism. Many of today's liberal pastors and priests will not admit they have lost faith, and as the high priest, Caiaphas, who was a Sadducee, only accepted the first five books of Moses (Torah). They did not believe most of what the Bible taught; so, they created a clever answer—a loophole—to give those who ask them if they believe the Bible is the Word of God. When asked, they will tell you they believe the Bible *contains* the Word of God. That is their way of thinking they have pacified you and avoided telling you they do not believe that the Bible is the *inerrant* Word of God.

The problem with this theory is who is to say which words are from God? By accepting this theory, there is no need to concern ourselves with the question of sin because now it becomes possible to disregard those troubling passages of sin in the Bible—depending, of course, on the sin you would like to indulge in without feeling guilty. This is a result and expansion of allegorical interpretation in the Church, which leads to replacement theology and allows us to either read into Scripture what we want it to mean or disregard the parts we do not like. By doing that, we can claim that the troubling passage was simply written by one of many men who wrote the Bible, and not God. That gives us the perfect excuse to pick and choose the Scriptures we like while rejecting those we don't, which is why some unscrupulous people and clergy say they believe "the Bible contains the Word of God," not "the whole Bible is the inerrant Word of God." Once we open the door to apostasy, anything is likely to happen.

What does God have to say about His word coming from uninspired men acting on their own and not from Him?

> knowing this first, that no prophecy of Scripture is of any private interpretation, for prophecy never came by the will of man, but holy men of God spoke *as they were* moved by the Holy Spirit. (2 Peter 1:20-21).

Remember, the thing which caused the separation of Adam and Eve from God and, therefore—the fall of humanity—was because they listened to the serpent in the Garden of Eden when he called God's Word into question (Genesis 3:1).

So it was that Caiaphas—being *theologically liberal* as well as a *politically motivated* High priest—realized Jesus could be a very great threat to him.

Consider Caiaphas' point of view. He was as powerful as the king and maybe even more so because, as God's high priest, he spoke for God—the ultimate authority! Caiaphas probably did not believe in a messiah or any resurrection, but the fact that many of the people did, presented a real problem for him. If they had accepted Jesus as the Messiah, then Caiaphas' authority would have been compromised because the Messiah was the only person who was not only equal, but also superior to the high priest in authority; thus, Jesus had to be eliminated.

Caiaphas addressed a special meeting of the Sanhedrin regarding Jesus' perceived threat to the status quo. The Sanhedrin (i.e., the Supreme Court of Israel) consisted of 71 men (Numbers 11:16), one from every district of the land. Predictably, there were great discussions and conflicting views—but putting a person to death just because some of the people thought He was the Messiah—did not go well with some. Fearing his influence might have been slipping away, Caiaphas argued that Jesus might lead the people in an uprising against Rome and bring down the full anger of Caesar and, therefore, should be eliminated. The bickering continued.

> Then Caiaphas, who was high priest that year, spoke up, "You know nothing at all! You do not realize that it is better for you that one man die for the people than that the whole nation perish" (John 11:49-50, NIV).

Therefore, it was decided that Jesus had to die. Charges were brought up before the Roman governor, Pilate, who found no wrong with Jesus and wanted to set Him free. The threat was too great for Caiaphas and the powers-that-be, so they demanded that Jesus be crucified. To make that happen, Caiaphas and the Sanhedrin rounded up a group of people—not unlike how today's community organizers gather up a group, many times by hiring them, to demonstrate for or against something. Consequently, it was Caiaphas' riffraff who assembled at Pilate's courtyard to demand Jesus' crucifixion.

> When Pilate saw he was getting nowhere, but that an uproar was starting, he took water and washed his hands in front of the crowd. "I am innocent of this man's blood," he said. "It is your responsibility!" All the people answered, "His blood is on us and on our children!" (Matthew 27:24-25, NIV.)

221

Notice how they justified letting Pilate give Jesus over to them to be crucified by telling Pilate not to trouble his conscience. They would take the blame—if there were to be any—on themselves and their children (a point well exploited by replacement theologians). Think about it. The small, but vocal group, was basically a "rent-a-mob"— not the entire country. The mob was comprised of those who did not believe Jesus was the real Messiah and, therefore, by them asking for the blood of someone whom they thought was just a liar or false prophet to be on their heads was meaningless. After all, why would God be angry with them for demanding the death of someone they believed to be a heretic? The reality, as we have shown, is that Jesus had thousands of Jewish followers, and this was only a small mob put together at the last minute by Caiaphas and the Sanhedrin to demonstrate against Jesus and bring about the end of His perceived threat to their power.

Some deceitful Christian Gentiles, in the centuries which followed, grabbed ahold of that verse, which described an event caused by a very small, but powerful group of Jesus' political enemies. Replacement theologians happily use the Matthew 27:24-25 passage to strengthen their false teaching that God was finished with all the children of Israel because *they* killed Jesus, making it—if not an obligation to avenge God— at least an excuse to root out the current generation of children of those Jews and let "God's judgment" fall on them. What a shameful misuse of Scripture! Remember that God made an everlasting covenant with Abraham and Sarah's descendants (Genesis 17), and the early Church Fathers were all Jews!

When studying the Scriptures, there is an important phrase that warns us: "A text without a context is a pretext for a proof text." That saying means we must be careful when looking at one or two passages or verses out of context by themselves because it can be deceiving. We must look at all the other verses surrounding the text to make sure it is precisely understood in light of the entire passage, chapter, book, and Bible as a whole. We cannot even begin to imagine how many millions of innocent Jews—men, women, and precious, innocent children—have been ostracized, tortured, and killed in the most ghoulish ways imaginable because of Matthew 27:25 being taken out of context when that small group of "rent-a-mob" Jews called for Jesus' blood to be "... on us and on our children!"

To be fair, when we consider how the Temple was destroyed in 70 A.D. and how the city of Jerusalem was so badly plowed under by the Romans, making it look as if nothing ever existed there, it sure seemed to give credibility to the false notion God had turned His back on Israel.[256]

A closer inspection of the Scriptures shows that Jesus prophesied the destruction of the Temple in 70 A.D. before His crucifixion—not because He was to die on the cross or because of a few rebellious Jews coming against Him—but as a result of Judah's rebellion against Rome (Luke 21:5-6; 23:24). Many people in Jesus' day, who believed He was the Messiah, also believed He would set them free from the rule of Rome, but the struggle against their Roman overlords continued with the ultimate result of Rome destroying both Jerusalem and the Temple in 70 A.D.

After the Jewish revolt of 135 A.D., Emperor Hadrian renamed Jerusalem, *Aelia Capitolina,* derived from his family name (Aelius) and its Capitoline Triad of gods, Jupiter, Juno, and his daughter, Minerva. As we mentioned earlier, Emperor Hadrian changed the name of Judea—as an insult to the Jews—to *Syria-Palæstina,* derived from the Philistines' homeland, Philistia (fil-**is**-tee-*uh*), who was hated, and by then, an extinct enemy of Israel.

As a result, there was even more reason to believe God was finished with the Jews—that is, unless one happened to know Scripture.

Without going into great detail, after Solomon died, his two sons, Rehoboam and Jeroboam, divided the Nation of Israel into two countries with Rehoboam ruling the Northern Kingdom of Israel and Jeroboam ruling the Southern Kingdom of Judea. About two centuries later, when the Assyrians captured Israel, there was still the Southern Kingdom of Judea left from that once proud and powerful nation. About a century later, Judea would also suffer wars and become a vassal state and pay tribute, in the form of taxes, to other countries—most notably, Babylon—followed by others, such as the Greek and Roman Empires.

While the prophet, Ezekiel, was exiled in Babylon—he was given a prophecy—which the Church ignored. God had predicted an event that

---

[256]Josephus, *The New and Complete Works of Josephus*, trans. William Whiston (Grand Rapids: Kregel, 1999), In the section titled *The Jewish War,* Book 7:1:1.

would occur some 2,500 years in the future. The event was the actual—not spiritual—return of Israel to their land. God also promised how the Nation of Israel would be reinstated—not as the divided kingdoms of Israel and Judea—but as a united Israel like it originally was under Kings Saul, David, and Solomon. That prophecy was not set in motion until after the Nazi Holocaust of the twentieth century.

Despite what seemed like the imminent end of all ethnic Jews on the planet, God's promise to Israel—through His revelation to the prophet, Ezekiel—was about to unfold. In the Bible, we read about the 1948 miraculous restoration of the land of Israel, as previously stated, some 2,500 years before that incredible event took place:

> The hand of the LORD was on me, and He brought me out by the Spirit of the LORD and set me in the middle of a valley; it was full of bones. He led me back and forth among them, and I saw a great many bones on the floor of the valley, bones that were very dry. He asked me, "Son of man, can these bones live?" I said, "Sovereign LORD, you alone know."

> Then He said to me, "Prophesy to these bones and say to them, 'Dry bones, hear the word of the LORD! This is what the Sovereign LORD says to these bones: I will make breath enter you, and you will come to life. I will attach tendons to you and make flesh come upon you and cover you with skin; I will put breath in you, and you will come to life. Then you will know that I am the LORD' " (Ezekiel 37:1-6, NIV).

Like Ezekiel's vision of the *Valley of Bones*, we see the skeletons and decomposing bodies of Jews slaughtered in the Nazi Holocaust.

The return of Israel as one nation and not a divided kingdom:

> The word of the LORD came to me: "Son of man, take a stick of wood and write on it, 'Belonging to Judah and the Israelites associated with him.' "Then take another stick of wood, and write on it," 'Belonging to Joseph (that is, to Ephraim) and all the Israelites associated with him.' "Join them together into one stick so that they will become one in your hand."

> When your people ask you, "Won't you tell us what you mean by this?" say to them, "This is what the Sovereign LORD says:" 'I am going to take the stick of Joseph—which is in Ephraim's hand—and of the Israelite tribes associated with him, and join it to Judah's stick. I will make them into a single stick of wood, and they will become one in my hand.'

> Hold before their eyes the sticks you have written on and say to them, "This is what the Sovereign LORD says:" 'I will take the Israelites out of the nations where they have gone. I will gather them from all around and bring them back into their own land. I will make them one nation in the land, on the mountains of Israel. There will be one king over all of them, and they will never again be two nations or be divided into two kingdoms' (Ezekiel 37:15-22, NIV).

That happened just as God predicted on May 14, 1948! God also had Ezekiel prophesy that King David's Throne (decedents of David's House) would be restored:

> My servant David will be king over them, and they will all have one shepherd. They will follow my laws and be careful to keep my decrees (Ezekiel 37:24, NIV).

Notice in these last verses, God told us not only how He would bring Israel back into the land, which He did on May 14, 1948, and that He would re-establish the throne of David. How can that be after 3,000 years? The answer is happening right now; it is called DNA. In an article by Nadine Epstein of the Eshet Chayil *(Women of Valor Foundation)*, she informs us about some important research that is currently being conducted. She quotes Susan Roth, who is a descendant of King David:

"If we could only find a DNA that is shared by all the descendants that would be unbelievable..." There was a king 3,000 years ago who pulled together 12 tribes and started a dynasty. There were always Jews in Israel but they were not always a nation because they were sent into exile. And they came back once and rebuilt the Temple and then the Romans came... [Susan] Roth envisions a royal House of David that takes its place alongside the current government of Israel. "Just like in England, where there is a queen who is a figurehead, there could be a king of Israel who is a figurehead," she says. "A king would be taken seriously and signify that Jews have been in Israel for over 3,000 years. The Knesset could run the country, but there would be a royal house that would bring legitimacy. The royal House of David could be a light unto the nation. It would bring about peace harmony and everything the world is waiting for because the world is in a terrible shape right now"[257] (bracketed clarification mine).

This is amazing! There is a modern-day effort to re-establish the throne of David, just as Ezekiel prophesied it would happen in the latter days. This is not unique just to Ezekiel. The Bible repeats this theme several times, including the promise made by the angel, Gabriel, when he told Mary before Jesus was born:

And the angel said unto her, "Fear not, Mary: for you have found favor with God. And, behold, you shall conceive in thy womb, and bring forth a son, and shall call His name Jesus. He shall be great, and shall be called the Son of the Highest: and the Lord God shall give unto him the throne of His father David: And He shall reign over the house of Jacob forever; and of His kingdom, there shall be no end" (Luke 1:30-33).

Consider that there must be a throne of David for Jesus to sit on when

---

[257]Nadine Epstein, "King David's Genes," *Moment Magazine,* March/April 2012. Web. 10 February 2016. *Moment Magazine,* North America's premier Jewish magazine, was founded in 1975 by Nobel Prize laureate, Elie Wiesel, and acclaimed writer, Leonard Fein. Fiercely independent, *Moment* is not tied to any organization, denomination, or point of view and offers a balanced accounting of the Jewish experience in America.

He returns, and it looks like there will be one—soon.

Last, although certainly not least, is the scriptural reference of God's continuing relationship with Israel, as we read in the book of Romans. It is wise to remember that the following passage we are revisiting was written many years *after* the circumstances, which led to the crucifixion of Jesus and His resurrection and ascension back to the Father.

Some of the Roman Gentiles questioned whether God was finished with the Jews because of the crucifixion—just like other Gentiles have continued to ask down through the ages. The Apostle Paul must have thought he was addressing that heresy once and for all when he wrote under the direction of the Holy Spirit:

> I ask then: "Did God reject His people" By no means! I am an Israelite myself, a descendant of Abraham, from the tribe of Benjamin. *God did not reject His people*, whom He foreknew (Romans 11:1-2a, NIV, emphasis added).

Because there was not an Israel anymore (i.e., Northern Kingdom) and Jesus was about to leave His disciples and ascend to the Father, many of His followers wondered when the kingdom of Israel and the throne would be restored. Jesus did not say Israel had fallen out of favor with God or say they should not look for it to be restored in their lifetime (notice the Southern Kingdom of Judea was still referred to as Israel (Matthew 20-21; 8:10, etc.):

> Then they gathered around him and asked him, "Lord, are you at this time going to *restore the kingdom to Israel*?" He said to them: "It is not for you to know the times or dates the Father has set by His own authority. But you will receive power when the Holy Spirit comes on you; and you will be my witnesses in Jerusalem, and in all Judea and Samaria, and to the ends of the earth" (Acts 1:6-8, NIV, emphasis added).

If this is not enough to convince you that we should seek guidance from the Bible when perplexing events arise, reflect on how almost every night on the news we see threats against Jerusalem—not just militarily—but

227

politically and economically as well, like the international BDS (Boycott, Divestment, and Sanctions) movement. We are also seeing many mainline Christian denominations (who insist God has turned His back on the Jews for killing Christ), divesting themselves of financial holdings related to Israel. Universities are canceling Jewish associations on campus, boycotting Israel, etc.—all being done to punish the Jews.

To make a point regarding the unexplainable importance of the small, out of the way capital known as "Jerusalem"—in a very tiny country called Israel that's only 60 miles wide at its widest and 9 miles wide at its narrowest points[258]—we will share a brief observation we made regarding this isolated, small town. Most cities of importance during the first century were usually on major waterways or oceans, which allowed them to be readily accessible for travel and commerce by boat. Important inland cities were aligned along trade routes located through flatlands or valleys. In mountainous countries, trade routes ran through canyons as much as possible because it made travel less cumbersome. It was also important for people traveling by land to have access to intermittent water wells and streams to refresh themselves and their animals.

Jerusalem sits on top of a mountain. I have been to Jerusalem and walked the Old City. At a brisk pace, it takes approximately 45 to 90 minutes, depending on whether the walk is around the original Old City of Jerusalem, which lay inside Hezekiah's walls, or the relatively more recent walls of the Old City.

Old City of Jerusalem   Photo courtesy of Eitan, f

The recent walls were built outside of Hezekiah's walls by the Ottoman Empire's Suleiman I from 1535 to 1538 A.D., as seen on in the photograph at the right. There were no main roads or waterways to reach Jerusalem,

---

[258]"Can Tiny Israel Afford to Surrender More Land?" Confidential Reporter. WEB. 1 Jan. 1970. "Israel is only 260 miles at its longest, has a 112-mile coastline, 60 miles at its widest, and is between three and nine miles at its narrowest. A high-powered rifle could launch a projectile right across the country."

and during the time of Jesus, travelers followed the coastline, cut over east, and climbed the mountain, or they could travel across the ridge of the mountain range running north and south through the land of Israel.

There are no oil wells, diamond, gold, or silver mines near Jerusalem—nor are there natural resources, which would make Jerusalem worth the trouble to conquer; however, during the Temple periods, there were more than ample amounts of gold and silver stored in the Temple, which also served as the nation's bank for securing the country's wealth, but that was not a natural resource. We concede that modern Jerusalem has expanded into a large capital city, a fact many countries have refused to acknowledge—including the United States' Islamic-leaning Barack Hussein Obama administration (2008-2016). In comparison, Jerusalem is not New York, London, Paris, Rome, Tokyo, Moscow, Beijing or Los Angeles, not to mention that Jerusalem is a capital city without an airport; so why is Jerusalem the most troublesome—as well as most talked about and controversial city—in the world today? The answer is in the Bible. God knew the whole world would become obsessed with Jerusalem and that all the nations of the world would come against her thousands of years before it would actually happen:

> And it shall happen in that day that I will make Jerusalem a very heavy stone for all peoples; all who would heave it away will surely be cut in pieces, though all nations of the earth are gathered against it (Zechariah 12:3, NKJV).

Jesus warned us of what it would be like in the End Times when He stated, "For there shall arise false Christs, and false prophets, and shall shew [show] great signs and wonders; insomuch that, *if it were possible, they shall deceive the very elect*" (Matthew 24:24, italicized emphasis added, bracketed clarification added).

You might ask where the false Christs are. They are all around us. They include (1) the late Reverend Sun Myung Moon (1920-2012) who claimed he was the reincarnated Christ;[259] (2) the Christ of the Mormons, who is one god in a lineage of many gods and whose brother is Satan. The

---

[259]Sun Myung Moon (2014, May 19), *Wikipedia, the Free Encyclopedia*, n.p. Web. 5 June 2014.

Mormons' Jesus has not only a father but also grandfathers, great grandfathers, and great-great-grandfathers ad infinitum.[260] The Jesus of Mormonism also married Lazarus' sisters, Mary and Martha, along with Mary Magdalene and possibly four other women and had children, some of whom today claim to be Mormon priests,[261] and (3) the Jesus Christ of Islam, who Muslims say is only a prophet of Allah and not the Son of God (Sûrah 17:111). There are other Christs like the Lord Maitreya, who was alleged to have appeared on June 11, 1988, by materializing suddenly and unexpectedly at a Christian prayer meeting in Nairobi, Kenya, and claimed to be the cosmic Christ.[262] There have been and will continue to be other false Christs.

Consider a cover story in the November 17, 2008, issue of *TIME Magazine,* where Nancy Gibbs (then *TIME Magazine's* Editor-at-Large) compared the messianic persona of Obama to Jesus.

In Islam, Muslims have their messiah; they say he is the rider on the white horse in Revelation 6 (one of the Four Horsemen of the Apocalypse) who will return with his subordinate, Jesus. [263] His is name is Muhammad ibn Hasan al-Mahdi (pronounced **Mah**-dee), and in the Shi'ite branch of Islam, he is also known as the "Twelfth Iman." According to an Ann Curry NBC interview on September 9, 2009, with Mahmoud Ahmadinejad (sixth president of Iran, 2005-2013), he is expected to return soon. Of course, Muslims would take great offense if one were to explain to them that the figure in Revelation 6, who is riding the white horse, is none other than the Antichrist.

Concerning the Jewish Messiah, while in Israel, we once observed a

---

[260]Lynn K. Wilder, Ph.D., "The Christian: Why I Left the Mormon Church to Follow Jesus," PremierChristianity.com/Past-Issues/2015/August-2015. This is from a reprint of the August 15, 2015, edition of the *Premier Christianity* magazine (UK). Lynn K. Wilder, Ph.D., was an ordinance worker in the Chicago temple of the Church of Latter Day Saints. Dr. Wilder was also a professor at Brigham Young University, the Church's leading education institution.

[261](LDS) Journal of Discourses, vol. 4, pages 259-260.

[262]*SHARE INTERNATIONAL* magazine, *Lord Maitreya,* June 5, 2014.

[263]J.P. Sloane, Ph.D., *A Simple Crash Course on Islam,* vol. I (Dallas: AvingtonHouse, 2015), 150-154, *Islam Exposed three-volume series.* In that book, we discuss the Mahdi in greater detail.

young, orthodox Jewish man pushing his child in a baby stroller. Strapped on his back was a portable, battery-operated speaker. He held a microphone in his hand, and as he proceeded to push the stroller along, he proclaimed for everyone to hear that the Messiah was coming soon. Are Christians, Jews, and Muslims all expecting the soon return of a messiah? It appears we might have arrived at the point in time spoken about in Matthew 24:24.

The basis of replacement theology rests on the opinion and traditions of people, not a biblical doctrine; so, who do we blame for killing Jesus? If we could have asked Jesus before the day of His Crucifixion, who was going to kill Him, what would His answer have been? As we discussed in Chapter 1—Jesus already answered that question in the Gospel of John:

> Therefore does My Father love Me, because I lay down My life, that I might take it [up] again. *No man* takes it from Me, but I lay it down of Myself. I have power to lay it down, and I have power to take it [up] again. This commandment have I received of My Father (John 10:17-18, bracketed clarifications mine, emphasis added).

It is important to remember that *no man* took Jesus' life. He is the controller of His own destiny. His blood atonement for *all* mankind was predestined from the beginning of time (Genesis 3:15), thousands of years before there were even Jews on the planet!

However, that still does not explain the destiny of the Jews and Israelites. Is God finished with them as the church has wrongly taught many Christians for thousands of years? Is there a light on this subject to be shed through the Bible? God promised Abraham:

> And I will establish my covenant between Me and thee and your seed after you in their generations for an *everlasting covenant*, to be a God unto you, and to your seed after thee (Genesis 17:7, emphasis added).

What part of "everlasting" does the replacement theologian not understand? What about the land of Israel still being a covenantal promise after all this time? The answer is found in the very next verse in Genesis 17:

> And I will give unto you, and to your seed after you, the land wherein

you are a stranger, all the land of Canaan, *for an everlasting possession*; and I will be their God (Genesis 17:8, emphasis added).

Again, we must ask, "What part of 'everlasting' does the supersessionist *not* understand?" Still, to this day, many continue to argue that God is done with the Jews. Consider that we have shown over and over again, in this book, how the Apostle Paul clearly addressed this subject when he wrote:

... Has God cast away His people? God forbid (Romans 11:1a).

These Scriptures have been available to biblical scholars throughout the ages if they had only studied the Bible more carefully. Think about it. If a just God was willing to spare Sodom and Gomorrah for the sake of 10 people (Genesis 18:22), then surely He would spare the Jewish people for the sake of hundreds (1 Corinthians 15:6), even thousands (Acts 2:41) who, in the first century, were devoted Jews that believed in Christ as their Savior (Acts 2:41; 21:20)!

Make no mistake. God has made unconditional promises to His beloved Israel, and because He is God, He cannot lie. The heresy of replacement theology does not come from the Bible; it comes from people:

God is not a man, that He should lie; neither the Son of Man, that He should repent: has He said, and shall He not do it? or has He spoken, and shall He not make it good? (Numbers 23:19.)

Throughout this book, we see the chilling and deadly results of the Church having embraced replacement theology throughout the ages. Consider if it were possible for God to break His word regarding the everlasting covenants He made with the Jews; then what assurance can we, as Christians, have that God will not also turn His back on us?

Do not be arrogant, but tremble. For if God did not spare the natural branches, He will not spare you either (Romans 11:21).

232

While God disciplines His children (Jeremiah 30:11),[264] it is not God who is against Israel, but Satan (1 Chronicles 21:1). Satan desires to subvert God's position in the cosmos[265] and to deceive those God wants to love by tricking them into serving him instead.

God's Signed Covenant Is Forever Sealed in the Mountains of Israel!

If God chose the Hebrews to be His people for all time (Genesis 17:7), would it be possible that He *sealed the deal* by signing His name as an everlasting covenant on the land He gave to the Jews?

We only have to look at the Bible:

> But unto the place which the LORD your God shall choose out of all your tribes *to put His name there*, even unto His habitation shall you seek, and there you shall come (Deuteronomy 12:5, emphasis added).[266]

It appears that is exactly what God did, but not in Greek, Latin, Arabic, or English—but Hebrew.

On the next page, we have a satellite photo taken from space. In that photo, just to the right and south of an Israeli town named *Bethel* (i.e., "House of God"), embedded in the mountains are four canyons, traced by the finger of God, spelling out the Hebrew Tetragrammaton, יהוה (i.e., *YAWA*, pronounced Yahweh). In the West, we know Him as "Jehovah" (although there is no "J" in the Hebrew alphabet). With the satellite photograph, we can see the actual canyons which form the Hebrew Tetragrammaton!

---

[264]"For I am with you," says the LORD, "to save you: though I make a full end of all nations whither I have scattered you, yet I will not make a full end of you: but I will correct you in measure, and will not leave you altogether unpunished" (Jeremiah 30: 11).

[265]"I will ascend above the heights of the clouds; I will be like the most High" (Isaiah 14:14).

[266]Note: God choosing to put His name in the land of Israel is repeated two more times in Deuteronomy 12:11; 21

In this satellite photograph,[267] we have placed (for comparison) the Hebrew Tetragrammaton, יהוה, in a white relief directly above the canyons, which also contains a Tetragrammaton in the mountains to the right of the little town of *Bethel* (i.e., "House of God"). We did this to aid those of you who are not familiar with Hebrew letters. Hebrew is read from right to left. Also, notice on the map the community of "Ramallah," the capital of the Palestinian Authority. *Ramallah* means "Mountain of Allah" (*Ram* means "mountain" and *Allah* is self-explanatory).

Consider: If the God of the Bible and Allah are the same person, and he chose Arabic and the Koran as his final revelation, why didn't the God of the Bible also write the name "Allah" in Arabic next to Ramallah or any other place on this planet for that matter?

<hr>

[267]"MAP 7.S-AB," *The Holy Land Satellite,* Atlas R.L.W. Cleave, ed. (Nicosia, Cyprus: RØHR Productions, Ltd., 1999), 81.

CHAPTER 8

WHERE IS GOD IN ALL THIS?

We have seen how replacement theology is the Church's dark and shameful history and how those representing Christ down through the ages have disgracefully mistreated their brothers—Christ's brethren—the Jews.

Consider: When Jesus rose from the dead and spent forty days with His disciples and His other followers—all Jews—He would have had plenty of time to teach them, as well as warn the rest of the Jews in Judea that "God was now through with Jews and that the Church would be replacing the Jews as His chosen people." Yet, Jesus never even hinted or even suggested such a foreign and unbiblical concept—and He had plenty of time to do so! As for the Holocaust deniers, like Mahmoud Abbas, the current President of the so-called nation of Palestine (as of this writing), their dispute is very similar to the time when Paul responded to those who argued that Jesus never rose from the dead. He challenged them, as we read in 1 Corinthians 15: 6, that they could get first-hand eyewitness confirmation of Jesus having been raised from the dead because there were many that were still alive, who not only saw Jesus, but talked with Him after He had risen! Likewise, today, when those like Mahmoud Abbas deny the Holocaust, we can respond as Paul did; that there are many still alive today who witnessed—and who are actual survivors—of that horrible Nazi Holocaust of the middle twentieth century.

During that dreadful Holocaust, the Nation of Israel had been off the world stage for two and a half millennia. At the time of Christ, Israel had been absent as a nation for five-hundred years. After such a long absence,

235

it didn't take the Gentile church long to completely do away with the Jews and start a new tradition by appointing themselves as God's chosen people, something God never intended. God is not bound by the traditions of the Church, which many times results in the perversion of Scripture because God is not mocked (Galatians 6:8). Regrettably, even with the Jews back in their land, and more returning every day, all is not well. In the passages of Scripture dealing with the Last Days, we still see Israel under attack.

Post-WWII and the 1972 Munich Olympic Massacre

Looking back at the twentieth century, we see that during 1938, preceding WWII, the Olympic games were held in Adolph Hitler's Berlin, Germany, but It would not be until 1972 that the Olympic Committee would allow the games to resume in Germany. It was during the 1972 Munich Olympics when eleven Israeli athletes were savagely murdered by the so-called Palestinian terrorist group, "Black September." They are the militant branch of the Palestinian group, Fatah, of which the Palestinian President, Muhammad Abbas (also known as "kunya Abu Mazen" (Arabic, أَبُو مَا زن, 'Abū Māzin), now heads. Fatah is also the current ruling political party of the so-called West Bank nation-in-waiting of Palestine. The terrorist group, Black September, was backed by PLO Chairman Yasser Arafat (1929-2004) and funded by Muhammad Abbas. Abbas replaced Arafat as Chairman of the PLO on May 8, 2005 (after a brief interim by Rawhi Fattouh), and became the president of Palestine on January 15, 2005.[268]

---

[268]The Editors of Encyclopaedia Britannica. "Munich Massacre MUNICH, GERMANY [1972]." *Encyclopædia Britannica*, Munich massacre. WEB. 31 May 2015. Palestinian terrorist attack on Israeli Olympic team members at the 1972 Summer Games in Munich....By 12:30 AM on September 6, the shooting had stopped, and the 20-hour reign of terror was over. Eleven Israelis had been killed, along with one Munich policeman, and five black September terrorists lay dead.

THE TWENTY-FIRST CENTURY USHERED IN
ST. MALACHY'S FINAL POPE ON MARCH 13, 2013

Background:

In 2005, Joseph Aloisius Ratzinger was elected Pope Benedict XVI, but in 2013, after serving eight years as pope, Benedict XVI amazed the world when he announced that he was stepping down. For a pope to step down is rare; it had only happened twice before. The first one was six hundred years ago, during 1415, when Pope Gregory XII stepped down to unite the Western Church, and (2) in 1294 when Pope Celestine V who, like Benedict, did so of his own accord. In 2013, Benedict XVI resigned because he said he had a "mystical experience" and felt prompted by God to step down at that time.[269] It does seem there is a divine power orchestrating those events. You are saying "divine power orchestrating those events," meaning a divine power had played a part in the stepping down of the tree popes you mentioned.

Consider: After centuries of anticipation, Pope Benedict's resignation put the selection of Malachy's 112th and final pope into motion. Just hours after Benedict's shocking resignation, the Vatican dome was struck by lightning from Heaven—not once—but *twice*. Many saw that as a bad omen.[270] What makes those events even more ominous to many of the faithful is that they all occurred on the very eve of the eighth, blood moon Tetrad of the Christian Era, which fell on Jewish holidays.

Even though Pope Emeritus, Benedict XVI, stepped down as pope, he is

---

[269]Hafiz, Yasmine, "Pope Benedict's 'Mystical Experience' Prompted Resignation. Said 'God Told Me To,' " *Huffington Post*. HuffPost.com, 21 Aug. 2013. Web. 11 Dec. 2014.

[270]Paul Cockerton, "Lightning Bolt Hit Vatican Not Once but TWICE Hours after Pope's Shock Resignation," *Mirror (UK)*, n.p. 12 Feb. 2013. Web. Dec. 2013.

still referred to as *His Holiness* and entitled to continue wearing the papal color of white, in addition to retaining the title of pope. Cardinal Jorge Mario Bergoglio followed Benedict XVI as pope.

A Name—Is a Name—Is a Name;
by Any Other, Could It Still Be the Same?

Before Cardinal Jorge Mario Bergoglio was elected to the papacy by the College of Cardinals, many were reminded of the prediction of Saint Malachy's remaining 112 popes, which would end with one named "Petrus Romanus" (i.e.,"Peter of Rome"). At the time when St. Malachy was given that prophecy, there had already been 154 popes, including the first and only one named "Peter," who was also the disciple of Jesus.

St. Malachy predicted that the line of popes would begin and end with the name "Peter"—a name that would not and had not been used by any other pope since the Apostle Peter—for a total of 266 popes. He predicted Peter of Rome (the 112th pope) as the one who would witness the tribulation and the destruction of the city of Rome. The Book of Revelation also deals with the End of the Age. In Chapter 17, it reveals a strange figure known as the "Whore of Babylon" who rules over spiritual Rome (vs. 9). As we read in our discussion of the sixteenth century, in order to deflect from the controversial pope and Church's role at the End of the Age prophesies, de Alcasar (1554-1613) had to create the theory of Preterism by deflecting those horrendous predictions, which were so embarrassing to the Church in Rome, and redirect them back to the first century.

> And this gospel of the kingdom shall be preached in all the world for a witness unto all nations; and then shall the end come.

> When you therefore shall see the abomination of desolation, spoken of by Daniel the prophet [Daniel 9:27], stand in the holy place (whoso reads, let him understand). Then let them which be in Judea flee into the mountains (Matthew 24:16, bracketed clarification mine).

For the first time in the history of the world, through the use of the Internet, radio, and television, the gospel is being preached all over the entire planet. That did not even come close to being true in 70 A.D.

Regarding Alcasar's prediction about the abomination of desolation, he had to revise the End Times biblical prophecy in order to create his doctrine of Preterism. We can agree from our study of the sixteenth century and Alcasar that there were Roman Temples in Jerusalem around 70 A.D., but no archaeological evidence of one on the Temple Mount. Even more important, as we read in Chapter 4, Roman sacrifices did not take place in a Hebrew Temple where both Daniel and Jesus predicted they would (Matthew 24:15-16). The Roman sacrifices were done in a new Roman structure dedicated to Roman gods and *never* to YHWH, which made it impossible to be a fulfillment of Scripture.

As for St. Malachy's prophecy, when the current and possibly last pope was elected in 2013, some cardinals strongly suggested that whoever was going to be designated should not take the name of St. Peter, prophesied by St. Malachy, in order to avoid being the final pope and bringing about Armageddon. Whether or not you believe that prediction, when the office of the pope fell to Cardinal Jorge Mario Bergoglio on March 13, 2013—in an effort to avoid the use of the name Peter—Cardinal Bergoglio chose to invoke the name of St. Francis of Assisi (Assisi being the city where Francis lived at the time and not his last name). Like Leonardo da Vinci, the end of one's name usually indicated where they lived. (In Italian, *da* means "from," and *di* means "of.") In Leonardo's case, he lived or was *da* (from) Vinci, Italy.

Did Cardinal Bergoglio cheat the prophecy by invoking the name of St. Francis? St. Francis is a nickname, possibly because his mother was French (i.e., a Frank) or because his father was away on business in France when he was born. The truth is that Francis is not even close to his real name, which is "Giovanni *di* Pietro (of Peter) *di* Bernardone" (of Bernardone[271]). As for his first name, "Giovanni," it is both an Italian *and* Hebrew name, which means "gift from God." In those two languages, it is very similar—

---

[271]Family names can refer to a place of origin, current abode, a clan or family group or a son of a person in a small town, such as "Johnson" (i.e., John's son) or occupation (i.e., "Cooper" (barrel maker).

meaning "God has shown favor or" "a favor from God."[272] Because Cardinal Bergoglio currently resides at the Vatican (which is in Rome), his true and accurate name should be "Giovanni Petrus Romanus" ("God has shown favor on 'Peter of Rome' "), so it would seem St. Malachy's 900-year-old papal prophecy has been fulfilled!

St. Malachy wrote a brief description of each pope and described the last—or—112th pope, whom he saw as the one ushering in Armageddon, "...who will feed his flock amid many tribulations, after which the seven-hilled city [Rome and the Vatican] will be destroyed, and the dreadful Judge [God] will judge the people. The End." (Bracketed clarifications mine.)[273]

This incredible prophetic event by a saint of the Catholic Church also coincided *on the eve of the biblical, blood moon Tetrad,* or *four blood moon cycles.* It seems as if End-Time predictions regarding people and events are falling into place.

While all this is interesting, you might ask, "What does St. Malachy's 112th pope have to do with the Jews?" Just four months before the first blood moon of the 2014 biblical Tetrad, the current 112th pope began a betrayal of Israel by inviting a "Palestinian" imam and rabbi for a prayer meeting at the Vatican to pray for peace in the Middle East, which on the surface seems harmless enough. The official stance of the Catholic Church under Pope Francis is that Muslims, Jews, and Christians worship the same God.[274] Never, in the history of the Roman Catholic Church, has a

---

[272]"Meaning of Giovanni—Italian Baby Name." "*Meaning of Giovanni - Italian Baby Name,*" n.p. Web. 10 Apr. 2016. "Giovanni (Italian) Giovanna (Hebrew) Meaning: Italian form of John 'God is gracious,' variant of John 'God has shown favor.' "

[273]Arthur Devine. "Prophecy." The Catholic Encyclopedia. Vol. 12. New York: Robert Appleton Company, 1911.

[274]Contrary to the pope, Muslims and Christians cannot be worshiping the same God because Christians worship Jesus as God! One of the reoccurring themes of the Koran (Qur'an) is that Allah has not taken to himself a son (Sûrahs 9:30-31; 19:88-92; 112:3, etc.). Nevertheless, Jesus claimed to be the Son of God and, therefore, God, as we read in the Gospel of John where Jesus said, "..do you say of Him whom the Father sanctified and sent into the world, 'You are blaspheming,' because I [Jesus] said, '*I am the Son of God*'?" (John 10:36, bracketed clarification mine, emphasis added.)

Muslim prayed or quoted from the Koran in a worship service at the Vatican as the Pope allowed in June of 2014.[275] Imagine, here we have one of the holiest sites in Christendom, and the pope invited a cleric from a religion, who not only denies that Jesus is the Son of God, but reduces Him to the level of an Islamic prophet—and one who plays third fiddle behind Muhammad and the Mahdi! The prayer invoked a section from Sûrah 2:284-286 in Arabic, which calls for Allah to grant victory over the infidels. One should not be surprised to learn that the prayer offered at the Vatican by this Palestinian imam was an appeal to Allah asking for a Palestinian victory over the small nation of Israel.[276] Unfortunately, this has not become an isolated event.

THE EIGHTH BLOOD MOON TETRAD OF THE
CHRISTIAN ERA (2014-2015 A.D.)

Pope Francis Petrus Romanus
Made a Treaty Between the Vatican and Israel's Enemy

On the Passover of April 15, 2014, and the Feast of Tabernacles on October 8, 2014, we saw the first two of the four blood moon Tetrads and the establishment of the ISIS Caliphate, which became ISIL (the Islamic State of Iraq and the Levant. The Levant includes all the land of Israel). Only three months after the first Blood Moon's appearance on July 8, 2014, enemies of Israel launched 40 missiles at her civilian populations from Gaza, which caused Israel to retaliate against the unprovoked bombings of its citizens by the Arab-Islamic led Hamas.

The next blood moon occurred on Passover, April 4, 2015, but just a few days before that ominous heavenly sign, another historical date coincidently occurred on April 2. It is known on the Hebrew calendar as "Nisan 13"—the very date when the Persian king, Xerxes, also known as "Ahasuerus," was deceived by his Prime Minister, Haman (Esther 3:7-12); he was tricked into signing a royal decree to allow for the destruction of

---

[275]Cheryl K. Chumley, "Vatican Makes History: Pope Allows Islamic Prayers, Koran Readings." *Washington Times*. The Washington Times, 9 June 2014. Web. 05 Nov. 2015.
[276]Daniel Greenfield, a Shillman Journalism Fellow, "The Vatican Falls for the 'Interfaith' Scam,' " *Frontpage Mag*, n.p. 22 June 2015. Web. 05 Nov. 2015.

all Jews. The outcome was bad for Haman but good for the Jews. It is remembered as the "Hebrew Feast of Purim." History seemed to repeat itself on April 2, 2015—the biblical anniversary of Nisan 13—when the president of the United States, Barack Obama, reached an agreement with the leader of Iran—the Old Persian Empire—regarding its nuclear weapons program, which did not bode well for Israel.

Pastor Mark Biltz observes:

> King Obama has issued his decree putting the Jewish nation at risk of annihilation on the very same day that King Ahasuerus' scribes came together and issued their statement to the rulers of every people of every province...to destroy, to kill, and to cause to perish, all Jews, both young and old, little children and women, in one day.[277]

Then on May 13, 2015—one month after the blood moon of Passover—Pope Francis exceeded the accepted, international protocol and essentially announced the Vatican would come alongside the enemies of Israel when he solidified his already cozy relationship with Muhammad Abbas—formally recognizing the West Bank and Gaza as a sovereign nation with Abbas as its president.[278] This assured that the Vatican would establish diplomatic ties and embassies with the pseudo-nation of Palestine, a nation that has *never* existed before in history.

As if that was not insulting enough to the small Jewish nation, Pope Francis went one step further and approved the pseudo-Palestinian's demands that Jerusalem should be divided, which gave the Temple Mount and East Jerusalem to the recently contrived Arab nation of Palestine[279] (something with which the United Nations is also in agreement).[280] The PLO has always insisted that Jerusalem must become

---

[277]Ibid. Opening quote in column from author and Pastor Mark Biltz of El Shaddai Ministries in Bonney Lake, WA

[278]"Vatican Recognizes State of Palestine in New Treaty," *Fox News*. FOX News Network, 13 May 2015. Web. 19 November 2015.

[279]NicoleWinfield, A.P., "Vatican Recognizes Palestine," *USNews*. U.S. News & World Report, 13 May 2015. Web. 31 May 2015.

[280]"General Assembly Votes Overwhelmingly to Accord Palestine 'Non-Member Observer State Status in United Nations | Meetings Coverage and Press Releases." *UN News Center*. United Nations, 29 Nov. 2012. Web. 22 June 2016. "The draft resolution on the Status of Palestine at the United Nations (document A/67/L.28)

their capital to show Islamic supremacy over the Jewish nation and all the biblical shrines and holy sites that are there. If the PLO were to gain control of this area, with the pope's blessings, the reality is that they would most certainly desecrate and eradicate East Jerusalem's many historic Jewish and Christian artifacts, just as they have done on the Temple Mount.[281] As a result, an Islamic-revisionist history of the region was solidified.

The pope also presented Muhammad Abbas with the "Angel of Peace" medal. It was reported that Pope Francis Petrus Romanus told Muhammad Abbas, "May the angel of peace destroy the evil spirit of war. I thought of you: may you be an angel of peace."[282] That is the same Muhammad Abbas we referred to at the beginning of this chapter, as the one who financed the Olympic *Munich Massacre* in 1972, and the same Abbas who allows his organization to remain in a perpetual state of war with Israel.[283] Palestine is the sworn enemy of Israel, and this type of betrayal of the brothers of Christ could only come about through replacement theology, with its sixteenth-century Preterist reinforcement by the Church in Rome. What is the real irony in all this? The fourth blood moon in this Tetrad followed the pope's actions by 19 weeks and coincided with the Feast of Tabernacles on September 28, 2015. That ushered in what seemed to indicate —the biblical End Times prophecy of the whole world coming against a Jewish Jerusalem (Zechariah 12:3)— had begun.

---

was adopted by a recorded vote of 138 in favor to 9 against, with 41 abstentions...." That was the first step in creating an actual State of Palestine, with Jerusalem as its capital.

[281]Mark Ami-El, *The Destruction of the Temple Mount Antiquities, by Mark Ami-El*, JERUSALEM CENTER FOR PUBLIC AFFAIRS, 1 Aug. 2002.

[282]Julie Stahl and Chris Mitchell, "Pope Francis Tells Abbas: Be an 'Angel of Peace.' " "*Pope Francis Tells Abbas: Be an 'Angel of Peace,' *" CBN News, 18 May 2015. Web. 31 May 2015.

[283]Eli E. Hertz. (n.p.): n. p. *Arab-Israeli Peace Agreements*. Myths and Facts. Web. 28 Apr. 2016. "Each Israeli concession was met with Palestinian non-compliance and escalating violence. Six times, Palestinians failed to honor their commitments and increased their anti-Israeli aggressions. Finally, they broke every promise they made and began an all-out guerrilla war against Israel and its citizens."

Still, while the events of the End Times are being played out, God is eternally committed to His people and the land of Israel. The Church has been grafted into Israel; it has not replaced it. Our salvation and roots are founded in Israel (Romans 11:17), and God, who cannot lie (Numbers 23:19), still stands by the covenant of blessings and curses He promised Abraham (Genesis 12:3).

Because President Donald Trump moved the U.S. Embassy to Jerusalem on May 14, 2018, and acknowledged Jerusalem as the eternal capital of Israel—exactly 70 years to the day of Israel's resurgence as a nation—it seems for the moment at least, that America did receive the blessing promised in Genesis 12:3.

There is no place in the Bible for the demonic Church tradition of replacement theology. Once more, we hear the prophetic echo of the Apostle Paul when he clearly stated:

> I say then, "Has God cast away His people?" God forbid. For I also am an Israelite, of the seed of Abraham, of the tribe of Benjamin (Romans 11:1).

> For I would not [want], brethren, that you should be ignorant of this mystery, lest you should be wise in your own conceits; that blindness in part is [has] happened to Israel, until the fullness of the Gentiles be come in.

> And so all Israel shall be saved: as it is written, There shall come out of Zion the Deliverer, and shall turn away ungodliness from Jacob: For this is my covenant unto them, when I shall take away their sins (Romans 11:25-27, bracketed clarifications mine).

For nearly two thousand years, in the name of the ungodly tradition of replacement theology, millions and millions of defenseless innocent Jews have been killed, mutilated, burned, or buried alive in the most despicable manner throughout the Church Age. The Bible never encourages anti-Semitism, nor did Jesus, as we pointed out earlier, during the forty days He spent in Jerusalem *after* He was crucified and returned to life! It is an ignorant conclusion perpetrated on the Church that began through bigoted Gentiles; however, in all fairness, we would be neglectful if we did not address some of the passages of Scripture which were inaccurately used (taken out of context) to justify that bigotry against the Jews:

After many days had gone by, *there was a conspiracy among the Jews to kill Him* (Acts 9:23, NIV, emphasis added).

As we learned earlier, "A text without a context is a pretext for a proof text" and that applies here. In our first proof text, it plainly states, "...there was a conspiracy among the Jews to kill Him." Historically, Jerusalem was made up of Roman occupiers who were only concerned with keeping the peace, while basically everyone else in Judea were Jews, some of whom the Bible tells us were politically motivated to end Jesus' life; therefore, we would not expect it to be the Syrians, Egyptians, or any other group who came against Jesus. Not surprisingly, those who came out against Jesus would have to have been the Jews because they were in Judea.

We are witnesses of everything He did in the country of *the Jews and in Jerusalem. They killed Him by hanging Him on a cross*, but God raised Him from the dead on the third day and caused Him to be seen (Acts 10:39-40, NIV, emphasis added).

In Acts 10, we read, "We are witnesses of everything He did in the country of the Jews and Jerusalem. They killed Him by hanging Him on a cross" (Acts 10:39-40, NIV). We have no problem with this statement as far as it goes because once again, most of the people living in Jerusalem *were* Jews; however, when Jesus was crucified, it was the time of the Passover, and there were many Hebrews, besides the native Jews (Judeans) in Jerusalem from around the world. As for the sentence which reads, "They killed Him by hanging Him on a cross," it is simply a generalization. Most people assume that the word "they" spoken of in this scripture were Jews—*when in reality*—*it was the Romans who actually hung Jesus on the cross.*

For you, brothers and sisters became imitators of God's Churches in Judea, which are in Christ Jesus: You suffered from your own people the same things those Churches suffered from *the Jews who killed the Lord Jesus* and the prophets and also drove us out. They displease God and are hostile to everyone in their effort to keep us from speaking to

245

the Gentiles so that they may be saved. In this way, they always heap up their sins to the limit. The wrath of God has come upon them at last (1 Thessalonians 2:14-16, NIV, emphasis added).

The third verse clearly makes the statement, "...the Jews who killed the Lord Jesus...," but in the context, we see a fuller picture of what is being shared with the reader:

We are witnesses of everything He did in the country of the Jews and in Jerusalem. They killed Him by hanging Him on a cross, but God raised Him from the dead on the third day and caused Him to be seen. He was not seen by all the people, but by witnesses whom God had already chosen [among the Jews]—[and] by us who ate and drank with Him after He rose from the dead (Acts 10:39-41, NIV, bracketed clarifications mine).

As we mentioned at the end of Chapter 1, when Jews are referred to in connection with the death of our Lord, it is because some Jews brought about the death of Jesus. Likewise, it was also Americans who brought about the deaths of Presidents Abraham Lincoln and John F. Kennedy.

Consider: Would it be fair if an American couple was visiting another country—or perhaps *relocated* to another country—and were accused by the locals of being *"president-killers"* because of the actions of a few Americans? Of course not! Neither is it fair to call all Jews *"Christ-killers"* because we know from Scripture Jesus had thousands of Jewish followers. Even the Apostle Paul stated long after Jesus went to be with the Father, "For I tell you that Christ has become a servant of the Jews" (Romans 15:8, NIV). Paul does not say anything about Jesus having a ministry to the Gentiles; in fact, Jesus confirmed that He was sent to the House of Israel, as we read in Matthew 15:

Leaving that place, Jesus withdrew to the region of Tyre and Sidon. A Canaanite woman from that vicinity came to him, crying out, "Lord, Son of David, have mercy on me! My daughter is demon-possessed and suffering terribly." Jesus did not answer a word. So His disciples came to Him and urged Him, "Send her away, for she keeps crying out after us." He answered, "I was sent only to the lost sheep of Israel."

The woman came and knelt before Him, "Lord, help me!" she said. He replied, "It is not right to take the children's bread and toss it to the dogs." "Yes it is, Lord," she said. "Even the dogs eat the crumbs that fall from their master's table." Then Jesus said to her, "Woman, you have great faith! Your request is granted." And her daughter was healed at that moment (Matthew 15:20-28, NIV).

Although Jesus was sent to His brethren, which is the whole House of Israel (of which the Jews comprise one-twelfth), we can also see His compassion toward the Gentiles. As we learn in Romans, we Gentiles become Jews by adoption (Abraham is our father in the faith, Romans 4:16) and, therefore, it is we who are the ones grafted into that great tree which is Israel:

If some of the branches [Jews] have been broken off, and you, though a wild olive shoot [Gentile], have been grafted in among the others [Jews] and now share in the nourishing sap from the olive root [covenants and blessing shared—not stolen from—Israel], do not consider yourself to be superior [replacement theology] to those other branches [the Jews]. If you do, consider this: you do not support the root, but the root supports you (Romans 11:17-18, NIV, bracketed clarifications mine).

Finding any Gentiles who followed Jesus during His ministry on earth would be difficult. As we have shown, there were a few: The Samaritan[284] woman at the well, the Canaanite woman, and the Roman Centurion. Even the Apostle Paul, cautioned us time and again:

For I am not ashamed of the gospel, because it is the power of God that brings salvation to everyone who believes: *first* to the *Jew*, then to the Gentile (Romans 1:16, NIV, emphases added).

---

[284]Samaritans were actually from the tribes of Ephraim and Manasseh, which were also part of the tribes of Israel. They became outcasts because of their apostate religious views when they refused to accept Jerusalem as the holy Throne of God, preferring instead, Mount Gerizim, where they built a competing Temple to the one in Jerusalem.

There will be trouble and distress for every human being who does evil: *first* for the *Jew,* then for the Gentile (Romans 2:9, NIV, emphases added).

But glory, honor and peace for everyone who does good: *first* for the *Jew*, then for the Gentile (Romans 2:10, NIV, emphases added).

What advantage, then, is there in being a Jew, or what value is there in circumcision? Much in every way! *First* of all, the *Jews* have been *entrusted with the very words of God* (Romans 3:1-2, NIV, emphases added).

We need to pay attention to every word which proceeds from the Father and particularly when God considers it worth stating more than once!

Despite the biblical admonition of ministering to the Jew first, so that they may have the benefit of first refusal or acceptance of the gospel message, there was never to be any negative reprisal if the Jews did refuse (Matthew 10:1-14). God is the judge (Romans 12:19), and He has a plan for all of Israel to be saved in the Last Days (Romans 11:25).

CHAPTER 9

THE NEVER-ENDING CYCLE OF HATRED TOWARD THE JEWS

The world has benefited immensely because of God's chosen people. In the fields of medicine and science alone, Jews have and continue to save innumerable lives as well as providing us with many means to live more comfortable lifestyles. Despite all the advancements Jews have contributed to humanity, today they are despised even more.

Toward the end of Chapter 3, we explained how "in their wisdom, the Jewish people knew the only thing they could take with them across borders, besides the clothes on their backs, was knowledge; therefore, the Jews placed a high premium on education." It is interesting to see how that has played out in the modern era. Jews comprise one-fifth of one percent of the world's population, but they have garnered a high percentage of awards in various fields. In the area of Nobel Peace Prize Awards alone, one out of every five recipients is a Jew. Consider this *New York Times* article:

> Jews are a famously accomplished group. They make up 0.2 percent of the world population, but 54 percent of the world chess champions, 27 percent of the Nobel physics laureates and 31 percent of the medicine laureates. Jews make up 2 percent of the U.S. population, but 21 percent of the Ivy League student bodies, 26 percent of the Kennedy Center honorees, 37 percent of the Academy Award-winning directors, 38 percent of those on a recent Business Week list of leading philanthropists, 51 percent of the Pulitzer Prize winners for nonfiction.[285]

---

[285]David Brooks, "The Tel Aviv Cluster," *The New York Times,* 11 Jan. 2010: A23.

Albert Einstein is probably one of the most well-known Jewish geniuses of our times and is best known for his *Theory of Relativity,* or $E=mc^2$, considered to be "the world's most famous mathematical equation."[286] Einstein is also perhaps one of the most well-known Nobel Laureates.[287]

Even today, at the dawn of the twenty-first century, the darkness of hate against the Jews still saturates the whole world. In *The Times of Israel* article titled, "Hating the Jew You've Never Met,"[288] Haviv Rettig Gur documented the following examples as researched by Israel's *Anti-Defamation League* (ADL) when they interviewed more than 53,000 people speaking 93 languages in 102 countries. The study pulls together "...a global picture of the web of stereotypes and hatreds through which a significant amount of how humanity views the Jews."

Some of the results from that survey are included here:

- 1.1 billion adults have at least some anti-Semitic views.
- The ADL survey presented 11 multiple-choice questions ranging from positive to negative. 74% of adult Middle Easterners selected the choice, which suggested: "Jews have too much power in international financial markets."
- 74% believe that the "Jews are responsible for most of the world's wars."
- 52% of Austrians and Germans believe "Jews talk too much about the Holocaust" (although many believe the youth are shedding their parents' anti-Semitic attitudes).
- "Britain, a hub of global efforts to delegitimize the Jewish state, is nevertheless one of the least anti-Semitic countries in the world, while Greece, Israel's newfound regional ally, is one of the most."
- "In the Muslim world, the survey found that Internet use is also a significant factor in a Muslim becoming anti-Semitic. The prevalence of anti-Semitic views grew by some 20 percentage points among Muslims who get their news primarily online."

---

[286]David Bodanis, *E=mc²: A Biography of the World's Most Famous Equation.* New York: Walker, 2000.

[287]Einstein received the 1921 Nobel Prize in Physics.

[288]Haviv Rettig Gur, "Hating the Jew You've Never Met," *The Times of Israel,* WEB. 15 May, 2014. ADL's globe-spanning study of anti-Semitism.

- 27% of people who have never met any Jews harbor strong prejudices against them.
- 77% of those who are anti-Semitic have never met a Jew.
- The survey also found that, as a general rule, the fewer Jews in a particular country, the more numerous the anti-Semites.
- Anti-Semitism is skyrocketing in precisely those parts of the world where Jews fled from or perished in the last century, primarily the Middle East and Eastern Europe.
- 85% of Greeks surveyed believe "Jews have too much power in the business world" (owning and running businesses).
- 82% of the Greeks believe "Jews have too much power in international financial markets" (stock markets and international banking).
- 82% of the 16 Arab countries surveyed hold anti-Semitic views. Palestinians are the most anti-Semitic people in the world (94%), Algeria (87%), Iraq (92%), Morocco (80%), and Lebanon (78%).

It is difficult to believe that in the twenty-first century, there are still those who claim the Jews perform human sacrifices (using innocent blood) to make their matzo. Even today, we do not have to look any further than those advocates of Islam who still promote the old blood libel falsehood, as revealed in a *Jerusalem Post* article dated April 13, 2014.

The on-line publication of the *Palestinian Initiative for the Promotion of Global Dialogue and Democracy* (MIFTAH) apologized and removed an article from its website stating that the Jewish blood libel is true.

> The Jerusalem Post article states, according to the *Israel National News,* [Dr. Hanan Ashrawi asked the rhetorical question] "Does [President] Obama in fact know the relationship, for example, between 'Passover' and 'Christian blood?!' Much of the chatter and gossip about historical Jewish blood rituals in Europe are real and not fake as they claim; the Jews used the blood of Christians in the Jewish Passover" (bracketed clarification mine).[289]

---

[289]"Elder Of Ziyon - Israel News: Passover Blood Libel in Hanan Ashrawi's 'Miftah' Website (UPDATE)." *Elder Of Ziyon - Israel News: Passover* Blood Libel *in Hanan Ashrawi's Miftah Website (UPDATE)*, 28 Mar. 2013. Web. 20 Oct. 2014. This is an anti-Jewish Muslim site referring to *the Jerusalem Post* article above quoting Al-Zaru where he asked, "... Does Obama in fact know the relationship, for example,

Hanan Ashrawi, a lawmaker for the Palestinian Authority, founded MIFTAH. When confronted, he apologized and told the Jerusalem *Post* that a low-level staff member inadvertently allowed it to be published. The "Jerusalem Post" reported:

"Dr. Hanan Ashrawi, as founder, has nothing to do with the day to day management at MIFTAH and was no way involved in this incident," the apology... said. According to the watchdog group, NGO Monitor, MIFTAH has received funding from the governments of Italy, Ireland and Norway, and from the United Nations Educational, Scientific and Cultural Organization (UNESCO).[290]

Two years after the blood libel insult and In keeping with the End Times prophecy, which tells of the whole world coming against Jerusalem (Zechariah 12:3), UNESCO decided that the holiest site in Judaism would no longer be referred to as the "Temple Mount."[291] For the Jews, this site is steeped in some 3,000 years of worship and biblical history exclusive to the children of Israel, as recorded in the Holy Bible. However, historical facts do not seem to matter for the world organization as the United Nations has officially renamed the Temple Mount the "Al Aqsa," in honor of a Christian Church that was rebuilt as a mosque 73 years *after* the death of Muhammad, which is now standing on that location. By renaming the Temple Mount, the "Al-Aqsa," the United Nations has rewritten history to fit their anti-Semitic political agenda. That is indeed the height of arrogance and stupidity since the city of Jerusalem is never mentioned in the Koran—one time!

---

between 'Passover' and 'Christian blood'...?! Or 'Passover' and 'Jewish blood rituals...?!' "

[290]Haviv Rettig Gur, "Hating the Jew You've Never Met." Tovah Lazaroff, "UNESCO Adopts Resolution Ignoring Jewish Ties to Temple Mount," *The Jerusalem Post*, n.p. 15 April 2016. Web. 03 June 2016. UNESCO's Executive Board in Paris on Friday adopted a resolution whose language ignores Jewish ties to its holy religious site of the Temple Mount and the Western Wall area in Jerusalem's Old City.

[291]The Dome of the Rock started construction around five years after the death of Muhammad by Caliph Umar (Omar). It was completed over a half century (59 years) after the death of Muhammad in 691. Next to it, Umar built a small prayer room that was rebuilt into the al-Aqsa Mosque in 705 A.D., some 73 years after Muhammad's death and around a century after his "Night Journey."

The Church must repent of this injustice to the Jews and combat the zeitgeist (spirit of the age) and tradition of hatred toward them. Whether some Gentiles (replacement theology advocates) like it or not—if we have accepted Jesus as our Lord and Savior—then we all have become Jews by adoption, and that dear friend *is the gospel truth*!

As the learned clergy looks on with approval, Jews are being burned alive.

Jesus said, "Truly I say unto you, inasmuch as you have done it unto one of the least of these My brethren [the Jews], you have done it unto Me" (Matthew 25:40, bracketed clarification mine).

CONCLUSION

In conclusion, we have seen the self-fulfilling argument made that God hates the Jews because they have suffered so much at the hands of those who live in the countries where they have wandered. Through the centuries, their abuse was thought to have been justified by the belief God was through the Jews. Those who assumed the Jews fell out of favor with God, point to all the persecutions and suffering they have experienced down through the ages as their proof Jews have lost God's favor. "Surely," they argue, "If the Jews were God's Chosen People, He would not have permitted them to suffer to the extremes they have." While this type of argument has been used as proof to support the view that the Jews have fallen out of favor with God, we only have to turn to the Bible—which we have done—to see that it does not establish replacement theology as a biblical concept, nor are the supersessionists' (replacement theologians) claims able to stand up in light of Scripture.

Consider: In the Bible, we are told about a man whose life, in many ways, paralleled the history of Israel. That man loved God with all of his heart, and because of his relationship with God, the Lord blessed him beyond measure. God provided a beautiful wife, seven healthy sons, and seven beautiful daughters. God also provided him with cattle and great wealth, just as He provided Israel with a land flowing with milk and honey (Exodus 3:8). Everyone knew he walked with God, just as the children of Israel are God's Chosen People (Deuteronomy 7:6). Then one day, Satan approached God and challenged Him regarding the faithful servant of His, like the time he used David to stand up against Israel (1 Chronicles 21:1).

Satan claimed that the only reason the faithful servant loved God was that God, more or less, bought his love through all the blessings He gave him. Satan told God this man of great wealth would turn on Him if he were to lose his family and wealth.

To make a long story short, God allowed Satan to destroy all He had blessed this man with, but stipulated that Satan could not kill him. Satan agreed, and soon that man—who everyone knew was a man of God—lost everything. His children were killed, and his land and wealth were removed. All he had left was his wife and health, but soon, his health began to fail. The God he had served so faithfully appeared to have turned His back on him and allowed him to lose everything dear, just as the Jews lost everything in 135 A.D. Even his wife claimed that God had turned His back on her husband and challenged him to curse God and die; just like many of the second century did, as well as the later Church Fathers who were hostile toward the Jews.

Then this miserable soul received a visit from several of his friends. After a while, his friends—having observed the miserable state their friend was in—*confronted* rather than *comforted* the man—by telling him—like the whole of Christendom throughout the centuries told the Jews—he must have done something awful for God to have turned His back on him like that. They challenged their suffering, old friend to think hard, and confess his sins against God, but the poor man kept insisting that his conscience was clear because he had always loved God. He would never turn his back on Him, in spite of all the bad things which had befallen him. However, his friends did not believe he had not sinned against God because God would not harm a good man or help an evildoer, but the man held fast. Even as his health was failing, he did not turn on God. Despite the devastation in his life, he still believed deep inside his soul that God was just, but then he too began to question himself wondering if maybe his friends could have been right—but what did he do wrong? Finally, because Satan could not break the man's love for God, the Lord brought a stop to all of his sufferings and restored him with double the blessings from what he had before—just like He will do for Israel (Luke 21:24; Romans 11:25-27).

That man's name was Job; his entire story is in the Book of Job. Job's blessings, suffering, and ultimate restoration is very similar to what the Jews have been experiencing through the centuries at the hands of Christians who argue that God has turned His back on the Jews, while at the same time ignoring the biblical promises that in the Last Days—like with Job—everything would be restored to them (Luke 21:24; Zechariah 12:10; Romans 11:26).

On May 14, 1948, we saw the countdown to the final events of the Last Days begin ticking down when Israel once more—against all the odds—became a nation again.

If we understand the Scriptures correctly, then there is no way to justify what has been done to the Jews by the Church in the name of Jesus.

The truth is, God is always the same and never changes (Malachi 3:6). God is not a man that He should lie (Numbers 23:19); therefore, when God makes an everlasting covenant with the children of Israel, it is an everlasting covenant (Genesis 17:7, 13, 19), no matter what anybody says or how they try to spin it. The Word of God is clear—anyone who harms Israel, the apple of God's eye—is poking his or her finger in God's eye!

> For thus says the Lord of hosts; after the glory has He sent me unto the nations which spoiled [plundered] you: for he that touches you touches the apple of His eye (Zechariah 2:8, bracketed clarification mine).

It Might Be That Replacement Theology *Is* Found in the Bible—Except, in Reality, It Is the Other Way Around!

Strange as it may seem, the Bible tells us that one group of people can assume another people's identity, thus passing the blessings that God promised the original group to be imparted to the new group as well. The difference is that the group being talked about are the Gentiles—Gentiles are the ones who can have their Pagan nature, history, and gods replaced. As we have already seen in the Scriptures, if you, as a Gentile, accept Jesus as Lord and Savior, your old nature is changed, and you become a new creature in Christ (2 Corinthians 5:17). Christians are those who are grafted into the tree that is Israel (Romans 11:17) and thereby become a part of Israel. Remember, if you as a Christian—are grafted into the tree of Israel, "... You do not support the root, but the root supports you" (Romans 11:18b, NIV). It would be foolish for the Gentile to take an ax to the root of the tree of which he has become a part because—if the tree dies—so will he!

The absolute truth of Scripture is that Christians are Jews by adoption. Consider this fact as the Apostle Paul wrote:

Therefore, the promise comes by faith, so that it may be by grace and may be guaranteed to all Abraham's offspring—not only to those who are of the Law but also to those who have the faith of Abraham. He is the father of us all. As it is written: "I have made you a father of many nations." He is our father in the sight of God, in whom he believed— the God who gives life to the dead and calls into being things that were not (Romans 4:16-17, NIV).

Jesus told the Jews, "Your father Abraham rejoiced at the thought of seeing my day; he saw it and was glad" (John 56, NIV). Why would Abraham be glad to see the day of Jesus—especially if it meant replacing all of his descendants with Christian Gentiles? Abraham knew that someday one of his sons, Jesus, would be born, and through Him, all the people of the world could be saved. Jesus said, "Do not think that I have come to abolish the Law or the Prophets; I have not come to abolish them, but to fulfill them" (Matthew 5:17); therefore, Jesus did not come to establish a *new* religion by abolishing the Jews or their religion, but He came to be the fulfillment of Judaism. The crucifixion of Jesus came as no surprise to Jesus or the Father. That was the plan from the start. "I know the end from the beginning, from ancient times, what is still to come. I say, 'My purpose will stand, and I will do all that I please' " (Isaiah 46:10, NIV).

In the beginning, after Adam and Eve sinned and fell from grace, God warned the evil serpent, "And I will put enmity between thee and the woman, and between thy seed and her seed; He shall bruise thy head, and thou shalt bruise His heel" (Genesis 3:15). The snake bruising His heel implies that the snake is deadly poisonous and would cause the woman's seed (i.e., Messiah) to die. "...He bore our griefs...and was stricken, by God...and wounded for our transgressions" (Isaiah 53:4-5). He was the perfect blood sacrifice as "...the Lamb of God, who takes away the sins of the world" (John 1:29b, NIV) and thus, defeated the serpent. God predicted the death of the Messiah, and for that reason, His covenant with the Jews never ended.

It is still the same religion of Abraham, Isaac, and Jacob, only now we have the New Covenant in Jesus as foretold by the prophet Jeremiah:

הִנֵּה יָמִים בָּאִים נְאֻם־יהוה וְכָרַתִּי אֶת־בֵּית יִשְׂרָאֵל וְאֶת־בֵּית יְהוּדָה בְּרִית חֲדָשָׁה

Translation:

> Behold, the days come, says the LORD, that I will make a *new covenant* with the house of Israel, and with the house of Judah" (Jeremiah 31:31, emphasis added).

The truth is, to become a Christian, we must accept the Jewish Messiah as our own, and this is where *real biblical Replacement Theology* comes into play. Because we are now Messianic Jews by adoption—we have truly received and *shared in* the covenant God made with Israel. God enables this accomplishment by allowing us to take off the old Pagan, Gentile garment of our ancestral heritage and put on the new Hebrew mantel of Christ! Based on Scripture, one *could* make the argument that the Gentile is being superseded (i.e., replaced), *not the Jew*!

What Does the Future Hold for Christians and Jews?

We wish we could say that soon, everyone will embrace the Jewish people with love and biblical brotherhood, but sadly, God, with His foreknowledge, told us that would not happen. With the onset of new and more sophisticated technology and education, we would like to believe that humanity will become more tolerant (in the traditional sense of the word) and put away old prejudices and hates, especially where the Jews are concerned. Unfortunately, that will not happen either. With the beginning of 2016, anti-Semitism in Europe reached 50% of the population, and hostility toward Bible-believing Christians is also rapidly increasing. We have witnessed the removal of the Ten Commandments and crosses that once peppered the American countryside, and now various statues focused on Satan are being displayed in public. One statue is that of a Baphomet, which is a Pagan/Wiccan, goat-headed god being worshiped by two adoring children.

Christmas in some cities is now referred to as a "Winter Celebration" or "Festival of Lights." In a 2014 *Washington Post* article by Abby Ohlheiser, we read:

> Michigan considered a nativity scene for the state capital this holiday season. Instead, they got the snake from the Garden of Eden sitting in front of a pentagram, offering a book representing "knowledge" as a gift.

A local chapter of the Satanic Temple in Lansing, Michigan, a group best known for testing the limits of the intersection of free speech and religious expression, and not for actually worshipping Satan, announced this week that its proposal for a small holiday display [representing Satan] was approved by the state. It was the second such display from a local chapter of the group to gain approval that year. In

The Temple of Satan's 9 foot tall display to be placed beside holiday displays. (Photo by Jonathan Smith, c. 2014)

Florida, the Satanic temple erected a holiday display in the Capitol rotunda, alongside those of several other religious and secular groups bracketed clarification mine).[292]

If that were not enough, in some American classrooms, we now have Satanic Clubs on campuses and are even offered to young children at the elementary school level.[293]

In many schools, K-12 and colleges, there are Mosque-like prayer rooms[294] for Muslim students, but nothing is allowed for Christians or Jews.

---

[292]Abby Ohlheiser, "Michigan's State Capital Will Host a Satanic Temple Display, but No Nativity Scene (for Now)," *Washington Post*. The Washington Post, 16 December 2014. Web. 1 February 2016.

[293]Rick Anderson, "Yes, an After-school Satan Club Could Be Coming to Your Kid's Grade School," *Los Angeles Times*, 19 Oct. 2016. Web. 17 Mar. 2017.

[294]Here are three examples of many: (1) Jerry Shaw, "5 Public Schools That Have Installed Muslim Prayer Rooms," *Newsmax*, Newsmax Inc. Newsmax Inc., WEB 25 Mar. 2015; (2) Stella Chavez, *All Things Considered: Concerns After Texas School Opens 'Prayer Room' That's Attracting Muslim Students* (National Public Radio, March 26, 2017), and (3) David Krayden, "Upstate New York School Offers Prayer Rooms for Muslim Students," *The Daily Caller*. The Daily Caller, WEB 27 May 2017.

European, fundamental Christians are being marginalized as the population of Europe becomes more atheistic, and church buildings are being converted into stores, bars, or mosques. (Muslims, in particular, like to convert Christian Churches to show the supremacy of Islam over Christianity.) In the United Kingdom, history textbooks still teach World War II, but not the Holocaust. An article in Britain's "Daily Mail" publication states, "The poll of 2,230 British Jews found 56% felt that anti-Semitism now echoes the 1930s, while 58% believed Jews might no longer have any long-term future left in Europe."[295] While this disturbing trend is getting attention, what does the Bible say about Israel and the Jews in the Last Days? Does their lot improve, or has replacement theology become so embedded in the world's psyche that anti-Semitism has become irreversible?

The Prophet Jeremiah warned of "Jacob's Trouble"

"How awful that day will be! No other will be like it. It will be a time of trouble for Jacob, but he will be saved out of it" (Jeremiah 30:7, NIV).

Remember, Jacob is the name of the son of Isaac who God renamed Israel, and it was his children who established the 12 tribes which made up the nation of Israel; therefore, this passage seems to indicate the nation of Israel will be poorly dealt with by the world in the Last Days.

Trouble During the End Times for Jews and Their Christian Allies

During the time of the Prophet, Daniel, King Nebuchadnezzar had a disturbing dream:

> ...a large statue—an enormous, dazzling statue, awesome in appearance. The head of the statue was made of pure gold, its chest and arms of silver, its belly and thighs of bronze, its legs of iron, its feet partly of iron and partly of baked clay (Daniel 2:31-33, NIV).

---

[295]Associated Press, "Many 'hold anti-Semitic Views," *Mail Online*. Associated Newspapers, 14 Jan. 2015. Web. 29 January 2016. Nearly half of Britains hold anti-Semitic views, new research suggests. A poll of more than 3,400 UK adults found 45% believed that at least one anti-Semitic view presented to them was "definitely or probably true," including one in eight people (13%) who thought Jews talked about the Holocaust to get sympathy.

The feet of that awesome statue represents the government's final days on planet earth. For centuries, it was a mystery why there was iron (understood to be the Revised Roman Empire) mixed with clay (theologians were not sure what the clay was supposed to represent). Many Bible historians have now concluded that the clay represents Islamic countries. Christianity and Islam do not mix; that is, unless you combine them (iron and clay) into a synthesized religion called Chrislam; yet despite their efforts, iron and clay still do not mix very well, and the feet of the statue, composed of the iron and clay, leaves the government vulnerable and very unstable.

Recently, the Muslim country of Turkey was admitted into the North Atlantic Treaty Alliance (i.e., NATO). This unusual marriage opened up a Muslim corridor for displaced Muslims as a means to invade Europe under the guise of being refugees from the turmoil in the Middle East. One might reasonably ask why they are migrating to a nominal, Christian realm with harsh winters and different climate conditions—which are so unlike the desert environments to which most of them are accustomed. Why not relocate within the familiar habitats of the Middle East and Africa with like-minded Islamic believers—especially when the Muslim countries have almost double the landmass of Europe? This infusion of Muslims into what was formerly known as "Christendom" has had a striking influence, especially against Jews in the region. Believers of Islam are taught from the Koran:

> O ye who believe! Take not the Jews and the Christians for friends. They are friends one to another. He among you who takes them for friends is (one) of them. Lo! Allah guides not wrongdoing folk (Sûrah 5:51).

The Koran makes it very clear: Any Muslim who makes friends of Jews and Christians is doing wrong; yet, this illogical immigration is not limited to just Europe. In America, hundreds and sometimes thousands of Muslims are given sanctuary each month while denying the same sanctuary for Middle Eastern Christians! In a report by the Assyrian International News Agency, we read:

...the U.S. State Department has made it clear that "there is no way that Christians will be supported because of their religious affiliation."[296]

How bad is it for Christians in Northern Iraq at the time of this writing? In the words of Archbishop Bashar Warda of Erbil in Northern Iraq:

Christianity in Iraq is going through one of the worst and hardest stages of its long history, which dates back to the first century. Throughout all these long centuries, we have experienced many hardships and persecutions, offering caravans of martyrs. Yet 2014 brought the worst acts of genocide against us in our history. We now face the extinction of Christianity as a religion and as a culture from Mesopotamia [ancient Iraq][297] (bracketed clarification mine).

This article goes on to say that the Rt. Rev. Julian M. Dobbs, Bishop of the Diocese of CANA East (Convocation of Anglicans in North America) "...revealed that the State Department advised him against setting up emergency housing for Christians in the region, saying it was 'totally inappropriate.' "[298]

Also important, it seems, is the resettling of the most vulnerable— Assyrian Christians in the United States. Donors in the private sector offered complete funding for the airfare and the resettlement in the United States of the Iraqi Christians who were sleeping in public buildings, on school floors, or worse. But President Obama's State Department—while they admitted 4,425 Somalis to the United States in just the first six months of 2015, and undoubtedly allowed members of ISIS through the Syrian and Iraqi refugee program—all paid for by tax dollars—told Lou Dobbs of Fox News that the State Department "would not support a special category to bring Assyrian Christians into the United States."[299]

---

[296]Faith J.H. McDonnell, "US State Department Says No to Iraqi Christians," Assyrian International News Agency, 17 May 2015. Web. 29 January 2016.
[297]McDonnell, "US State Department Says No to Iraqi Christians."
[298]Ibid.
[299]Ibid.

As if this was not bad enough, Kirsten Powers reported in "USA Today" how then-President Obama and the Prime Minister Renzi of Italy shrugged off an incident regarding the murder of Christians whose only crime was praying to Jesus. Miss Powers began her April 23, 2015 article with this provocative question:

> What do you call it when 12 men are drowned at sea for praying to Jesus?

> Answer: religious persecution.

> Yet, when a throng of Muslims threw a dozen Christians overboard a migrant ship traveling from Libya to Italy, Prime Minister Matteo Renzi missed the opportunity to label it as such. Standing next to President Obama at their joint news conference Friday [April 17, 2015], Renzi dismissed it as [a] one-off event and said, "The problem is not a problem of [a] clash of religions"[300] (bracketed clarification mine).

Prime Minister Renzi must have taken a page from his friend, Obama, who cannot even utter the words "Muslim terrorists," and like his predecessor, former President George W. Bush proclaimed, "Islam is a religion of peace." That is something you would be hard-pressed to find in the Koran and the Hadith.

As for what we can soon expect for the small nation of Israel, despite President Trump having relocated the U.S. Embassy to Jerusalem, will not be pretty. Elected officials in Washington D.C., as well as international powers, will continue to try and divide or destroy the land of Israel through boycotts, missile attacks, and demands of land for peace. Sadly, peace will not come as politicians, along with Islamic religious strife, will continue to tear away at land of Israel. Yet God, who is not mocked (Galatians 6:7), will one day soon call all the nations of the world to accountability in the Valley of Jehoshaphat for the crime of dividing God's land of Israel (Bible: Joel 3:2; Tanak (תנ״ך), Joel 4:2).

---

[300]Kirsten Powers: "Christians Thrown Overboard Left to Drown by Obama," *USA Today*, Gannett, 21 Apr. 2015. Web. 26 Jan. 2016. Obama only mentions Christians to lecture them, rather than defend them from persecution.

These events have not taken God by surprise because 2,500 years ago He predicted they would happen. We can read in Zechariah 12:3 how God predicted the whole world would one day come against Jerusalem. Nevertheless, as we previously discussed, some Preterists say this already happened in 70 A.D., which, of course, cannot be truthful because the whole world did not come against Jerusalem back then; only Rome did. There were still more countries outside the Roman Empire, such as Russia to the North, China to the northwest, and India to the southwest, as well as Japan and the Americas to the far west, just to mention a few countries of the world who were not included in the 70 A.D. assault on Jerusalem. That assault will happen in the future, perhaps in such a time as this—if the anti-Semitism and overwhelming amount of sanctions against Israel within the United Nations is any indication!

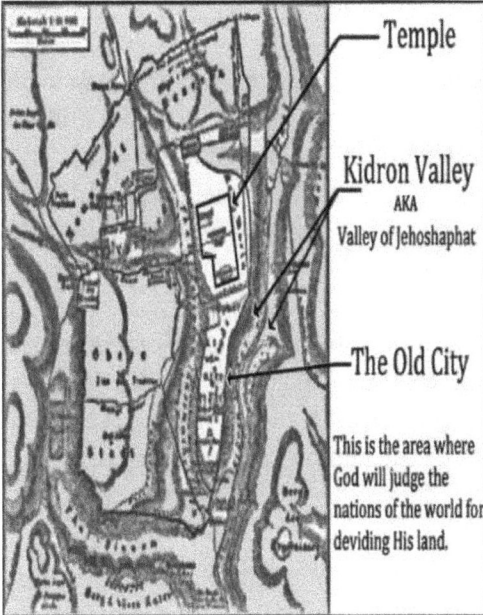

Map labels: Temple; Kidron Valley AKA Valley of Jehoshaphat; The Old City; This is the area where God will judge the nations of the world for deviding His land.

Zechariah warned us that during the time of the end:

> I will gather all the nations to Jerusalem to fight against it; the city will be captured, the houses ransacked, and the women raped. Half of the city will go into exile, but the rest of the people will not be taken from the city (Zechariah 14:2).

The New Testament refers to this period as the "End Times," which will culminate with the *Battle of Armageddon*.[301] Muslims also have an End Times prediction against the Jews, which seems to coincide with the

---

[301]Megiddo is a town which guards the Western pass through the Carmel Ridge of what is now the Jezreel Valley. It is located on the mountain of Har (Ar) Megiddo (Mountain of Megiddo). Har-Megiddo evolved into its Greek name of Armageddon. We first saw that biblical town when Joshua defeated the king of Megiddo in Joshua 12:7, 21b

Battle of Armageddon, which explains why there can never be peace between Muslims and the tiny nation of Israel:

> Judgment Day will come only when the Muslims fight the Jews and kill them until the Jew hides behind the tree and the stone, and the tree and the stone say: "Oh Muslim, oh servant of Allah , there is a Jew behind me, come and kill him"—except for the Gharqad tree [a boxthorn tree cultivated by Jews] (Hadith, Sahih Muslim, Book 41, No. 6985, bracketed clarification mine).

These battles will finally climax when all the nations are forced to face God, as we previously discussed. It will take place in the Valley of Jehoshaphat, now referred to as the Kidron Valley, which closely runs North and South near the East side of the Old City of Jerusalem.

As *Bible-believing* Christians, we too now face a world of hostility, not unlike what has befallen our Jewish brothers and sisters. It benefits us to remember God's eternal covenant with Abraham, which was passed down through Isaac and his descendants (Genesis 17:19;21) when He promised, "I will bless those who bless thee and curse those who curse thee" (Genesis 12:3). We are to come alongside our biblical brothers and sisters by supporting them and the very small Nation of Israel the best we can. Does this mean we have to agree with everything the nation and the people of Israel do? Of course not. I do not always agree with my wife or daughter, and they do not always agree with me, but we love each other and stand by one another, so it is with Christians who read and believe the Bible (including both the Old and New Testaments). We must stand with Israel and bless them. Remember, it is we who are the ones grafted into the ancient tree, Israel:

> If some of the branches [which are the Jews] have been broken off, and you, though [you are] a wild olive shoot, [and] have been grafted in among the others and [thus allowing you to] now share in the nourishing sap from the olive root [of Israel], do not consider yourself to be superior to those other [Jewish] branches. If you do, consider this: You do not support the root, but the root supports you (Romans 11:17-18, NIV, bracketed clarifications mine).

As we just affirmed, it is good for us to remember that it is we who are nourished by the roots of Israel (vs. 17b). The Bible also indicates, with the closing of time, things are not going to get any better for the Jews or for those of us who are committed Bible-believing Christians. We cannot change the demonic hatred toward Israel, but what we can do is be a blessing to them. We should be thankful for all the Hebrew prophets through whom God gave us the Holy Scriptures, as well as providing us with our Savior. It would also be very prudent for us to realize that if the tree dies, so will we!

SUMMARY

God is not through with Israel, nor will He ever be. In fact, the very gates of Heaven bear the names of each of the tribes of Israel on them, which will be established on earth at the End of the Age when heavenly Jerusalem will descend to earth in all its glory.

The Apostle John describes it like this:

> And he [the angel] carried me away in the spirit to a great and high mountain, and showed me that great city, the holy Jerusalem, descending out of Heaven from God,
>
> Having the glory of God: and her light was like unto a stone most precious, even like a jasper stone, clear as crystal;
>
> And had a wall great and high, and had twelve gates, and at the gates twelve angels, and names written thereon, which are the names of the twelve tribes of the children of Israel (Revelation 21:10-12, bracketed clarification mine).

Consider: Because God is consistent—if He had replaced Israel with the Church—wouldn't He have removed the 12 names of the 12 tribes of Israel from the gates of Heavenly Jerusalem?

Ultimately, answering the following two questions can clear up all those shameful years of bloody and unjust treatment of the Jews:

- **Who really did kill Jesus? We *all* killed Jesus.**

- **Why did Jesus die?   FOR YOU!**

APPENDIX

SOME CHRISTIANS NOT ONLY FROWN ON ACKNOWLEDGING JEWISH HOLIDAYS, BUT THEY ALSO DRAW THE LINE AT CELEBRATING CHRISTMAS AND EASTER.

Some Christians also want to extend Replacement Theology to the celebrations of both Christmas and Easter and replace them with no celebrations. They insist that those holidays have Pagan origins, and should not be celebrated by true Christians. While we will not deny that there are some areas of Pagan influence surrounding these holidays, a Christian does not have to avoid them any more than a Christian has to avoid enjoying the biblical feasts found in the Bible.

In Chapter 2, we addressed the revision of the Hebrew/Christian celebration of First Fruits becoming Easter. We also discussed a fourth-century manuscript (which is no longer in existence) known as the "Chronography of 354 A.D.," also referred to as the "Calendar of 354." This beautiful, expansive calendar contained full-page illustrations and other beautiful artwork that was commissioned for a well-to-do Roman Christian known as "Valentinus." What also made this beautiful calendar so special was that it contained the earliest, documented reference to the Christ (Messiah) Mass (celebration) or Christmas celebration.

During that same time, Christmas was acknowledged as a liturgical feast of the Roman Catholic Church,[302] which coincidently, fell very close to the

---

[302]Western countries now use the Gregorian calendar (1582 AD) initiated by Pope Gregory XIII. It was designed to change the date of Easter so it would not coincide with the Passover. While we do not take issue with the celebration of *Easter*

celebration of *Saturnalia* on the Roman calendar, an event which honored the Roman "god," Saturn, and was similar to the Mardi Gras celebrations we see today. Predictably, that resulted in some Christians having concerns regarding the Pagan trappings attached to those holidays.

Therefore, as we mentioned above, those Christians who want to avoid celebrating Christmas and Easter make legitimate points that the many of the cherished symbols of the Christmas season are rooted in Paganism, which honors Pagan gods. Some examples are:

- Despite the resemblance to St. Nicholas (270 A.D.—342 A.D.), the Bishop of Myra,[303] some argue that Santa Claus is actually the Norse god, Odin (other Pagan gods and goddesses are cited as well).

- The Christmas tree, as we know it, began in seventeenth-century Germany, but its origins go back even further than the Christmas celebration.

- The evergreen fir tree has long been used in Pagan winter festivals around the winter solstice. The branches from the fir trees were also used to decorate homes of Pagans as a reminder that spring was not far away.

- Mistletoe has its origins in the ancient Druids who believed that it had magical powers; by hanging it in their homes, it would bring good fortune and keep evil spirits away.

These are but a few of the Pagan roots, which can be found in the symbols surrounding the Christian holiday. Because of their Pagan symbols, some

---

in our house, we refer to it as *Resurrection Sunday*. As for Christmas, it is our favorite holy day of the year, and we start preparing our hearts around the beginning of summer. The day after Halloween, a holiday my family and I *do not* celebrate—we decorate our house for the Christmas season. We begin the 12 days of Christmas counting from December 25 through January 5. On the following day, January 6, we put away our decorations. NOTE: Some of the Eastern Orthodox Churches celebrate Christmas around January 7th.

[303]"Who Is St. Nicholas?" *St. Nicholas Center*, Web. 1 Jan 2016.

Christians refuse to celebrate Easter and Christmas, claiming that it violates two of the Ten Commandments, which state:

> Thou shall have no other gods before Me. Thou shall not make unto you any graven image, or any likeness of anything that is in Heaven above, or that is in the earth beneath, or that is in the water under the earth (Exodus 20:3-4).

Understandably, sincere Christians do not want to take the chance of honoring Pagan gods; therefore, we should not ostracize our brothers and sisters who choose differently. I think most of us would agree that today's commercial aspects of the holidays are simply designed to make money, not glorify God. I simply ignore that aspect of the holidays and see the Christmas trees, decorations, and music, which brightens the stores for what they really are—the heralding of the coming of the Lord. Sadly, however, in our politically correct society, it is becoming rarer to hear a friendly store employee greeting their customers with "Merry Christmas!"

In our home, we never think of Pagan gods when we look at our lovely tree and decorations. They add beautiful aesthetics to this wonderful season we have set aside to celebrate the birth of Christ. For us, the evergreen tree is a symbol of Christ's everlasting love, and the eternal life promised to us with the advent of the baby Jesus. I think how beautiful Heaven must be when I look at our home all decked out for Christmas. As for our brothers and sisters who want no part of acknowledging *any* Pagan god, it should be pointed out that they do so daily, even though it is unintentional.

During the second century, when the Church shifted from being mostly Jewish to becoming mostly Gentile, it rejected how the Jews referred to the days of the week—preferring instead to use the names Gentiles used for the days of the week—names which honored Pagan gods. Therefore, whenever one of our well-intentioned, legalistic brothers and sisters are asked what day it is, and they tell you its name, they are acknowledging and honoring the name of that day's god!

The Church Aligned Itself with the Pagan Week

The Jews referred to their days in reference to where they were in regards to the Sabbath Day. The day after, the Sabbath was called *Yom Reeshone* (i.e., "First Day"). The Pagans, on the other hand, named each day with a name honoring one of their gods or goddesses, as noted in Table 3.

Table 3. Names of the Pagan and Hebrew Days of the Week and Their Meanings

SECULAR NAME OF DAYS	PAGAN GOD IT HONORS	HEBREW NAME OF DAYS	HEBREW MEANING
Sunday	The Sun god	Yom Reeshone	First Day
Monday	Moon goddess	Yom Shaynee	Second Day
Tuesday	The god, Tyr	Yom Shlee'shee	Third Day
Wednesday	The god, Odin	Yom Revee'ee	Fourth Day
Thursday	The god, Thor	Yom Khah'mee'shee	Fifth Day
Friday	The goddess, Freya, Odin's wife	Yom Ha'shee'shee	Sixth Day
Saturday	The god, Saturn	Shabbat	Rest Day

Adoption of the Pagan week is arguably another area where it might have been better if the Church had stayed with its Jewish roots!

SOURCES CITED

Abel, Ernest L. *The Roots of Anti-Semitism* Cranberry: Associated University Press, Inc., 1975.

Ami-El, Mark. *The Destruction of the Temple Mount Antiquities,* by Mark Ami-El. Jerusalem Center for Public Affairs, 1 Aug. 2002.

Analytical Greek Lexicon. The 7th ed., s.v. Grand Rapids: Zondervan, 1972.

Anderson, Rick. "Yes, an After-school Satan Club Could Be Coming to Your Kid's Grade School." *Los Angeles Times.* 19 Oct. 2016. Web. 17 Mar. 2017.

Avraham, Rachel. South African MP*:* "Israel Is Not an Apartheid State." *United with Israel.* Web. 18 May 2014.

Aelia Capitolina. *Wikipedia, the Free Encyclopedia.* May 13, 2013. Web. 15 May 2014.

Aharoni, Yohanan, and Shmuel Aḥituv. *The Jewish People: An Illustrated History.* New York: Continuum, 2006.

Algemeiner Journal. Aug. 19, 1994.

Associated Press. "Many 'hold Anti-Semitic Views.' " *Mail Online.* Associated Newspapers. 14 Jan. 2015. Web. 29 Jan. 2016.

Baer, Yitzhak. *History of the Jews in Spain* trans. Louis Schoffman. Philadelphia: Jewish Publication Society of America, 1961.

Bainvel J., tr. by Tomas Hancil. "Tradition and Living Magisterium." *The Catholic Encyclopedia,* vol. XV, 1912 by Robert Appleton Company. Online Edition, 2003 by K. Knight. TheNihil Obstat, October 1, 1912. Remy Lafort, S.T.D., Censor Imprimatur + John Cardinal Farley, Archbishop of New York.

Bard, Mitchell. "United Nations: The U.N. Relationship with Israel." *The U.N.-Israel Relationship*. American-Israeli Cooperative Enterprise. Updated July 2015. Web. 10 Feb. 2016.

Barker, Kenneth, Gen. Ed. T*he New International Version Study Bible*. Grand Rapids: Zondervan, 1983.

Bernis, Jonathan. "A Rabbi Looks at the Lost Tribes of Israel." *A Rabbi Looks at the Lost Tribes of Israel*. *Jewish Voice*, n.p. Web. 27 Apr. 2016.

Bishop, Chris. *SS Hitler's Foreign Divisions; Foreign Volunteers in the Waffen-SS, 19400-45*. London: Amber Books Ltd., 2015.

"Blood Libel." (2014 May 9). *Wikipedia, the Free Encyclopedia*. Web. 15 May 2014.

Blum, Julia. "Two Goats of Yom Kippur." *Biblical Hebrew and Holy Land Studies Blog - IIBS.com*. 13 Oct. 2016.

Bodanis, David. *E=mc²: A Biography of the World's Most Famous Equation*. New York: Walker, 2000.

Boteach, Rabbi Shmuley. "The World's Oldest Hatred." *Levitt Letter* (Sept. 2010).

Boycott, Divestment, and Sanctions (2016 Feb. 5). In *Wikipedia, The Free Encyclopedia*. Web. Feb. 11, 2016.

Brecht, Martin. *Martin Luther*. tr. James L. Schaaf. Philadelphia: Fortress Press, 1985–93.

Brooks, David. "The Tel Aviv Cluster." *The New York Times*. 11 Jan. 2010.

Campbell, Mike. "Meaning, Origin and History of the Name Luke." *Behind the Name*. Web. Oct. 26, 2011.

"Can Tiny Israel Afford to Surrender More Land." *Confidential Reporter*. Web. 1 Jan. 1970.

Cassius. *Roman History*. Harvard Univ. Press, 2001.

Chavez, Stella. *All Things Considered: Concerns After Texas School Opens 'Prayer Room' That's Attracting Muslim Students.* National Public Radio. March 26, 2017.

"Children's Memorial." *Yadvashem.org,* www.yadvashem.org/remembrance/commemorative-sites/children-memorial.html.

Chumley, Cheryl K. "Vatican Makes History: Pope Allows Islamic Prayers, Koran Readings." *Washington Times.* The Washington Times. 9 June 2014. Web. 05 Nov. 2015.

Cleave, R.L.W. *The Holy Land Satellite Atlas, vol. 1.* Nicosia: ROHR Productions, 1999.

Cloud, David. *The Bible Version Question and Answer.* London: Way of Life Literature, 2006.

Cockerton, Paul "Lightning Bolt Hit Vatican Not Once but TWICE Hours after Pope's Shock Resignation." *Mirror (UK),* n.p. 12 Feb. 2013. Web. Dec. 2013.

Crawford, Jamie, CNN National Security Producer. "Palestinians Seeking Statehood: What's at Stake—CNN .... President Ahmadinejad of Iran... 'Push Israel into the Sea.' " [journal on-line]; *NN.* CNN. 16 Sept. 2011. Web. 8 Dec. 2011.

Davidson, Robert, and Alfred Robert Clare Leaney. *Biblical Criticism.* Harmondsworth: Penguin, 1970.

Devine, Arthur. "Prophecy." The Catholic Encyclopedia. Vol. 12. New York: Robert Appleton Company, 1911.

Dinnerstein, Ph.D., Leonard. "Leo Frank Case." *New Georgia Encyclopedia,* 14 May 2003. Web. 17 August 2014. Last edited by NGE Staff on June 5, 2014.

"Dogmatic Constitution on Divine Revelation." *Dei Verbum #9, Vatican Council II.* As quoted in Birch D.A. *Trial, Tribulation & Triumph.* Queenship Publishing Co, 1995.

Dorell, Oren. "Israel: Peace Deal Requires Recognition of Jewish State" *USA Today*. 2 Dec. 1015. Web. 3 Feb. 2014.

Durant, Will J. *The Story of Civilization: Part III Caesar and Christ* New York: Simon & Schuster, 1944.

_____ *The Age of Faith*. New York: Simon & Schuster, 1950.

Dubnow, Simon. *History of the Jews in Russia and Poland: From Earliest Times Until the Present Day*. 2 vols. Tr. in Russian by I. Friedlander. Philadelphia: The Jewish Publication Society of America, 1923.

Editorial Team, *Israel My Glory*. "Who Are the Refugees?" *Israel My Glory* (2003): 41. Print. This article first appeared in the Jan./Feb. 2003 issue of *Israel My Glory* magazine, published by the Friends of Israel Gospel Ministry. Copyright 2016 by the Friends of Israel. All rights reserved. Used by permission.

Edmunds, Donna Rachel. "UN's Human Rights Council Condemns Israel More than Rest of World Combined - Breitbart." *Breitbart News*, n.p. 25 June 2015. Web. 27 Apr. 2016.

Ehrman, Bart D and Daniel B. Wallace. *The Reliability of the New Testament*. Edited by Robert B. Stewart, (Minneapolis: Augsburg Fortress Press, 2011), 118.

Elder Of Ziyon - Israel News: Passover Blood Libel in Hanan *News: Passover* Blood Libel *in Hanan Ashrawi's "Miftah" Website* (update). 28 Mar. 2013. Web. 20 Oct. 2014.

Elon, Amos. Founder*: Meyer Amschel Rothschild and His Time* (New York: HarperCollins, 1996).

Encyclopedia Britannica, 14th ed. s.v. "Emperor Trajan."

Epstein, Nadine. "King David's Genes." *Moment Magazine*. Mar.-Apr.2012. Web. 10 Feb. 2016.

Ehrman, Bart D., and Daniel B. Wallace. *The Reliability of the New Testament*. Edited by Robert B. Stewart. Minneapolis: Augsburg Fortress Press, 2011.

Falcon, Ted, and David Blatner. *Judaism for Dummies.* Indianapolis: Wiley Publishing, Inc., 2001.

Father Stephen. "St. John Chrysostom's Christmas Homily." *Glory to God for All Things*, 23 Dec. 2008. Web. 22 Nov. 2015.

Flannery, Edward. *The Anguish of the Jews: Twenty-Three Centuries of Mahwah*: Paulist Press, 2004.

Fiske, Gavriel. "Israel Said Willing to Give up 90% of West Bank." *The Times of Israel*. 6 Feb. 2014. Web. 2 Dec. 2015.

Freund, Michael. "Passover Blood Libels, Then and Now." *Jerusalem Post*. Jan. 2014. Web. 13 Aug. 2014.

Garcia, Charles. "Was Columbus Secretly a Jew? - CNN.com." CNN. Cable News Network. 24 May 2012. Web. 1 May 2015.

Gayford, Martin. "Roman Catholicism--Founder: Emperor Constantin" [article online]. Nov. 8, 2011.

Geary, Patrick J., ed. *Readings in Medieval History.* Toronto: Broadview Press, 2003.

"General Assembly Votes Overwhelmingly to Accord Palestine 'Non-Member Observer State' Status in United Nations | Meetings Coverage and Press Releases." *UN News Center*. United Nations. 29 Nov. 2101. Web. 22 June 2016.

Gibson, Shimon, Ph.D. *The Cave of John the Baptist.* New York: Random House, 2005.

Gilbert, Lela. "Jews, Christians and UNESCO's Jerusalem Resolution." *Fox News*. Fox News Network. 21 Oct. 2016. Web. 04 Nov. 2016.

Glass, Andrew. "Egypt, Israel Finish Peace Treaty, March 26, 1979." *Politico*, n.p. 26 Mar. 2014. Web. 2 Dec. 2015.

Gonen, Rivka. *Contested Holiness: Jewish, Muslim and Christian Perspectives on the Temple Mount in Jerusalem*. Jersey City: KTAV Publ., 2003.

Gorelik, Vadim (Вадим Горелик) "Как товарищи Махмуд Аббас и Евгений Примаков Холокост отрицали" (Eng. "Comarades Mahmoud Abbas' and Yevgeniy Primakov's denial").

Gottschalk, H. L. *The Encyclopedia of Islam*. New Edition: H-Iram, ed., vol. III. New York: Brill, 1986.

Graetz, Heinrich Hirsh. *History of the Jews*. 5 vols. Philadelphia: The Jewish Publication Society of America, 1898.

Greenfield, Daniel, a Shillman Journalism Fellow. "The Vatican Falls for the 'Interfaith' Scam." *Frontpage Mag*. n.p. 22 June 2015. Web. 05 Nov. 2015.

Grosser, Paul E. & Edwin G. Halperin. *Anti-Semitism: Causes and Effects*. New York: Philosophical Library, 1978. (See "Jewish Persecution"| Timeline of Judaism | "History of AntiSemitism.")

Grossman, David. *Anti-Semitic Stereotypes without Jews: Images of the Jews in England, 1290-1700*. Detroit: Wayne State University Press, 1975.

Grosser, P.E. and E.G. Halperin. *Anti-Semitism: Causes and Effects*. New York: Philosophical Library, 1978.

Gur, Haviv Rettig. "Hating the Jew You've Never Met." *The Times of Israel*, n.p. 15 May 2014. Aug. 19, 2014. ADL's GLOBE. Globe-spanning study of anti-Semitism.

Grun, Bernard. *The Timetables of History* 3rd revised edition. New York: Simon & Schuster/Touchstone Book, 1991.

"Hebrew Roots/Neglected Commandments/Idolatry/Easter." *Wikibooks, The Free Textbook Project*. 29 Mar. 2016, Web. 23 Apr. 2016.

Hafiz, Yasmine. "Pope Benedict's 'Mystical Experience' Prompted Resignation, Said 'God Told Me To.' " *Huffington Post.* HuffingtonPost.com. 21 Aug. 2013. Web. 11 Dec. 2014.

Hertz, Eli E. (n.p.): n. g. *Arab-Israeli Peace Agreements.* Myths and Facts. Web. 28 Apr. 2016.

"History - Historic Figures: Titus (39 AD - 81 AD)." *BBC*, The British Broadcasting Corporation, 2014,

"History of Ancient Israel and Judah" [Wikipedia on-line]; n.p. Web. 16 Nov. 2011.

"History of Israel: League of Nations: Creating a Mandate State. "*Stand for Israel.* Web. 14 May 2014.

Hitler, Adolf. *Mein Kampf,* vol. I, Ch. X.

Holweck, Frederick. "The Feast of the Assumption." The Catholic Encyclopedia, vol. 2. New York: Robert Appleton Company, 1907.

"House of Wisdom." In *Wikipedia, The Free Encyclopedia,* n.p. Web. 24 Apr. 2016.

Isaac, Jules, *The Teaching of Contempt Christian Roots of Anti-Semitism.* New York: McGraw Hill Book Co., 1961.

Ishaq, Ibn, Sirat Rasul Allah. *The Life of Muhammad,* tr. A. Guillaume. New York: Oxford University Press, 1980.

"Ispahan." *JewishEncyclopedia.com: The unedited full-text of the 1906 Jewish Encyclopedia, n.p.* Sept. 2, 2014.

Isseroff, Ami. "Rindfleisch Pogroms." Zionism and Israel— Encyclopedic Dictionary, 29 Mar. 2009. Web. 27 Nov. 2015.

"Jewish Persecution" | Timeline of Judaism | "History of AntiSemitism." *Judaism.* Web. Sept. 2015. "Simple to Remember: History of Jewish Persecution/Jewish Persecution."

"Josephus." *The New and Complete Works of Josephus.* Trans. William Whiston. Grand Rapids: Kregel, 1999.

(LDS) *Journal of Discourses*, vol 4. "Luke" [*Wikipedia* on-line]; Web. 26 Oct. 2011.

"Rooms for Muslim Students." *The Daily Caller*. The Daily Caller. WEB 27 May 2017.

Lane, William L. *The Gospel According to Mark: The English Text with Introduction, Exposition, and Notes*. 2nd ed., Grand Rapids: Eerdmans, 1974.

Lazaroff, Tovah. "UNESCO Adopts Resolution Ignoring Jewish Ties to Temple Mount." *The Jerusalem Post*, n.p.. 15 Apr. 2016. Web. 03 June 2016.

McCarthy, Rory. "East Jerusalem Should Be Palestinian Capital, Says EU Draft Paper." *The Guardian*. Guardian News and Media. 2 December 2009.

McDonnell, Faith J.H. "US State Department Says No to Iraqi Christians." "*US State Department Says No to Iraqi Christians*." Assyrian International News Agency, 17 May 2015. Web. 29 Jan. 2016.

"Meaning of Giovanni - Italian Baby Name." *Meaning of Giovanni - Italian Baby Name*, n.p. Web. 10 Apr. 2016.

Medoff, Dr. Rafael. "FDR and the 'Voyage of the Damned.' " *The Jewish Press RSS*, n.p. 14 Nov. 2011 Latest update: Apr. 29, 2013. Web. 18 Aug. 2014.

Meshoe, Dr. Kenneth. "Pro-Palestinian Ads Misrepresent Apartheid." *The San Francisco Examiner*. Published, May 15, 2013. Web. 22 May 2014.

Michael, Robert. *A History of Catholic Antisemitism: The Dark Side of the Church*. New York: Palgrave Macmillan, 2011.

Medieval Sourcebook: *A Blood Libel Cult*: Anderl von Rinn, d. 1462. Fordham University; May 14, 2014.

Meotti, Giulio. "Churches Against Israel." *Levitt Letter* (Sept. 2011).

"Military." *Jerusalem Must Be Capital of Both Israel and Palestine, Ban Says*. UN News Service. 28 Oct. 2009. Web. 20 Oct. 2014.

Mindel, Nissan. "The Martyrs of Blois—(circa 1171)—Jewish History." *The Martyrs of Blois—(circa 1171)—Jewish History*, Kehot Publication Society. 15 Aug. 2014.

Minor, Jack. "Obama's Iran Deal Falls on Ominous Bible Date." *WND*. WorldNetDaily.com. 6 Apr. 2015. Web. 20 Nov. 2015.

Munificentissimus Deus 40, 1 Nov. 1950.

Ohlheiser, Abby. "Michigan's State Capital Will Host a Satanic Temple Display, but No Nativity Scene (for Now)." *Washington Post*. The Washington Post. 16 Dec. 2014. Web. 1 Feb. 2016.

Ogilvie, Sarah A. and Scott Miller. *Refuge Denied: The St. Louis Passengers and the Holocaust. Madison*: Univ. of Wisconsin, 2006.

Omer-Man, Michael. "This Week in History: The Jews of Basel Are Burnt." *This Week in History: The Jews of Basel Are Burnt*. The Jerusalem Post. 14 Jan. 2011. Web. 7 Sept. 2014.

"On the Keeping of Easter. Nice. A.D. 325." *The Seven Ecumenical Councils of the Undivided Church*. Ed. Henry R. Percival, MA, DD. 2nd ed., vol. 14. Peabody: Hendrickson, 2004. 54. Nicene and Post-Nicene Fathers.

Parkes, James. *The Jew in the Medieval Community: A Study of His Political and Economic Situation*. New York: Hermon, 1976.

Poliakov, Leon. *The History of Anti-Semitism*. Trans. Richard Howard. New York: Vanguard Press, 1965.

Powers, Kirsten. "Kirsten Powers: Christians Thrown Overboard Left to Drown by Obama." *USA Today*. Gannett. 21 Apr. 2015. Web. 26 Jan. 2016.

Roberts, D.D., Alexander, James Donaldson, LL.D, ed's. *Ante-Nicene Fathers,* vol. 1 (Peabody: Hendrickson Publ., 2004), 199-200, Ch. 11.

_____. *Ante-Nicene Fathers,* vol 1. "The Epistle of Ignatius to the Philippians." Peabody: Hendrickson Publ., 2004.

_____. *Nicene and Post-Nicene Fathers,* vol. 2. "The City of God." Peabody: Hendrickson Publ., 2004.

_____. *Ante-Nicene Fathers,* vol. 4. Tertullian, Part (IV). *Minucius, Felix, Commodian, Origen.* Peabody: Hendrickson Publ., 2004.

_____ *Ante-Nicene Fathers,* vol 4. "Origen Against Celsus." Peabody: Hendrickson Publ., 2004.

Rubinstein, W. D. (1996). *A History of the Jews in the English-Speaking World: Great Britain.* New York: Macmillan Press, 1996.

"Palestinian Authority PM Salam Fayyad Proclaims Historic Jerusalem the Capital of 'Palestine,' " n.p. Web. 8 December 2011.

"Palestinian NGO Apologizes for Posting Jewish 'Blood Libel' Article." *Algemeiner.com RSS.* 3 Apr. 2013. Web. 4 Aug. 2014.

Parks, James. *The Jew in the Medieval Community.* New York: Hermon Press, 1976.

Poliskov, Leon. *The History of Anti-Semitism in Germany.* New York: Vanguard Press. 1965.

Publications Relating to Various Aspects of Communism (1946), by United States Congress, House Committee on Un-American Activities. Issues 1-15, p. 19 comments attributed to Goebbels.

Rocca, Francis X., Joshua Mitnick. "Vatican to Sign First Treaty with 'State of Palestine,' " Wall Street Journal. 13 May 2015. Web. 16 May 2015.

Roth, Cecil. *Encyclopedia Judaica:* "Forced Baptism," n.p. Web. 25 Apr. 2016.

_____*A History of the Jews in England.* Oxford: Clarendon Press, 1965.

Rothschild family (2014, May 8). In Wikipedia, *the Free Encyclopedia,* n.p. Web. 11 May 2014.

Roxanne at Ariel Ministries. E-mail correspondence dated June 29, 1999, regarding a previous response by Arnold G. Fruchtenbaum, Th.M., Ph.D., regarding whether or not Luke was a Jew.

Runciman, Steven. *A History of the Crusades*, vol. II: *The Kingdom of Jerusalem.* London: Cambridge University Press, 1957.

Runes, Dagobert. *The War Against the Jews*. New York: Philosophical Library, 1968.

Schaff, Philip, D.D., LL.D. and Henry Wace, D.D., *Nicene and Post-Nicene Fathers: A Select Library of the Christian Church, Second Series,* vol. 1. Hendrickson Publishers, 2004.

Schama, Simon. *The Story of the Jews: Finding the Words (1000 BCE–1492),* vol 1. London: The Bodley Head, 2013.

Schwartz, Sharon. The BLAZE: "Ukrainian Jews Reportedly 'Flooding' Israeli Consulate to Get Out of Country in 2014." Web. 9 May 2014.

Secrets of Great British Castles: The Tower of London, season 1, Ep. 2. A Sideline Production/GroupM Productions Ltd., 2015.

Seif, Ph.D., Jeffery. <staff@levitt.com> (E-mail correspondence dated August 1, 2011.) "First major incident of anti-Semitism."

Share International magazine, "Lord Maitreya."Web. 5 June 2014.

Shaw, Jerry. "5 Public Schools That Have Installed Muslim Prayer Rooms." *Newsmax*, Newsmax, Inc. Newsmax, Inc. WEB. 25 Mar. 2015.

Slavik, Diane. *Cities through Time: Daily Life in Ancient and Modern Jerusalem*. Geneva: Runestone Press., 2001.

Sloane, J. P., Ph.D. *A Simple Crash Course on Islam*, vol. 1. Dallas: AvingtonHouse, 2015. *Islam Exposed*.

Sobel, Jerrold L. *Articles: There Was Never a Country Called Palestine*. *American Thinker*. 12 Feb. 2012. Web. 27 Apr. 2016.

"Sun Myung Moon" (19 May 2014). *Wikipedia, the Free Encyclopedia*. Web. 5 June 2015.

"SS Exodus" (8 Aug. 2014). *Wikipedia, the Free Encyclopedia.* 18 August 2014.

Stahl, Julie, and Chris Mitchell. "Pope Francis Tells Abbas: 'Be an Angel of Peace' " *Pope Francis Tells Abbas: Be an 'Angel of Peace.'* CBN News. 18 May 2015. Web. 31 May 2015.

"Strasbourg's Jews Fearful, but Staying Put in France." *Euronews,* (European News), 16 Mar. 2015. Web. 14 Feb. 2016.

Terry, Michael, edit. *Readers Guide to Judaism.* New York: Routledge, 2000.

Tenney, Merrill C., Walter M. Dunnett. *New Testament Survey, Revised.* Grand Rapids: Wm. B. Eerdmans Publ., 1988.

Thatcher, Oliver J., trans, and Edgar Holmes McNeal, eds. *A Source Book for Medieval History.* New York: Scribners, 1905.

The Editors of Encyclopædia Britannica. "Marcus Minucius Felix." *Encyclopedia Britannica Online,* n.p. WEB. 19 June 2016.

_____."Migration Period." *Encyclopedia Britannica Online.* Encyclopedia Britannica, n.p. 18 May 2016 last update. 26 Jul. 2016.

_____."Munich Massacre. Munich, Germany [1972]." *Encyclopaedia Britannica,* Munich massacre, n.p. WEB. 31 May 2015.

The Gutenberg Galaxy: The Making of Typographic Man (1st ed.), Toronto: University of Toronto Press, 1962.

The Jewish Black Book Committee, *The Black Book: The Nazi Crime Against the Jewish People,* New York: Suell, Sloan and Pearce, 1946.

The Holy Land Satellite, Atlas R.L.W. Cleave, ed., Nicosia, Cyprus: RØHR Productions, Ltd., 1999.

The House of Rothschild: Money's Prophets, 1798–1848, vol. 1. Niall Ferguson, 1999. Tertullian [database on-line]. Web. 11 Nov. 2011.

Tikkanen, Amy. "MS St. Louis." *Encyclopædia Britannica*, Encyclopædia Britannica, Inc., 28 Mar. 2019.

Twain, Mark. "Concerning the Jews." *Harper's Magazine*, 1899.

Thurston, Herbert. "Catholic." *The Catholic Encyclopedia*, vol. 3. New York: Robert Appleton Company, 1908. WEB. 15 Aug. 2016.

Tzu, Sun, *The Art of War* (Restored Translation). Tr. Lionel Giles, Lionel Giles, n.p. Pax Librorum, 2009.

"UNESCO Votes to Admit Palestine" [database on-line]. (Peabody: Hendrickson Publ., 2004). Web. 8 Dec. 2011.

"Vatican Recognizes State of Palestine in New Treaty." *Fox News*. FOX News Network, 13 May 2015. Web. 19 Nov. 2015.

Vocelle, L.A. "CATS AND WITCHCRAFT (Part 3-Malleus Maleficarum)." *THE GREAT CAT*, WEB 28 Mar. 2016.

Wallmann, Johannes. "The Reception of Luther's Writings on the Jews from the Reformation to the End of the Nineteenth Century." *Lutheran Quarterly* n.s. 1 (Spring 1987).

"Who Is St. Nicholas?" *St. Nicholas Center*. Web 1 Jan 2016.

William, Warren. *Who Changed Text and the Why*. Augsburg: Fortress Press, 2011.

Watt, W. Montgomery. *Muhammad at Medina*. Oxford: Clarendon Press, 1956.

Wilder, Ph.D., Lynn K. "The Christian: Why I Left the Mormon Church to Follow Jesus." This is from a reprint of the August 15, 2015 edition of the "Premier Christianity" magazine (UK).

William I 'the Conqueror' (r. 1066-1087). The Official Website of the British Monarchy, n.p. Web. 25 Jan. 2016. The Royal Household © Copyright 2008/09 the Royal Household © Crown Copyright.

Wilken, Robert L. Tertullian. *Encyclopedia BritannicaOnline*. Encyclopedia Britannica, n.p. Web. 02 Nov. 2016.

Winfield, Nicole, A.P. "Vatican Recognizes Palestine." *US News*. U.S. News & World Report. 13 May 2015. Web. 31 May 2015.

Working Group I. To the Fourth Assessment Report of the Intergovernmental Panel on Climate Change [Solomon. *What Caused the Ice Ages and Other Important Climate Changes before the Industrial Era?*] (n.p.): National Oceanic and Atmospheric Administration. Web. 26 Apr. 2016.

"Yad Vashem." *Wikipedia*, Wikimedia Foundation, 18 Mar. 2020.

ABOUT THE AUTHOR

As a student of history and theology, J.P. Sloane has researched not only the diversity of Christianity, but he has also explored the various other religions, sects, and cults in order to understand how they interact, challenge, and influence each other. It was because of his quest for knowledge that he embarked on over 30 years of higher education taking advantage of several scholastic opportunities afforded him, which includes enrollment at the following schools from which he has since graduated: Purdue University, through a program sponsored by *the Indiana Council of Churches*, the Institute of Charismatic Studies at Oral Roberts University, the Moody Bible Institute and the Institute of Jewish-Christian Studies. He earned a B.A., *Summa Cum Laude*, from the Master's University where he also studied at their IBEX campus in Israel. While at Masters, he earned an M.A. in Biblical Counseling. At Trinity Theological Seminary he earned a Doctorate of Ministry as well as a Ph.D., *With Distinction*, in Religious Studies.

Throughout the years, Dr. Sloane has appeared on such television programs as *The 700 Club, the PTL Club, Lester Sumrall Today, Richard Roberts Live,* LeSea Broadcasting's *Harvest* and Trinity Broadcasting Network's *Praise the Lord,* to name a few.

Publications in which Dr. Sloane appears include, *Who's Who in the World* and *Who's Who in America*. He is also featured in the *Dictionary of International Biography* and *2000 Outstanding Intellectuals of the 21st Century* (Cambridge, England).

Continued...

Dr. Sloane is seen working at the "John the Baptist" dig during his

undergrad work in Israel, under the direction of the *Israeli Antiquities Authority* and supervision of Dr. Shimon Gibson (Adjunct Professor of Archaeology at the University of North Carolina at Charlotte).

This site is located in the orchards of Kibbutz Tzuba, near the village of Ein Karem—also believed to be the traditional birthplace of John the Baptist (located west of Jerusalem). "From a historical point of view, the uniqueness of this cave is that it contains archaeological evidence that comes to us from the very time of the personalities and events described in the Gospels … (in) the cave is the earliest ever Christian art depicting John the Baptist as well as the three crosses of the crucifixion."[304]

---

[304]Shimon Gibson, Ph.D., *The Cave of John the Baptist* (New York: Random House, 2005), back cover.

www.ingramcontent.com/pod-product-compliance
Lightning Source LLC
LaVergne TN
LVHW011218080426
835509LV00005B/189